AMERICAN
HERITAGE

June 1962 · Volume XIII, Number 4

Per ardua ad astra, c. 1870

The halls of Matthew Vassar's college for young ladies, which last year celebrated its centennial, had not yet acquired their mantle of ivy when this picture was taken. The scene is the observatory; the cast, fourteen female students of astronomy (and, inexplicably, one small and uninterested boy lounging on the steps). The figure barely visible in the open second-floor window at right is their teacher, the famous astronomer Maria Mitchell, who once turned out the whole college in the middle of the night to observe a meteor. A good thing, too: using the telescopes in broad daylight, as some of the girls are seen doing here, would have given them an extremely limited view of the cosmos.

AMERICAN HERITAGE

The Magazine of History

PUBLISHER
James Parton

EDITORIAL DIRECTOR
Joseph J. Thorndike, Jr.

SENIOR EDITOR
Bruce Catton

EDITOR
Oliver Jensen

ASSOCIATE EDITORS
Robert Cowley
E. M. Halliday
Richard M. Ketchum
Joan Paterson Mills
Robert L. Reynolds

ASSISTANT EDITORS
Meryle Evans, Stephen W. Sears

CONTRIBUTING EDITOR
Margery Darrell

LIBRARIAN
Caroline Backlund

COPY EDITOR
Beverly Hill
ASSISTANT: Suzanne Adessa

SENIOR ART DIRECTOR
Irwin Glusker

ART DIRECTOR
Murray Belsky
STAFF PHOTOGRAPHER: Herbert Loebel

ADVISORY BOARD
Allan Nevins, *Chairman*
Carl Carmer   Alvin M. Josephy, Jr.
Albert B. Corey   Richard P. McCormick
Christopher Crittenden   Harry Shaw Newman
Marshall B. Davidson   Howard H. Peckham
Louis C. Jones   S. K. Stevens
Arthur M. Schlesinger, Sr.

AMERICAN HERITAGE is published every two months by American Heritage Publishing Co., Inc., 551 Fifth Avenue, New York 17, N.Y. Correspondence about subscriptions should be addressed to: American Heritage Subscription Office, 383 West Center Street, Marion, Ohio. Single Copies: $3.95. Annual Subscriptions: $15.00 in U.S. & Canada; $16.00 elsewhere.

An annual Index of AMERICAN HERITAGE is published every February, priced at $1.00. A Cumulative Index of Volumes VI–X is available at $3.00.

AMERICAN HERITAGE will consider but assumes no responsibility for unsolicited material. Title registered U.S. Patent Office. Second class postage paid at New York, N.Y.

Sponsored by

American Association for State & Local History · Society of American Historians

CONTENTS   *June 1962 · Volume XIII, Number 4*

COVER: Dolley Madison still lived near the White House when Andrew Jackson departed and the little widower Martin Van Buren moved in with his four young sons. The place needed a woman, she decided, and within a year she had married off her beautiful young cousin, Angelica Singleton, to the President's eldest son, Abraham, who served as his father's secretary. Angelica made a gracious hostess for her father-in-law, who appears in the background of Henry Inman's portrait in a Roman bust. The portrait is reproduced through the courtesy of the White House, where it hangs today. A study of Van Buren's long struggle to achieve his four years there begins on page 28. *Back Cover:* This cartoon from the humorous magazine *The Verdict,* for July 16, 1900, comes from the Butterfield Collection, subject of the article that begins on page 32.

Even tests made back in the 1920's, before Sacco's execution, point to his gun as a murder weapon. This highly magnified composite picture brings together half of a test shell (top) fired from Sacco's pistol and half of Shell W (bottom), found near the murdered guard, so arranged as to show clearly how a pattern of vertical scratches, or markings, meet and match across the bases of the two shells. While the shells do not otherwise make a complete fit, having been fired on a different axis, these telltale markings prove to the satisfaction of experts that both shells struck the same breechblock. And each pistol's hand-finished breechblock is as individual as a man's fingerprint.

Four years ago Mr. Russell claimed in our pages that the central figures in the famous trial at Dedham had been unjustly executed. Now he has restudied the long record, held new ballistic tests, and reached a dramatic new conclusion. Should not the verdict be, he asks:

SACCO *GUILTY,*
VANZETTI *INNOCENT?*

By FRANCIS RUSSELL

The murders for which Nicola Sacco and Bartolomeo Vanzetti were convicted and finally executed were quick, simple, and brutal. On the afternoon of April 15, 1920, in the small shoe manufacturing town of South Braintree, Massachusetts, a paymaster, Frederick Parmenter, and his guard, Alessandro Berardelli, were shot and robbed as they walked down Pearl Street with the Slater & Morrill Shoe Company payroll—some fifteen thousand dollars in two metal boxes.

The paymaster and the guard, each carrying a box, had crossed the railroad tracks near the front of the Rice & Hutchins factory when two strangers who had been leaning against the fence there suddenly stepped toward them. The strangers were short, dark men. One wore a felt hat and the other, a cap. In a flash the first man whipped a pistol from his pocket and fired several shots into Berardelli. The guard dropped to the ground. Parmenter, a step in advance, turned and when he saw what was happening, started to run across the street. Before he reached the other side he was shot twice. He dropped his box and collapsed in the gutter. Witnesses—of which there were a number in the factory windows and along Pearl Street—were afterward uncertain whether one man or two had done the shooting, but most thought there had been two.

With Parmenter and Berardelli lying in the gravel, one of their assailants fired a signal shot, and a Buick touring car that had been parked near the Slater & Morrill factory now started jerkily up the rise. As it slowed down, the two bandits picked up the money boxes and climbed into the back seat. Berardelli had managed to get to his hands and knees. Seeing him wavering, a third man sprang from the car and fired another shot into him. It was a death wound.

The Buick continued along Pearl Street with five men in it, a gunman in the front seat firing at random at the crowd drawn by the sound of the shots. No one was hit, although one bystander had his coat lapel singed. The car gathered speed, swung left at the top of Pearl Street, and one of the men in the rear seat threw out handfuls of tacks to hinder any pursuit. The speeding car was noticed at intervals along a ten-mile stretch of road; then it vanished. Two days later it was found abandoned in the woods near Brockton, a dozen miles away.

Berardelli died within a few minutes, the final bullet having severed the great artery issuing from his heart. Parmenter too had received a fatal wound, a bullet cutting his inferior vena cava, the body's largest vein. He died early the following morning. At the autopsy two bullets were found in Parmenter and four in Berardelli. The county medical examiner, Dr. George Burgess Magrath, removed the bullets from Berardelli's body, scratching the base of each with a Roman numeral. The bullet that had cut the artery and that, from the angle of its path, he determined must have been fired while Berardelli was down, he marked III. It had struck the hipbone obliquely and was slightly bent from this glancing contact.

Of the six bullets, five had been fired from a .32 caliber pistol or pistols with a right-hand twist to the rifling. These bullets were of varied manufacture—three Peters and two Remingtons. The remaining bullet, the one Dr. Magrath marked III, was a Winchester of an obsolete type having a cannelure, or milling around the edge. It had been fired from a .32 caliber pistol with a left-hand twist. Only a Colt, among American pistols, had such a reverse twist. Four spent cartridges of the same caliber as the bullets were picked up in the gravel near Berardelli's body. Two of these were Peters, one a Remington, and one a Winchester later known as Shell W.

No weapons were found on the bodies, although Berardelli customarily carried a revolver with him. On March 19, 1920, he had taken his gun to the Iver Johnson Company in Boston to have it repaired. According to his wife, it needed a new spring. Lincoln Wadsworth, in charge of the repair department, recorded that on that day he had received a .38 caliber Harrington & Richardson revolver from Alex Berardelli and had sent the gun upstairs to the workshop. There the foreman, George Fitzemeyer, for some reason marked it as a .32 caliber Harrington & Richardson requiring a new hammer and ticketed it with a repair number.

No one at Iver Johnson's recorded the revolver's serial number. The store manager testified a year later at the trial that the company did not keep a record of deliveries of repaired guns, but he was certain this particular revolver had been delivered. All weapons in the repair department not called for by the year's end were sold and a record made of each sale. Since Berardelli's revolver was no longer in the store, and there was no record of its being sold, the manager insisted it must have been called for.

Several witnesses of the shooting said at the inquest that they saw one of the bandits stoop over Berardelli. Peter McCullum, peering out of the first floor cutting room of Rice & Hutchins after he heard the shots, saw a man putting a money box into the Buick while holding a "white" revolver in his other hand. A Harrington & Richardson revolver was nickel-plated and might well have seemed white in the sunlight. This may have been Berardelli's. It seems unlikely that the guard would have accompanied the paymaster

---

Mr. Russell's previous article on Sacco and Vanzetti appeared in the October, 1958, issue of AMERICAN HERITAGE *under the title "Tragedy in Dedham." Challenged by many readers at the time, he began to reread the vast transcripts of the case and the endless motions, arguments, and investigations that filled the long years between the crime in 1920 and the execution in 1927. Out of his researches, interviews with surviving witnesses, and ballistics tests has grown a book, also called* Tragedy in Dedham, *which the McGraw-Hill Book Company of New York will publish in August. This article, which confines itself to the ballistic evidence, was prepared especially for* AMERICAN HERITAGE.

without being armed. And if he had a revolver, it is possible that one of the men who shot him may have reached down and taken it.

Sacco and Vanzetti were arrested almost by chance on the night of May 5, 1920. They had met earlier in the evening at Sacco's bungalow in Stoughton—a half-dozen miles from South Braintree—with two anarchist comrades, Mike Boda and Ricardo Orciani, to arrange about gathering up incriminating literature from other comrades for fear of government "Red" raids. Until a few months before this, Boda had been living in West Bridgewater ten miles away with another anarchist, Ferruccio Coacci, who had been taken away for deportation on April 17. Not until Coacci was at sea did the police come to suspect that he and Boda might have been concerned in the South Braintree holdup. Boda had left an old Overland touring car in a West Bridgewater garage to be repaired, and the four men were planning to pick it up that evening. Orciani and Boda left Stoughton on Orciani's motorcycle. Sacco and Vanzetti went by streetcar. Once they had arrived, Boda was unable to get the car from the forewarned proprietor. As the men argued, the proprietor's wife telephoned the police.

Sacco and Vanzetti were arrested in Brockton while riding back to Stoughton on the streetcar. The police found a .32 caliber Colt automatic tucked in Sacco's waistband. In the gun's clip were eight cartridges, with another in the chamber. Sacco had twenty-three more loose cartridges in his pocket. These, though all .32 caliber, were of assorted makes—sixteen Peters, seven U.S., six Winchesters of the obsolete type, and three Remingtons. Vanzetti was found to be carrying a Harrington & Richardson .38 caliber revolver, its five chambers loaded with two Remington and three U.S. bullets.

The day following their arrest the two men were questioned at some length by the district attorney, Frederick Katzmann. Sacco told Katzmann he had bought his automatic two years before on Hanover Street in Boston under an assumed name. He had paid sixteen or seventeen dollars for it, and at the same time he had bought an unopened box of cartridges.

Vanzetti said he had bought his revolver four or five years before, also under an assumed name, at some shop on Hanover Street and had paid eighteen dollars for it. He had also bought an unopened box of cartridges, all but six of which he had fired off on the beach at Plymouth.

At their trial fourteen months later the two men told very different stories. They both admitted they had lied when they were first questioned, but explained that they then thought they were being held

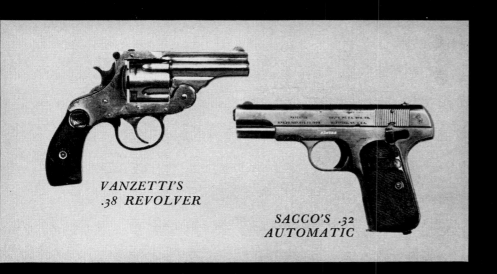

VANZETTI'S
.38 REVOLVER

SACCO'S .32
AUTOMATIC

Among the key items which Mr. Russell discusses are the two pistols and the four bullets taken from the body of the murdered guard. The magnified base views show the numbers scratched in them by the medical examiner; much controversy once raged about whether the "III" on the misshapen "mortal bullet" differs in style from the other numbers. The lead core of III is concave, whereas the others are flat, for, as the side views show, the bullets are of various makes. When Mr. Russell re-examined them last year they were still in sealed envelopes, ticketed (right) for shipment to the Lowell Committee. He then made new tests, one of which appears below, on October 11, 1961, as Colonel Frank Jury, New Jersey firearms expert, fires Sacco's pistol into wadded cotton at the Massachusetts Department of Public Safety ballistics laboratory.

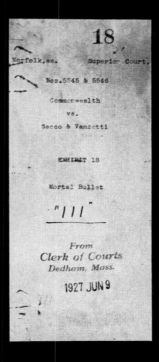

18

Norfolk, ss.   Superior Court.

Nos. 5545 & 5546

Commonwealth

vs.

Sacco & Vanzetti

EXHIBIT 18

Mortal Bullet

"III"

From
Clerk of Courts
Dedham, Mass.

1927 JUN 9

I

II

III

IIII

BULLET BASES

SAME BULLETS: SIDE VIEWS

I   II   III   IIII

Vanzetti (left) and Sacco, in court before sentencing

because they were anarchists. They had lied, they said, partly because they were afraid and partly to protect their comrades. Indeed they had good reason to feel apprehensive about their anarchism, for there were rumors of new government Red raids, and only a few days before their arrest their comrade Salsedo had died mysteriously in New York while being held by federal agents.

Sacco's revised trial story was that he had bought the pistol in 1917 or 1918 in the small town where he was working. He had bought a box of cartridges on Hanover Street shortly afterward. The man who sold him the box filled it with various makes because of the wartime scarcity of cartridges.

Vanzetti now said that he had bought his revolver a few months before his arrest. Often he carried a hundred dollars or more with him from his fish business, and he felt he needed a gun to protect himself because of the many recent holdups. He had bought the revolver from a friend, Luigi Falzini. It was loaded when he bought it, and he had never fired it.

Falzini appeared in court, identified the revolver by certain rust spots and scratches as having belonged to him, and said he had bought it from Orciani. Another witness, Rexford Slater, testified that the revolver had originally belonged to him and that he had sold it to Orciani in the autumn of 1919.

Orciani had been arrested the day following the arrests of Sacco and Vanzetti. However, as he was able to provide a timecard alibi for his whereabouts on April 15, he was released. During the early part of the trial he acted as chauffeur for one of the defense attorneys, but although he was in the courthouse almost daily, he did not take the stand. Yet he was, as the district attorney pointed out in his summing up,

the missing link in the revolver's chain of ownership.

At the trial the prosecution contended that the automatic found on Sacco was the one that had fired Bullet III and that Vanzetti's revolver had been taken from the dying Berardelli. Several days before the ballistics testimony, two experts for the prosecution, Captain William Proctor of the Massachusetts State Police—then no more than a detective bureau—and Captain Charles Van Amburgh from the Remington Arms Company in Connecticut, fired a number of test shots from Sacco's automatic into oiled sawdust. Proctor and Van Amburgh were joined in these experiments by a defense expert, James Burns. After the test bullets were recovered they were then compared with Bullet III.

The trial testimony of the firearms experts on both sides was involved and confusing, "a wilderness of lands and grooves" as one reporter noted. In the opinion of the Gunther brothers, whose book on firearms identification has become a legal classic, all the ballistics evidence offered was so primitive as to be worthless.

Each tooled gun barrel, with its hundreds of minute striations, is unique. The one certain method of determining whether two separate bullets have been fired through any particular barrel is the use of a comparison microscope. Through this instrument the ends of the two bullets are brought together in one fused image. If the striations match, then it is practically certain that both bullets were fired from the same weapon.

Today the comparison microscope is the standard method of bullet identification. In 1920 it was just beginning to come into use, but it was not used in the Sacco-Vanzetti trial. There the experts attempted to measure the bullets with calipers and compare them with measurements made of a cast of the barrel of Sacco's pistol. It was a useless, haggling proceeding.

No one disputed that Bullet III had been fired from a Colt automatic, but Captain Proctor told District Attorney Katzmann before the trial that he did not believe it had been fired from Sacco's Colt. The prosecution was aware of Proctor's doubts when the captain was questioned in court. "My opinion is," Proctor said with a prearranged ambiguity that escaped the defense, "that it [Bullet III] is consistent with being fired by that pistol." The prosecution claimed that the Winchester cartridge among the four picked up near Berardelli had also been fired in Sacco's pistol. Comparing this cartridge with one fired on the test range, Proctor again used the word "consistent." Privately he had from the time of their arrest expressed doubt that Sacco and Vanzetti were guilty.

Two years after the trial he signed an affidavit saying that he had used the ambiguous phrase "consistent with" at Katzmann's request, but that if he had been asked directly in court whether he believed that Bullet III had been fired from Sacco's Colt, he would have replied No.

Captain Van Amburgh was scarcely more emphatic in his trial testimony: "I am inclined to believe," he said, "that the Number III bullet was fired from this Colt automatic pistol." Burns and a second defense expert, J. Henry Fitzgerald of the Colt Patent Firearms Company, denied this. In their opinion neither Bullet III nor Shell W, the Winchester cartridge, had any connection with Sacco's pistol.

Fitzemeyer, the Iver Johnson foreman, when handed Vanzetti's revolver on the witness stand and asked if it had been repaired recently, replied: "Well, a new hammer, I should call it, a new hammer."

In the summer of 1924 Captain Van Amburgh was appointed head of the newly formed ballistics laboratory of the Massachusetts State Police. Fortunately for his new career the repercussions of his blunder in the Harold Israel case had not yet reached Massachusetts. On February of that same year Father Dahme, a priest in Bridgeport, Connecticut, had been shot and killed as he was taking his customary evening walk. A week later a drifter by the name of Harold Israel was picked up by the police in nearby Norwalk. In Israel's pocket was a loaded .32 caliber revolver. Several witnesses identified him as the man they had seen shoot Father Dahme. Van Amburgh was called in to examine the ballistics evidence. He fired Israel's revolver and compared a test bullet with one taken from Father Dahme's body. Both bullets, he reported, had come from the same weapon. Later, however, five experts from the Remington Arms Company plus another from the New York Police Department examined the bullets and were of the unanimous opinion that the bullet that had killed Father Dahme could not have been fired from Israel's revolver. Israel was then released.

Captain Van Amburgh remained head of the state police laboratory until his retirement in 1946. During his earlier years there he developed a device called a spiralgraph with which he was able to make strip photographs of bullets as they revolved on a turntable. By comparing the strips of two bullets, he maintained he could determine whether or not they had been fired from the same gun. Later he made such comparative photographs of Bullet III and the test bullets of the Sacco-Vanzetti case. These photographs he used for demonstrations when he testified in the 1923 Hamilton-Proctor motion, one of the many filed requesting a new trial for Sacco and Vanzetti.

The Hamilton-Proctor motion was based in part on Captain Proctor's affidavit as to what he had really believed when he testified at the trial, although Proctor himself had died before the motion could be argued. In addition to his affidavit, there was further evidence offered by a post-trial defense expert, Dr. Albert Hamilton, that Bullet III could not have come from Sacco's Colt.

Dr. Hamilton would never have been engaged by the lawyers for Sacco and Vanzetti if they had known more about his background. His doctor's degree was self-awarded. He had started out in Auburn, New York, as a small-town druggist and concoctor of patent medicines. Over the years behind the counter he developed expertness at a second career, advertising himself in a publicity pamphlet as a qualified expert in chemistry, microscopy, handwriting, ink analysis, typewriting, photography, fingerprints, toxicology, gunshot wounds, guns and cartridges, bullet identifi-

CONTINUED ON PAGE 107

BOSTON *Globe*

The great funeral procession for Sacco and Vanzetti moves up Hanover Street in Boston after their execution in 1927. To thousands of the deeply committed it was a moment of sorrow and angry frustration; argument gave way to faith, and the dead anarchists were elevated into a kind of sainthood.

In his sixties, John Frost took up his brushes to record—in brilliant colors and

HISTORY IN

*Frost's composite view of Marblehead in the Revolution shows Colonel Glover's Marbleheaders (in blue)
holding the near shore; their anchored ships fly the Pine Tree flag. The British occupy Marblehead Neck
across the bay. Beyond, two naval duels, which occurred six months apart in 1775–76, are in progress.*

HOUSE PAINT

On a warm summer day in 1926, in the little town of Marblehead, Massachusetts, a gray-haired old man walked from store to store distributing handbills. "Mr. J. O. J. Frost," they read, ". . . has opened his new art building containing about eighty paintings depicting his life on the Grand Banks and in the town of Marblehead. There will be a charge of twenty-five cents to see these paintings . . ."

The painter, handbill distributor, and exhibitor were one and the same—Frost himself—and the "art building" was a simple structure he had built behind his house at No. 11, Pond Street. On opening day, having shined up the premises and decked himself out in an immaculate white suit, he sat down to await his first customer. No one came—on that day or the next or the next—and precious few quarters ever found their way into his little cardboard collection box. Disappointed, the old man was not deterred from his painting. When he died two years later, he left behind more than 100 scenes—executed in ordinary house paint on scraps of pine or wallboard and even on the walls of his kitchen—recording the long and illustrious history of his native town. It was an extraordinary body of work, begun only when Frost was nearing seventy and carried on without benefit of formal art training. Yet the simple directness and primitive charm of his pictures have since commanded handsome prices and brought to their humble creator a measure of posthumous fame. In the preparation of this article, AMERICAN HERITAGE gratefully acknowledges the assistance of Mrs. Albert L. Carpenter of Jamaica Plain, Massachusetts, who furnished much of the material on the artist's life and extended permission to reproduce from her collection several of his paintings.

Few men were better qualified, by background at least, to chronicle Marblehead's past. John Orne Johnson Frost was born there in 1852, of a family that had put down roots in Massachusetts' rocky soil in 1634. At sixteen he shipped out on a fishing schooner bound for the Banks. He might have continued in that hard, hazardous, and unrewarding calling except that upon returning from his first trip in 1868 he met and fell in love with Annie Lillibridge, a pretty, brown-haired teen-ager; at her urging, he quit the sea after one more voyage. For almost a quarter of a century following their marriage in 1873, John Frost ran a restaurant in Marblehead; afterward, as the town developed into a summer colony for wealthy families from nearby Boston, he and Annie gradually transformed her hobby, growing flowers, into their livelihood.

Not until after Annie died in 1919 did Frost attempt his first painting; he took up a brush apparently in an effort to fill the void left by her passing. His son and daughter-in-law offered to keep house for him, but he preferred to live alone as he worked. "I know the compass I have steered by for almost half a century is not lost, but invisible," he said, "and that is enough to sustain me in anything I undertake to do." He had always been fascinated by Marblehead's history, and he set out, using whatever materials came to hand, to record it all before he died. During his last years he suffered from severe anemia; his fingers would bleed, so that holding a brush was difficult. But he persisted, despite the apathy of Marbleheaders, often forgetting to eat and sometimes fainting at his work. He finished his last painting only three weeks before he died—on November 3, 1928.
　　　　　　　　　　　　　　　—Robert L. Reynolds

J. O. J. Frost

FRONT-STREET-LATER—
HIS SON. 1664
SQUAW. SACHEM
1684
TOWN OF
MARBLEHEAD

***Frost's chronicle of Marblehead begins** with the arrival in 1625 of the white man. His very first painting (right), done in 1920, shows the crude camp of a pioneer variously known in local tradition as Dolliber, Doliver, or Doluber, who rebelled against the strict Puritanism of Salem and put to sea in a little boat, towing behind him a huge hogshead. Beaching his craft at the future site of Marblehead, then an outlying section of Salem township, he set up housekeeping in the hogshead and lived peacefully among the friendly Naumkeag Indians. A few years later Dolliber was joined by other dissenters from Salem and, still later, by fishermen from the Channel Islands of Jersey and Guernsey. Thus Marblehead was founded on a tradition of independence and nonconformity, traits which distinguish its natives to this day. In 1648 Salem faced up to the inevitable and granted the obstreperous fishermen their independence, and in 1684—as Frost recorded in the painting above—they secured title to the land by paying the Naumkeags the sum of $80 ("nine pence per Cow in Money" from each cattle-owning resident). That was more than three times what the Dutch had paid for Manhattan 58 years before, but if the Marbleheaders had known it, they would have said their lands were worth more. The deed, bearing the signatures of the white witnesses and the X's of the red, is still preserved in the town offices.*

As these two paintings clearly reveal, John Frost knew almost nothing of such elementary artist's skills as perspective. The treaty picture demonstrates another characteristic of his work: his scrupulous determination to include the facts that caught his childlike fancy, even if—as in this instance—it meant painting in the names and dates. History, not fine technique, was always his primary goal.

COLLECTION OF MAXIM KAROLIK

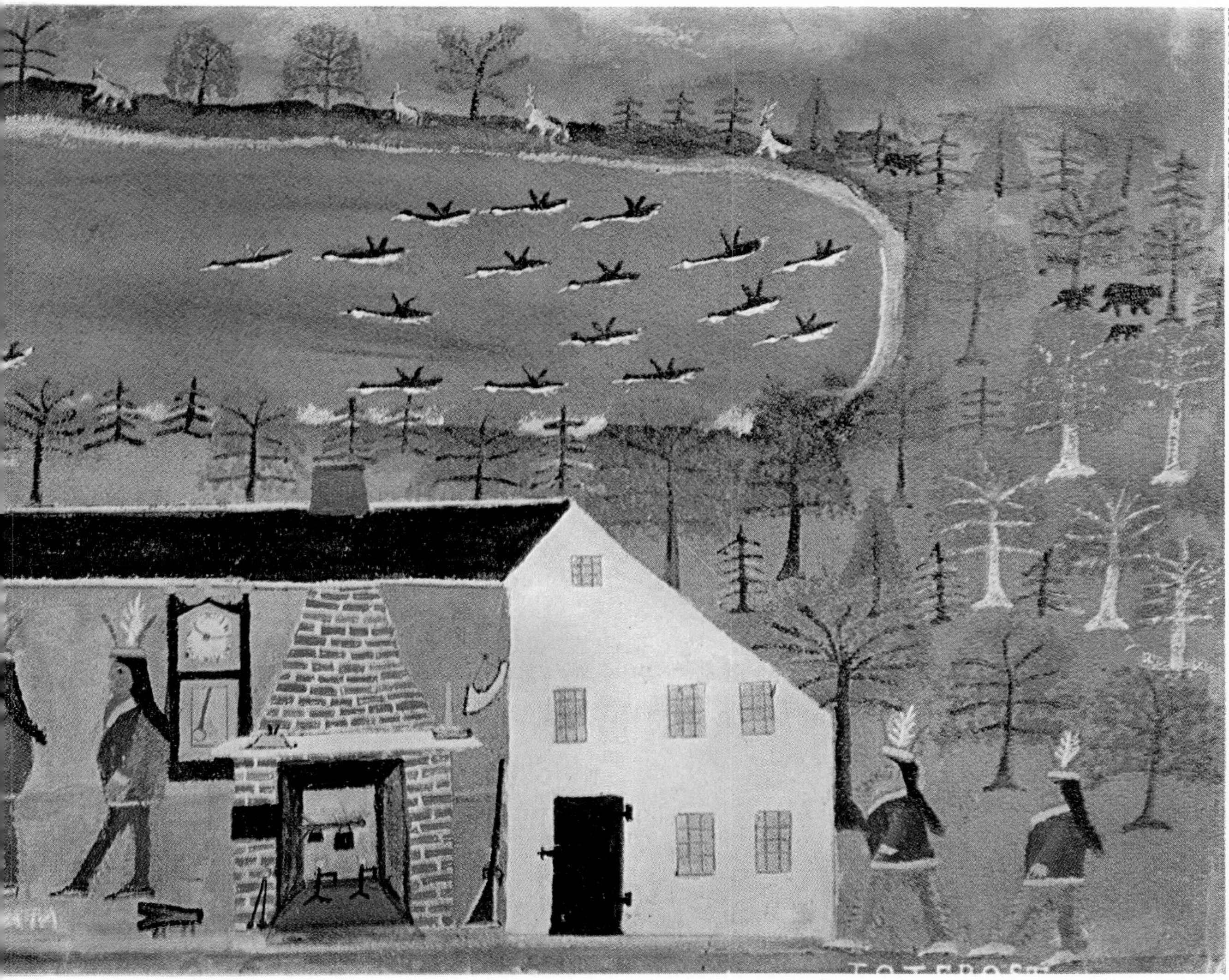

COLLECTION OF MRS. ALBERT L. CARPENTER

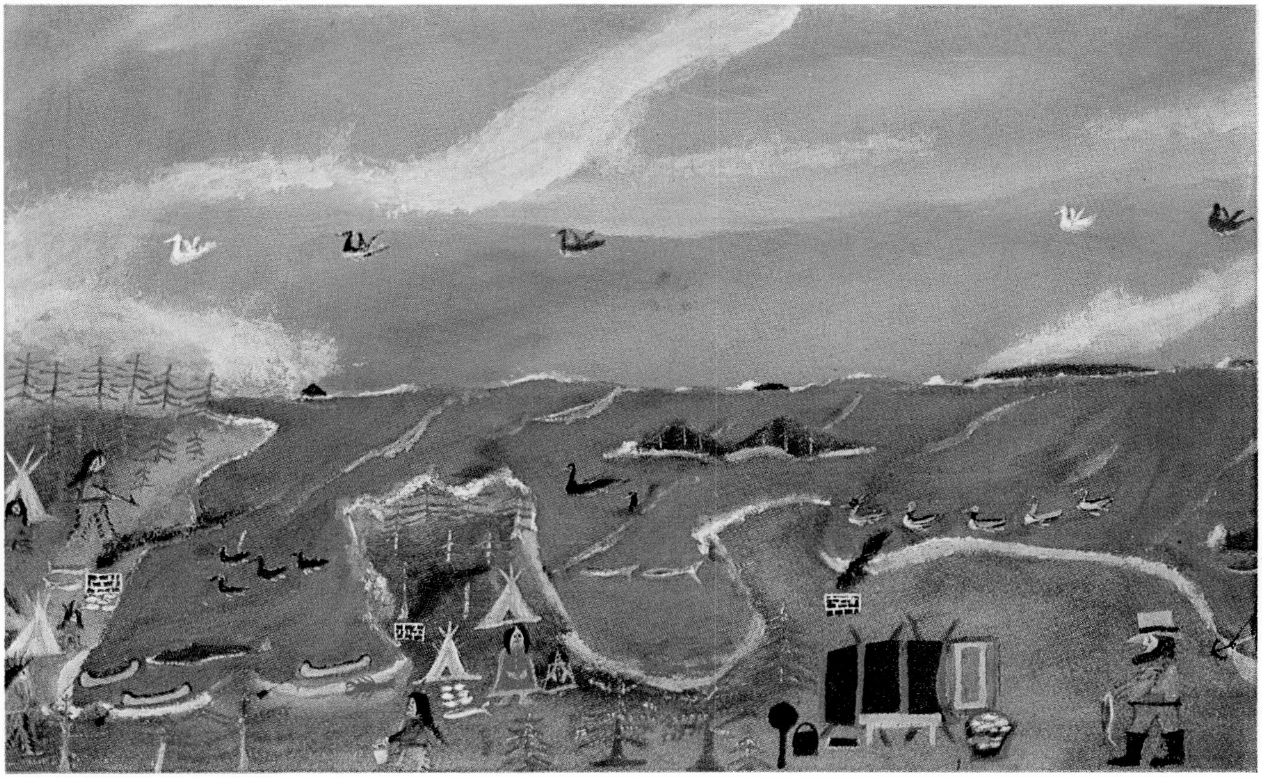

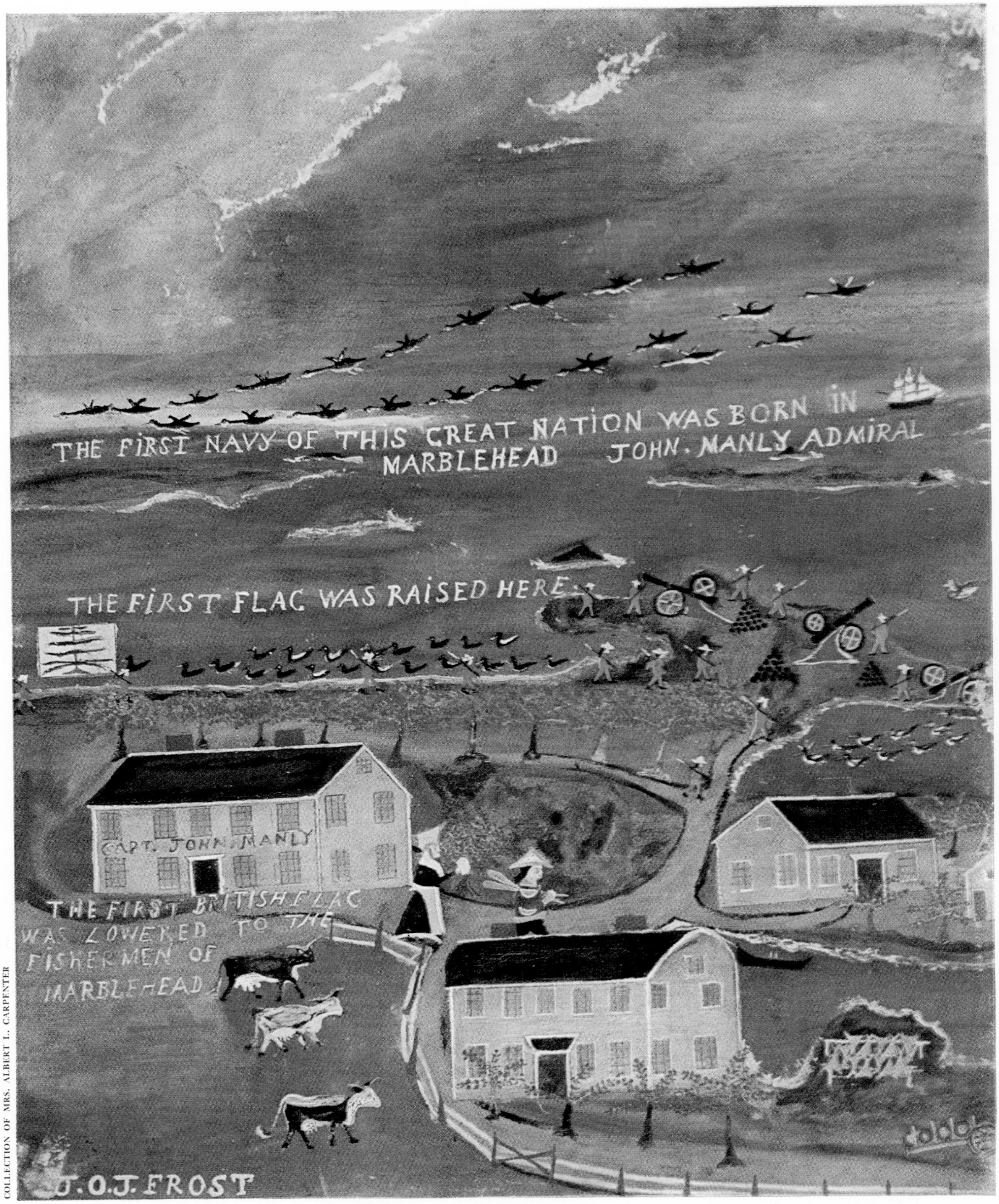
THE FIRST NAVY OF THIS GREAT NATION WAS BORN IN
MARBLEHEAD
JOHN. MANLY ADMIRAL
THE FIRST FLAG WAS RAISED HERE
CAPT. JOHN. MANLY
THE FIRST BRITISH FLAG
WAS LOWERED TO THE
FISHERMEN OF
MARBLEHEAD
J.O.J. FROST

COLLECTION OF MRS. ALBERT L. CARPENTER

In growing colonial Marblehead (above), British soldiers rode in the streets, and a British flag flew atop the King George Tavern. Evidently Salemites and Marbleheaders had patched up their differences, for a road between them had been built; evidently, too, all was not bliss in this Eden: Marblehead early found need for a poor farm and a work house. Still, when the Revolution came, few places of its size made a comparable contribution to liberty. Young Frost grew up hearing tales of the war from oldsters and from his own mother, who had seen Lafayette on his grand tour of America in 1824–25. Frost's claim (left) that Marblehead was the birthplace of the U.S. Navy has merit; John Manly (or Manley) of Marblehead is reputed to have been Washington's favorite captain in the tiny fleet—forerunner of the Continental Navy—assembled in 1775 to prey on British shipping. Manly's schooner, the Lee, is shown on page 10 capturing the British brigantine Nancy; John Glover's famous amphibious regiment of Marblehead fishermen ferried Washington's army across the Delaware for his surprise attack on Trenton (see "Soldier in a Longboat," AMERICAN HERITAGE, February, 1960). In 1772 Marblehead had only 5,000 inhabitants; when the world turned upside down at Yorktown, there were 378 widows in Marblehead, and 672 children who would never see their fathers again.

The Civil War: If John Frost's personal knowledge of the Revolution was limited to tales and legends, his experience of the Civil War was much more direct. He was nine years old when the scene above—men of Marblehead answering President Lincoln's call for volunteers—took place in 1861. It is one of his finest paintings. Though he recalled with pride that these soldiers were "the first to reach Faneuil

16

Hall in the state," he also saw the war—at least from the perspective of old age—in a strongly moralistic light. He showed
the women and children of Marblehead (left) bidding their
men a tearful farewell and saying, "We don't want war. We
love our homes." At far right war profiteers, motivated by
"selfishness and greed," reach for their ill-gotten gold, saying,
"Let's have war." And in the sky above is a pacifist slogan.

17

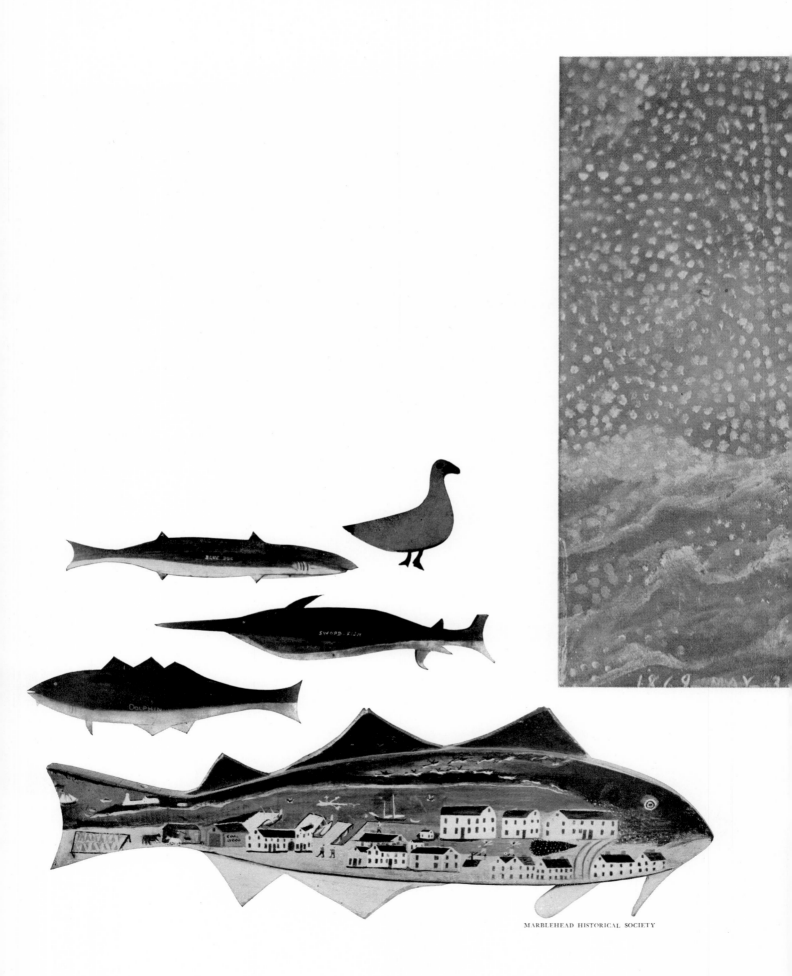

MARBLEHEAD HISTORICAL SOCIETY

WESTERN·EDGE·OF·THE·GRAND·BANKS

Marblehead began its existence as a fishing village, and for a long time its major source of livelihood was the sea. Frost's own memories of his two journeys to the Grand Banks remained vivid all his life and inspired some of his best work. The picture above, painted half a century after the event on wallpaper mounted on wallboard, commemorates the terrible morning of May 3, 1869, when Frost's vessel, the schooner Oceana, was caught in a blizzard. In his journal he recalled that he couldn't see the bow from the stern. "[The snow] cut your face and [it was] so cold we had to go down in the cabin and stay ten minutes at a time and warm yourself, then go up and let one of the others come down. If there had been [other] ships or ice bergs we couldn't have seen them. We were hove to under a close reefed foresail just trusting to luck."

As New England whaling crews made scrimshaw from the teeth, tusks, or jawbones of whales, John Frost as an old man carved in wood the fish and sea birds he had seen on his voyages or in the waters around Marblehead. Some of these, like the codfish at left, he decorated with quaint harbor scenes. His carvings, like his paintings, bear the unmistakable stamp of an authentic folk artist.

19

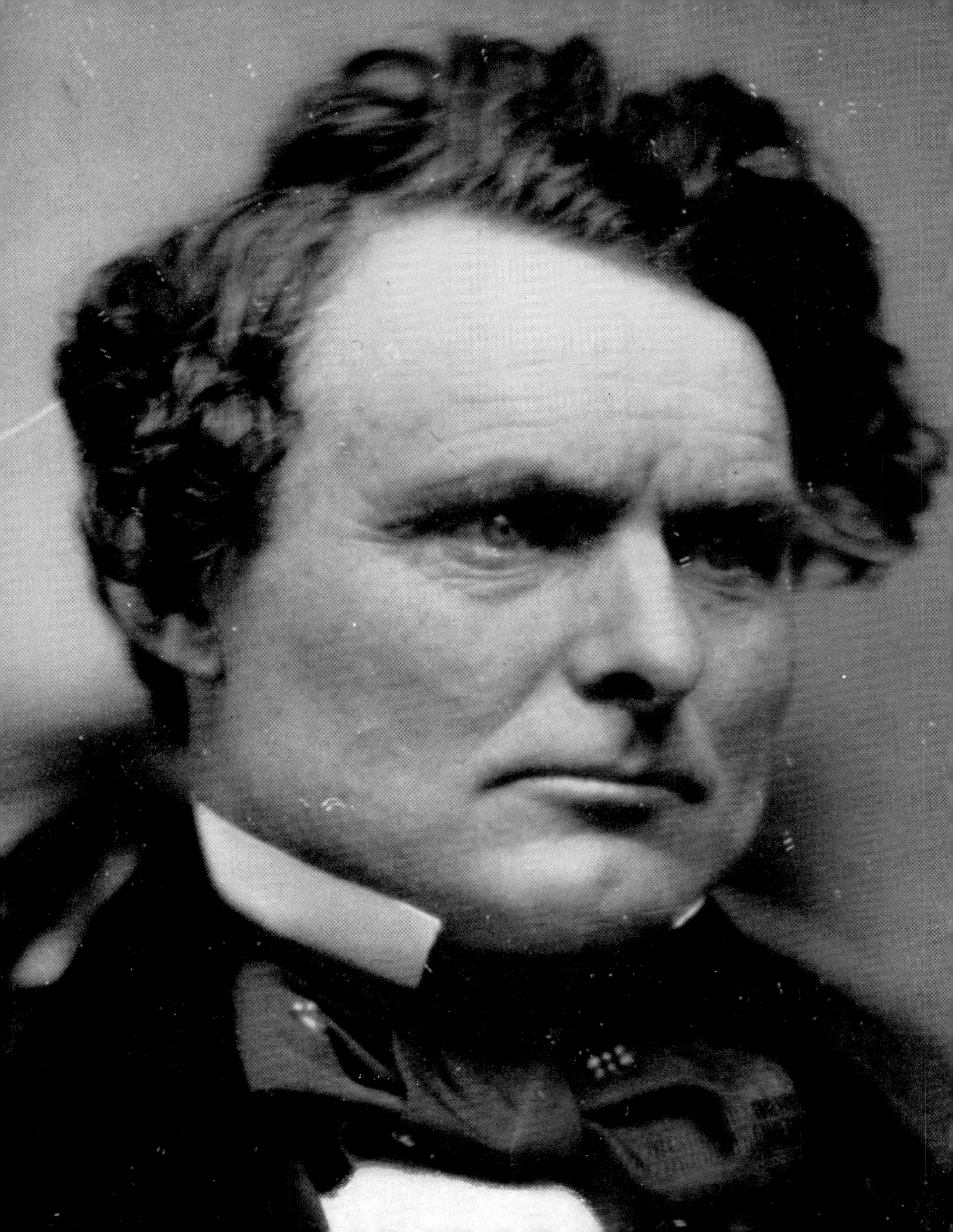

FACES FROM THE PAST—VII

Three decades of his life had been devoted to a single passion—a passion that took him to the very pinnacle of success. Then the era he had helped to create began to fade, and one could see in his face an awareness of the onrushing winds of change. The year was 1855, and the burst of genius and energy which had made America, for a time, the greatest maritime power in the world was being drowned by forces beyond anyone's ability to control.

From Nova Scotia, in 1826, Donald McKay had come to New York—his passage on a coaster paid with the savings of his mother and father and brothers—and at the age of sixteen he signed an indenture to Isaac Webb, the ship-builder. The terms were harsh: he was to work from sunrise to sunset, six days a week, for $1.25 a day. As soon as he was released from the agreement, McKay took a job in another shipyard, and by night drew plans, studied mathematics, modeled hulls, and talked to the men who sailed the oceans of the world. By the time he was thirty-four he had his own shipyard in East Boston and was beginning to make a name for himself constructing packets; five years later, in 1850, he launched his first clipper ship, the *Stag Hound;* the next year the *Flying Cloud* came down the ways.

The clippers which Donald McKay and his fellow builders produced were not only the fastest ships afloat; they were incomparably beautiful—a reflection of the American's love of speed and grace, of his preference for the new and daring over the old and established. Long, thin-waisted craft, towering above everything else in port, their bowsprits forming great arches along the bustling waterfronts, they could be spotted even by the greenest landsman. Once at sea, they were driven by as tough and skillful a lot of skippers as ever lived; until they reached Cape Horn and the savage battle that might last for weeks against the shrieking westerly gales, they carried every yard of canvas that could be spread —including, sailors said, the captain's long drawers.

Donald McKay's *Flying Cloud,* 1,783 tons, set sail on her maiden voyage from New York on June 3, 1851, with Josiah Cressy in command and his wife as navigator. In the Atlantic squalls the ship lost most of her top hamper and sprung the mainmast; a mutiny nearly broke out; then she ran head-on into screaming southwest winds and thick snow while rounding the Horn, and the men were sent aloft—up and up, one hundred feet above the dark, surging water—to make repairs while the ship rolled and tossed in the wild storm. But eighty-nine days and twenty-one hours later the ship came flying through the Golden Gate—a record east-west passage that would be equaled only twice by sailing vessels (once by the *Flying Cloud* herself). After unloading, she headed west again—this time to China for a cargo of tea—and when she returned to New York, only ninety-four days out of Canton, the city went wild, Captain Cressy was given a hero's welcome, and Donald McKay's name was on every merchant's lips. But McKay was not satisfied.

In 1852 he built the 2,400-ton *Sovereign of the Seas* on his own account, since no one was willing to order so large a ship, and he gave her command to his brother Lauchlan. There was a public holiday in Boston when she was launched, another celebration in New York while she was being loaded for California, and when she arrived in San Francisco after a harrowing voyage, she showed a clear profit of nearly $100,000. The next year the *Sovereign* sailed from the Sandwich Islands to New York in eighty-two days, her log showing a run of 421 miles during one twenty-four-hour period—and this voyage was accomplished with a green, shorthanded crew and a sprung fore-topmast which prevented Lauchlan McKay from carrying all the sail he wanted. From that moment, world attention centered on Donald McKay and his ships. No other builder produced such a tonnage of clippers; no vessels were more successful than his. Instinctively, he gave them beauty along with strength and speed—even their names had music to them. In 1852, in addition to the *Sovereign of the Seas,* he launched the *Bald Eagle* and *Westward Ho.* In 1853 came the huge *Great Republic,* the *Empress of the Seas, Star of Empire, Chariot of Fame,* and *Romance of the Seas.* Yet none quite satisfied him: "I never yet built a vessel that came up to my own ideal," McKay said; "I saw something in each ship which I desired to improve."

But by 1855 there was neither time nor opportunity to improve the clipper ships. Six extreme clippers had been launched in 1854—three at McKay's shipyard—but none was ever laid down again in the United States. For too long America's attention had been focused on the West. Young men whose minds and energies would have turned naturally to the sea a century earlier were engaged now in staking out claims and building towns. Steam was replacing sail; even in their heyday the clippers met more and more steam-powered craft, and were escorted in and out of port by stubby, snorting tugs. Man was beginning to achieve a mastery of sorts over the elements. The clipper had been his supreme, barehanded challenge to nature—a dare to come and do her worst.

For a few years the great ships held on. They were put to work hauling coal and coolies, guano and lumber; but before long they were rotting at dockside or in some lonely backwater anchorage. Donald McKay had seen this coming, and he turned his talents to steam and to building iron-clads; but things were never the same with him again, and in 1869 he sold the famous shipyard. For a while he lived on a farm, and when he died in 1880 he was buried in New-buryport, just in sight of the ocean which his beautiful ships had ridden for those few glorious years.

—*Richard M. Ketchum*

21

When Pancho Villa sacked an American town, Pershing was ordered to find him and bring him to book. But the orders failed to say where —or how

By LEON WOLFF

BLACK JACK'S MEXICAN GOOSE CHASE

arly in March, 1916, Francisco "Pancho" Villa's riders were operating closer to the United States border than ever before and almost daily firing upon our patrols from across the barbed-wire line, causing several American enlisted men to become quite dead as a result. On the first day of March a family of ranchers named Wright was kidnapped near Juárez, whereupon Mr. Wright had been murdered and his wife, Maud, taken by the raiders to face a perhaps even more harrowing denouement. But this was merely the latest of many incidents affecting relations between Mexico and the United States.

All told, about 170 American citizens had been killed by Mexican bandits, or factional troops, during recent years. Admittedly, most of the victims had died in Mexico, which had been in the throes of revolution since 1910. Under such circumstances, any adjacent foreigners are very likely to get hurt. But how to explain Villa's recent plundering of Nogales, Arizona? What on earth was the meaning of it? And it was followed by the horrible affair at Santa Isabel, Chihuahua, in January, when a group of Villistas had stopped a train, ordered out the American passengers (nineteen employees of a mining company), and killed all but one. For what purpose? Nobody north of the border knew for certain, but the United States went wild with fury, and Senate Republicans petitioned the President to send our Army and Navy into action.

Was Pancho deliberately seeking United States intervention? He was not the man he used to be, but he still controlled 5,000 mounted irregulars; he was still the military emperor of Chihuahua, and quite openly he was threatening to kill all U.S. citizens in his state. A State Department agent named Carothers had already predicted that if the revolutionary wing received no support from Uncle Sam in its machinations against Venustiano Carranza (Mexico's official First Chief) the irresponsible Villa would surely bring matters to a head by attacking some American town. As a result of this warning and recent depredations, six troops of the 13th U.S. Cavalry had been dispatched to Columbus, New Mexico, two miles north of the border. On March 7, Colonel H. J. Slocum, commanding, was advised that Villa and a large force were two miles south of the Border Gate.

Regrettably, next evening less than 200 of Slocum's men were in Columbus proper. Others were garrisoned at Bailey's Ranch and Gibson's Ranch, three and fourteen miles west, respectively, and some officers were in El Paso, where they had been playing polo that afternoon. When at 2:30 A.M. Villa and a thousand men swept into the town from three directions, shouting *"Viva Villa! Viva Mexico! Muerte a los ameri-*

canos!" the cavalry regiment was badly split and taken by surprise. First to die was the sentry guarding the officer of the day's shack. Within minutes the chatter of small arms, the pounding of hoofs, the yelling of the raiders, and the crackling of flames were mingling with the cries of women and babies to create a hellish cacophony. The town grocer, James Dean, was shot down in the middle of Main Street. As the Ritchie Hotel burst into flames, Mr. Ritchie ran out, and was held at gunpoint by the Mexicans. He begged for his life, offering all the money on his person: fifty dollars. They divested him of it and then killed him anyway.

Meanwhile American cavalrymen were bringing down substantial numbers of Villistas, partly with four machine guns, two of which soon jammed. (Splendid guns for fighting a war "between sun-up and sun-down," subsequently remarked the New York *Sun*.) The sergeant of F Troop was heard to call out: "Pick your men, there is hardly any more ammunition." Lieutenant W. A. McCain killed one Mexican with his pistol butt. Another died at the end of a baseball bat. Villa's men emptied Mr. Walker's hardware store of saddles and other goods. Riderless horses and unmounted men darted in all directions, surrealistically illuminated by the flames of the Lemmon Store and the Ritchie Hotel, while most unarmed residents of the town tried to flee. Hidden within houses and behind improvised barricades, the white troopers and armed civilians took a murderous toll of the raiders. A sixteen-year-old boy named Arthur Ravel was grabbed by two Mexicans and walked down the main street, past the groaning, dying body of Mr. Ritchie. En route one was killed. The other cautioned Arthur to keep walking. Near the town drugstore, the remaining Mexican was also shot down. Saved by someone who knew how to handle a rifle, the boy ran for cover.

Several Villistas were caught in a crossfire as they crouched in clear sight against a kitchen wall. Direct hits and ricochets almost wiped them out. Mrs. Wright, a hysterical witness of the orgy, had been thrust into a nearby ditch. When Pancho Villa happened to ride by, she caught his eye and begged to be let free. He motioned her curtly toward the burning town. She ran to the house of a woman friend, whose husband lay dead on the threshold. It was now almost dawn, Mexican bugles were sounding retreat, and the remaining men of the 13th Cavalry were approaching Columbus in the best tradition of a television western, except that they were too late. As Major Frank Tompkins and other avengers clattered down the main

Villa (third from right, below) rose to command among his rough-hewn peers by his bold tactics and his knack for handling men and supplies. But by the time of the Columbus raid, his forces had shrunk to a fraction of their former strength.

BROWN BROTHERS

street, past the smouldering wreckage, past scores of brown and white bodies sprawled in the dust, eighteen gringos were dead and about twice that number wounded. The cavalrymen pursued the Mexicans over the border, breaking through three rear-guard blocks, and later claimed that they killed 120 of them.

Six days later, a punitive column under Brigadier General John J. "Black Jack" Pershing also crossed the border after Villa. The fat was in the fire.

Now we were involved in the tag end of a foreign revolution, militarily penetrating a foreign land with which we were at peace; we had been intolerably provoked, and our motives were pure; still, here was Pershing in Mexico with 6,600 men at a time when our involvement in the great European conflagration seemed increasingly likely. Germany, although the evidence that she was financing Villa is questionable, was of course delighted.

A punitive expedition is not technically an act of war, provided that the acting Power is strong and civilized, while the chastised nation is backward and weak. Certainly Mr. Wilson, although he and Sr. Carranza disliked and mistrusted each other, did not desire hostilities with Carranza's government, which he had recently recognized after two years of "watchful waiting"; and the Columbus raid was an outrage which cried aloud for vengeance. On the other hand it was fairly well understood by 1916 that Villa was an enemy of his own government. Was it not President Carranza's job to punish him for the Columbus affair?

In 1914 Mexico's reactionary President Huerta had resigned as a result of pressures from Washington, and we must revert to this point in order to envision the circumstances a year and a half later. Major General Hugh Scott, U.S. Chief of Staff, was strongly backing Villa for the presidency, and so was Secretary of State Bryan, who considered him an "idealist" because he neither drank nor smoked. General Villa was then the strongest war lord in Mexico. His personal army had swelled to about 50,000 men who were on the verge of taking Mexico City; but it was Venustiano Carranza—a huge, egotistical politician with moderate views on the land question—who took control of the Mexican government August 20, 1914. Immediately he advised President Wilson to remove his troops from Veracruz, where a large U.S. force had been stationed all through the late spring and summer.* After three

* On April 10, some U.S. sailors had been arrested by the Mexicans and quickly released, with an official apology. But the American commander also demanded a 21-gun salute to the Stars and Stripes; when Huerta refused, Wilson backed the demand, Congress backed Wilson, and on April 22, the day after a German ship arrived at Veracruz with arms for Huerta, U.S. troops entered the city. In the action, 126 Mexicans were killed.

The Mexican campaign was a contest between two radically different bodies of horse-soldiers: Pershing's disciplined U.S. cavalrymen (above) and Villa's hard-riding irregulars (right). The Villistas had two advantages that in the end proved decisive—they knew the country intimately, and they enjoyed the steady and more-than-tacit support of its people.

months of prodding and veiled insults, Wilson did so. By this time the two presidents had come to despise each other in earnest. "I have never known a man more impossible to deal with," complained the American. And too late he learned that Carranza's intention was to reserve all petroleum and mineral rights for the benefit of the Mexican people. Suddenly Carranza was issuing a stream of legal decrees which were virtual death warrants against U.S. property interests in Mexico. The man, it turned out, was a thief, a communist, a double-dealer. Mr. Wilson refused to recognize him or his government.

Meanwhile Pancho had been awarding himself various small titles, such as general-in-chief of the Mexican armies and president of Mexico. As 1915 dawned, civil war between Carranza, Villa, Zapata, Obregón, and other gun-happy generals was in full swing; more U.S. citizens were being killed below the Rio Grande; and Mr. Wilson was writing furious notes to the de facto First Chief in which he warned that U.S. rights must be respected, that Carranza must terminate his antireligious program and plans for expropriating U.S. property, and so on. He advised all Americans to leave Mexico. Forty thousand out of fifty thousand departed before the end of the year. In Chihuahua, General Pancho Villa had reached his apogee of power when suddenly he was dealt two mortal blows.

First came a military catastrophe. In the past Villa

had shown talent as a resourceful tactician with a sense for communications and for handling large masses of supplies. Except for a couple of drawn engagements, he had not once been defeated in battle since the revolution had begun. In the autumn of 1915, he attacked Carranza's army in an impregnable position at Agua Prieta (south of Douglas, Arizona) and was thrown back with fearful losses. Four times Villa sent his screaming cavalry head-on against the barricaded *Federales,* in futile charges which cost him over 5,000 men. Demoralized and with the cream of its fighters gone, the rebel army melted away as it retreated toward the mountains. What had happened? President Wilson, having extended *de facto* recognition to Carranza's government, had allowed Carranza's troops and supplies to utilize U.S. railroads from Laredo and El Paso to Douglas. The same privilege had been denied Villa's men; outnumbered, they had been drawn into a trap.

At this Villa flew into a maniacal rage and swore that he would revenge himself upon the gringos. General Scott, too, was perturbed. When early in 1915 Villa had demanded the confiscation of U.S. property in areas he controlled, Scott had talked him out of it. Now Scott said:

We permitted Carranza to send his troops through the United States by our rails to crush Villa. I did what I could to prevent this . . . I had never been put in such a position in my life. After Villa had given up millions of dollars at the request of the state department . . . they made him an outlaw. He was a wild man who . . . might very well have thought that I double-crossed him . . .

The last straw had been Wilson's grudging recognition of Carranza's government that October. By 1916 Pancho was financially squeezed, down to a few thousand ragged die-hards, terrorizing the north of Mexico, merciless in his treatment of white men—the victim, in short, of official U.S. policy.

At the time General Villa was thirty-eight years old, an inch or two under six feet, slightly obese, with a handlebar mustache and narrow, murderous eyes. His real name was Doroteo Arango, which at an early age he had changed to Francisco Villa (the "Pancho" came later), the name of a celebrated outlaw of former days. From birth he and his family were impoverished mestizo serfs who planted cotton at Hacienda Rio Grande under the godlike supervision of Don Arturo López Negrete and his degenerate son, Leonardo. Pancho was in and out of jail for years on minor offenses until Leonardo deflowered his sister, Mariana. An artist with *la pistola,* Villa killed him in a stately duel of the usual western type, fled, and joined up with various bandit gangs which infested northern Mexico. Though semiliterate, he gradually rose to high command among the anti-Huerta revolutionaries.

25

His appetite for women ran in odd directions; he was known to violate fourteen-year-old Mexican girls and respectable middle-aged women, sometimes American. At the same time he was devotedly married to a placid woman (she had to be placid) named María Luz Corral. He was at the mercy of children, whom he loved and for whom he would do anything. Mad for money wherewith to acquire women and power, he spent it uncaringly in any amount.

His political views were vaguely left-wing. Mainly they ran along the lines of redistributing the swollen estates. The masses loved him and considered him a kind of Robin Hood. A nurse in El Paso described him as a "nice-looking, fair-skinned and blue-eyed man . . . he plundered and robbed the wealthy, but he was a humanitarian and distributed the loot to the poor. People would line up in long queues and he would give them money and food." He combined courage with cruelty. Once when being interviewed by a newspaperman, he was bothered by the shouting of a drunken soldier. Villa walked to the window, killed the man with a shot, and then resumed his talk.

Carranza he hated, not only because the First Chief was a conservative by Villa's rough standards but because he was a pompous civilian who had achieved power without fighting Huerta. Concerning their first meeting, Villa later said,

I embraced him energetically, but with the first few words we spoke my blood turned to ice. I saw that I could not open my heart to him. . . . He never looked me in the eye and during our entire conversation emphasized our differences in origin . . . lectured me on things like decrees and laws which I could not understand . . . There was nothing in common between that man and me . . .

Sartorially Pancho was no prize. During the early years of the revolution he had been resplendent in a general's gold-braided uniform, but after years of fighting he had tired of appearances. Usually he affected a brown turtle-neck sweater under a sweat-stained sombrero. Sometimes he wore an unpressed suit, a vest, and a shirt minus a tie.

Frequently he lived in El Paso in a hideout at Second and El Paso streets, visited the Juárez race track with such notables as General Scott, Colonel Matt Winn of Kentucky Derby fame, Tom Mix (later to be an actor), various gringo aerial pilots such as Mickey McGuire and Wild Bill Heath, Captain Sam Dreben ("the Fighting Jew"), and Colonel Giuseppe Garibaldi of the Italian liberator's family. He was never without a bodyguard. He embraced no religion. Most officers caught by his men were killed. Once when over-running Juárez, he personally supervised the execution of seventy-five Federalists. Another atrocity was described by a doctor in La Colorada:

Presently there appeared a group of men accompanied by soldiers on the opposite side of the arroyo . . . Villa arose and . . . spoke a few words, which I did not hear, to the soldiers, and the men were immediately lined up against the wall. Villa then personally shot and killed these eight men with his shooting iron, turned to us and said, "This is what

happens to enemies of Pancho Villa. People are your friends or your enemies. There can be no neutrals . . ."

He walked in a slouch. On horseback he was grace personified. He spoke little. Usually he was expressionless, except for an occasional grin which became a sinister trademark in U.S. cartoons. He loved dancing; at one wedding he danced for thirty-six hours. "He is the most natural human being I ever saw, natural in the sense of being nearest to a wild animal," wrote an observer; another said that "he was as unmoral as a wolf." A journalist described his eyes as "never still and full of energy and brutality . . . intelligent as hell and as merciless."

This was Francisco "Pancho" Villa—social revolutionary, rapist, commander of cavalry, megalomaniac —the unbalanced and almost brilliant idol of northern Mexico. It was Pershing's job to get him dead or alive.

The man who led the third and last U.S. invasion of Mexican soil was born in 1860. Both Major General Scott, Chief of Staff, and his assistant, Major General Tasker Bliss, had recommended Pershing for the assignment over the man on the spot (Major General Frederick Funston), who outranked him. Commissioned in the cavalry in 1886, he was immediately put to work against the Sioux and Apaches. During the Spanish-American War he had served at Santiago ("the coolest man under fire I ever saw," noted his commanding officer), and next performed brilliantly in the Philippines at the turn of the century, climaxing his efforts in 1903 by subduing the fanatical Moros of Mindanao. Three years later President Roosevelt promoted him to brigadier general from the rank of captain, passing him over 862 senior officers.

By 1915 he and his contingent were garrisoned at Fort Bliss. While not adequately equipped (threequarters of their saddles were defective, trucks were lacking, replacement supplies were inadequate, there were too few light guns), these men were reasonably well trained, although most of them were recruits. Pershing was not charming, nor was it his job to be charming. He was severe but fair, tall, slender, grayhaired, immaculately tailored, well-modulated in speech. He lived by a code of ethics so honorable as to be almost incomprehensible to lesser men. It is hard to imagine two humans more different than this one and Villa.

One morning that August Pershing received a tele-

In the saddle Villa was superb, but in the seats of power he and men like Emiliano Zapata, here seen at his left during their brief tenure of the National Palace, were victims of their own ignorance and the plotting of jealous rivals. They were likely to die just as they had lived—violently.

phone call from San Francisco informing him that his wife and three of their four children had just died in a fire which had swept their wooden house in the Presidio. By October he was back on duty, somewhat more silent but otherwise unchanged. Only in letters to friends did he express emotion. "I shall never be relieved of the poignancy of grief . . . It is too overwhelming!" The training and inspections went on, even more intensively. "I shall be tied down with this border patrol indefinitely. I am working just as hard as possible and am really fortunate to have something to do." So ended a bad year for Pershing and Villa; and ten weeks later came the nightmare in Columbus. . . .

The idea was to catch Villa unawares. On March 10 the White House stated that he would be captured "by a swift surprise movement." Five days later, after mountains of newspaper publicity, Pershing's column proceeded south from Columbus. ("Whose fault is it," fumed the *Army & Navy Journal*, "that the Army was obliged to advertise for 54 motor trucks before it could venture across the frontier?") What followed was to be an ironic footnote to the cavalry tradition established by Stuart and Sheridan in the Civil War, and given added luster by Chaffee, Lawton, and other Indian fighters.

Republican periodicals were especially outraged over the massacre. The New York *Tribune* stated that "the Bryan-Wilson policy . . . of dodging the duty of protecting them [U.S. citizens in Mexico] when living, and of avenging them when dead, has borne its perfect fruit." Shrieked the editorial voice of William Randolph Hearst, who preferred to have us embroiled with Mexico rather than fighting alongside the British he abhorred: "California and Texas were part of Mexico once . . . What has been done in California and Texas by the United States can be done ALL THE WAY DOWN TO THE SOUTHERN BANK OF THE PANAMA CANAL AND BEYOND."

And he further suggested: "Our flag should wave over Mexico as the symbol of the rehabilitation of that unhappy country and its redemption to humanity and civilization." From New Mexico's distraught Senator Ashurst (who had known some of the Columbus victims) came a demand for more "grape shot" and less "grape juice"—referring to the nonalcoholic soirees conducted by that contemptible pacifist, Mr. Bryan. "Nothing less than Villa's life can atone for the outrage," declared Pulitzer's New York *World*.

Army recruiting stands were hastily erected to sign up 20,000 volunteers. In Chicago an enormous banner reading "Help Catch Villa" was carried behind a military band. The volunteers did not materialize as anticipated. After a trickle of 1,269 had responded, Con-

CONTINUED ON PAGE 100

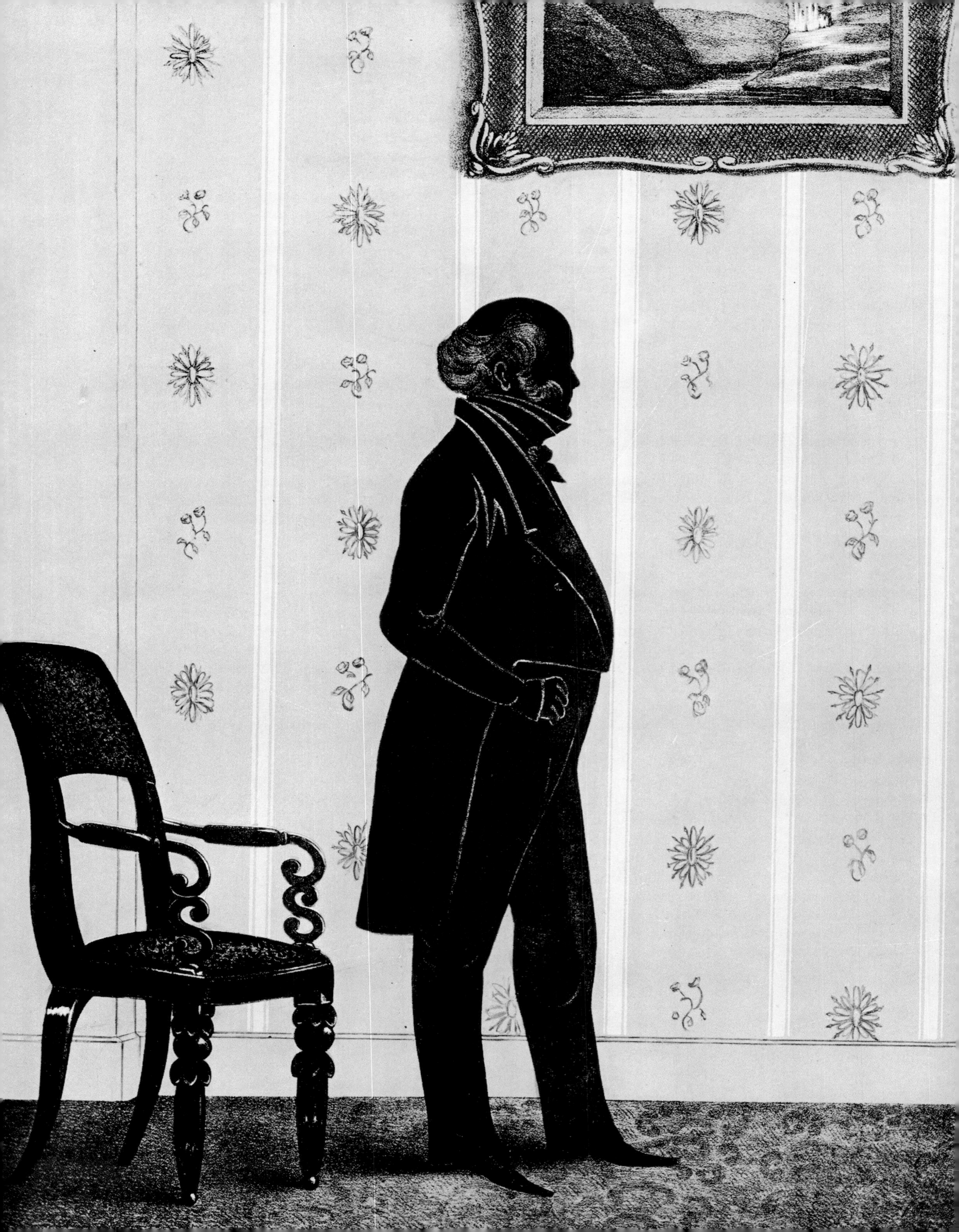

The
RISE
of the
LITTLE
MAGICIAN

Martin Van Buren, Andrew Jackson's right-hand man, was a master of political intrigue who let nothing block his one unwavering ambition—the Presidency. But sometimes he was too smart for his own good

By LOUIS W. KOENIG

Early one spring evening in 1829, a brougham, handsomely carved and immaculately kept, jogged at a dignified pace down Pennsylvania Avenue toward the White House. Within was a solitary figure sitting with the pompous grace of a Hindu rajah. He was the new Secretary of State, Martin Van Buren of New York, just arrived after a hard journey from Albany through the wilderness and cities of the seaboard. Recollections of that journey made his solitude welcome. He had much to think about. For the step he was to take this evening, in committing his services to the new President, defied the urgent warnings of many friends whose judgment he had leaned upon from the day he had become a figure in national politics. They considered him foolhardy to join this administration, and the force of their reasons still haunted his mind. The Cabinet, they unanimously contended, was packed with the minions of Vice President John C. Calhoun, who proposed to dominate the administration and advance ruthlessly to his long-cherished goal, the Presidency itself. In such company, Martin Van Buren and his political future would be hopelessly submerged.

The alarums of his friends were still ringing in Van

Buren's ears even as his carriage entered the White House grounds and approached the front portico. A lackey was on hand to open the door and help him alight. The figure that emerged was in dress and form most outstanding—scarcely more than five and a half feet and free of the corpulence that afflicts middle age. It was a pleasantry of Washington society that he wore a corset. Everything about his features seemed exaggerated; his hair was emphatically yellow and curly, parted over the right temple and combed back in wavy masses, hiding his ears. His forehead was of great proportions. Red sideburns came to the point of his jaw. His long and aggressive Roman nose suggested the fox, and his guileless, deep-set blue eyes seemed to promise, as the mood required, easy laughter and prodigious determination. His clothes were a cartoonist's delight. For years his dandylike dress had been the butt of political broadsides, and on this evening he sustained his reputation: he wore a snuff-colored coat, white trousers, lace-tipped cravat, yellow gloves, and morocco shoes.

Into the White House this impeccable little creature walked, with light tiny steps. The doorman ushered him through the vestibule to the President's office and opened the door. In the dim light of the single candle that lit that enormous room, he saw a haggard face from which bereavement had drained all spirit. For

A silhouette done from life depicts the dandylike figure of Martin Van Buren which was long the satirist's delight.

Andrew Jackson had just buried his beloved wife, and that event—coupled with the torment of ceaseless physical illness—had left him with the countenance of Job: cadaverous eyes with anguished lines beneath them, and withered white hair. But when Jackson rose, there occurred a miraculous transformation from despair and exhaustion, and his affectionate and eager greeting melted every anxiety in Van Buren's mind. Leaving his own misfortunes unmentioned, Jackson inquired anxiously about Van Buren's recent illness and, noticing his weariness, insisted that all business be postponed until the next day. Paternally, he ordered Van Buren to bed. In that short interlude, from those few gestures, Van Buren considered his decision vindicated.

The new Secretary of State had been born December 5, 1782, in a long, low, one-and-a-half-story clapboard farmhouse in Kinderhook, New York. His parents were second-generation Dutch-Americans, who regularly spoke the ancestral language at the dinner table. The father, Abraham, a farmer and tavern operator, was one of the few local residents well-to-do enough to meet the stiff suffrage requirement—ownership of land valued at a hundred pounds over and above encumbrances. At school age, Martin was enrolled in the Kinderhook Academy, where he compiled a good record. His heart was set on entering Columbia College, when his father's finances went into an unexpected tailspin and the boy was forced to go to work. The change of plan left its scar. Forever after, Van Buren venerated the learning that had been denied him—so much so that he developed a conspicuous sense of intellectual inferiority.

His dandyish dress had origins in his youth, too. His schooling ended, family friends secured a clerkship for him in the offices of Francis Sylvester, first lawyer of Kinderhook. Van Buren showed up for his job in coarse homespun linens and woolens made by his economy-minded mother. His employer, appalled by this ungainly apparition, finally took his clerk aside and ardently lectured him on the importance of proper dress. Next day Van Buren had undergone a sartorial transformation that left Sylvester gasping: he was decked out in a complete gentleman's outfit consisting of a black broad-brimmed cocked hat, a waistcoat with layers of frilly lace, velvet breeches, silken hose, and huge flashing silver buckles.

Although Van Buren rose rapidly in the legal profession, politics was his consuming passion. He so excelled at composing differences in the local Democratic caucus that he was rewarded with a major plum—election at twenty-six as surrogate of Columbia County. A year later, in 1809, he cut short his honeymoon with Hannah Hoes to go off into the deep snows for the hustings. In 1812, Van Buren was elected state senator.

Simultaneously, Van Buren was ascending to a leading place in party councils, owing not so much to his devotion to policy as to his gifts at political management. He presided over an enormously successful Democratic organization, the "Albany Regency," a handful of state leaders who traded jobs in the executive branch for votes in the legislature and made their bargains stick.

In 1821, after a term as New York's attorney general, Van Buren stepped onto the national political stage when the Regency boosted him into the United States Senate. By every appearance, his coming made no great splash. Though Van Buren toiled with exemplary diligence on the finance and judiciary committees, he became identified with no significant legislation. He spoke infrequently on the floor and seldom with much impact, his pianissimo style of oratory being hopelessly drowned out by the organ tones of titans like Daniel Webster, Robert Hayne, and John C. Calhoun.

As head of the prevailing party in New York, however, he became a leading influence in the congressional caucus and in the wide-open presidential race of 1824. In choosing among the many candidates entreating his support, Van Buren, in the manner of his hero, Thomas Jefferson, aimed to link the power of

The rejected Minister, We never can make him President, without first making him Vice president this week

A cartoon that appeared in 1832, shortly after the Senate's rejection of Van Buren as Minister to Great Britain, ribbed him for his efforts to "reach the throne" on Jackson's back.

New York with that of the South. Accordingly he came out for the leading southern candidate, William H. Crawford, a Georgian who had been Secretary of the Treasury in the Monroe Cabinet.

Van Buren's first venture in the "art and business of President-making," as he called it, was totally disastrous. Hardly had Crawford announced his candidacy when he was felled by a general paralytic stroke. His nervous system was shattered; he permanently lost the use of his lower limbs and temporarily, his sight and speech. Still, pressed by Van Buren, Crawford stayed in the race. The candidate's distraught promoters labored overtime at hiding his distress from public view. He made no speeches; a tightly covered coach carried him about when travel was unavoidable. Whenever a meeting with impressionable visitors was necessary, they were ushered into a room so darkened by heavy curtains and dimmed lights that the pitiful Crawford, propped between several devoted associates, was scarcely visible. Hardly had a visitor settled into his chair when he was, on some pretext or other, whisked out. Notwithstanding these precautions, rumors got around that Crawford was a very sick man. In desperation, Van Buren attempted a bold eleventh-hour deal: he offered Henry Clay of Kentucky the Vice Presidency if he would support Crawford. Clay turned him down cold.

The sly maneuver and the ruthless machination provide the basis for much of Martin Van Buren's lasting political reputation. All his nicknames—and no other public figure in his time or perhaps since has had so many—betoken the unprincipled political trickster. "The Little Magician" and "the Red Fox of Kinderhook" he was first called in New York politics, and later "the American Talleyrand." DeWitt Clinton spoke of Van Buren as "the prince of villains" and "a confirmed knave." Calhoun, a later foe, said of him: "He is not . . . of the race of the lion or of the tiger; he belonged to a lower order—the fox."

In his private ruminations following the calamitous elections of 1824, Van Buren decided to hitch his wagon to the rising star of Andrew Jackson. In the three-way race among Jackson, Crawford, and John Quincy Adams, the hero of New Orleans had, after all, garnered the largest popular vote, and had lost to Adams only when the election was thrown into the House of Representatives. For the next several years, Van Buren worked quietly and successfully to bring the Crawford men into Jackson's fold. In 1828, Old Hickory triumphed at the polls and fittingly offered "the Magician," who in the same year became Governor of New York, the choicest spot in the new administration, the post of Secretary of State.

By every indication, Van Buren proposed to be far more than a mere presidential counselor: he intended to do nothing less than succeed General Jackson in the Presidency itself, and, everything considered, this steadily burning ambition was altogether reasonable. It was widely believed that Jackson did not have long to live. The creeping dropsy, the racking cough, the wizened frame signified a man whose days were numbered. There was, further, an enthralling statistic in Van Buren's favor: in the twenty-eight years subsequent to 1800, four secretaries of state had become President.

Van Buren was not the only party of interest hungering for the succession. His most redoubtable competitor was John C. Calhoun, a man of consuming drive, maturer national political experience, and wider public fame. The Van Buren-Calhoun competition was hardly a matter of conjecture; it was starkly manifested even before the inauguration when both camps launched a series of maneuvers designed to control the selection of the Cabinet. Van Buren trained his guns on the two departments richest in patronage, the Treasury and the Post Office. To his great chagrin, both posts went to loyal Calhounites. As Secretary of War, Jackson chose his longtime friend from Tennessee, John H. Eaton, whose preference between Van Buren and Calhoun was not at all clear. The two other members of the Cabinet, the Attorney General and the Secretary of the Navy, were mediocrities who, when the cards were down, were expected to throw in with Calhoun. However, Van Buren's companionship was much welcomed, both during business hours and after, by a President just emerging from the pit of tragedy. Van Buren was also a widower (Hannah had died in 1819), and Jackson found in him the solace of shared experience. The New Yorker was a constant visitor at the Executive Mansion. Unconstrained by the demands of family, he could respond to every beck and call.

Van Buren moved easily in the considerable circle of personalities residing in the White House. In its size and essential informality, the circle was unprecedented. Besides the President, it included his nephew and confidential secretary, the astute and discreet Andrew Jackson Donelson, and his wife Emily, a spare, aristocratic beauty who presided expertly as official White House hostess. Also in residence were the President's old friend and political bodyguard, William B. Lewis; Mrs. Donelson's attractive cousin, Mary Eastin (Van Buren's eldest son, Abraham, was courting her); and the President's adopted son, Andrew, and his family. Together, the several families contributed four children to the White House population. These were considerably augmented by other

CONTINUED ON PAGE 88

PICTURES PAPERS IN THE

Born in the 1840's, the era of the woodblock and the "view taken from nature," early pictorial journalism left behind a matchless treasure of history

By ROGER BUTTERFIELD

On May 30, 1842, a young Englishman named John Francis drew a pistol from his waistcoat pocket and fired a shot at Queen Victoria as she rode by in an open carriage. A police constable grabbed the would-be assassin just as he pressed the trigger, so his bullet whizzed harmlessly through the air. His effort made history nonetheless, for it became the subject of the first spot news picture in the world's first pictorial newspaper, the still surviving—and still great—*Illustrated London News.*

This pioneer picture is reproduced in the portfolio that accompanies this article. Pictorial journalism, as a distinct profession, technique, and business, is now 120 years old. Its newest productions are not necessarily its most handsome or entertaining—as the display of older American papers on the opposite page may suggest.

Of course some people have always expected that a public fed on pictures would stop reading words entirely. Pictorial journalism was still very young when William Wordsworth wrote a gloomy sonnet entitled "Illustrated Books and Newspapers":

> Now prose and verse sunk into disrepute,
> Must lacquey a dumb Art that best can suit
> The taste of this once-intellectual Land.
> A backward movement surely have we here,
> From manhood,—back to childhood. . .
> Avaunt this vile abuse of pictured page!
> Must eyes be all-in-all, the tongue and ear
> Nothing? Heaven keep us from a lower stage!

Yet in spite of the Poet Laureate's disdain, and much justified criticism over the years, the pictorial press as an institution has never stopped expanding. In numbers of individual papers and variety of interest, it probably reached its peak in the 1880's and 90's. But in total circulation and its mastery over popular taste, it was never more imposing than it is today.

To historians all this is useful, and is even becoming essential. The intimate manuscript letters and diaries through which so much of the past is studied are rarely produced in this mechanized age. But intimate photography is everywhere, even behind the President's rocking chair, and with it now is the electronic ear of television, which records whatever it hears. These instruments cannot read man's secret thoughts—at least not yet—but they perpetuate more facts about his activities than any previous period dreamed of.

The connection between picture news and history was stressed from the beginning. In the preface to the very first volume of the *Illustrated London News,* for the year 1842, is this charming example of Victorian promotion copy:

What would Sir Walter Scott or any of the great writers of modern times have given . . . for any museum-preserved volume such as we have here enshrined. The life of the times—the signs of its taste and intelligence—its public monuments and public men—its festivals—institutions—amusements—discoveries—and the very reflection of its living manners and costumes—all . . . these would have lain hid in Time's tomb or perished amid the sand of his hour-glass

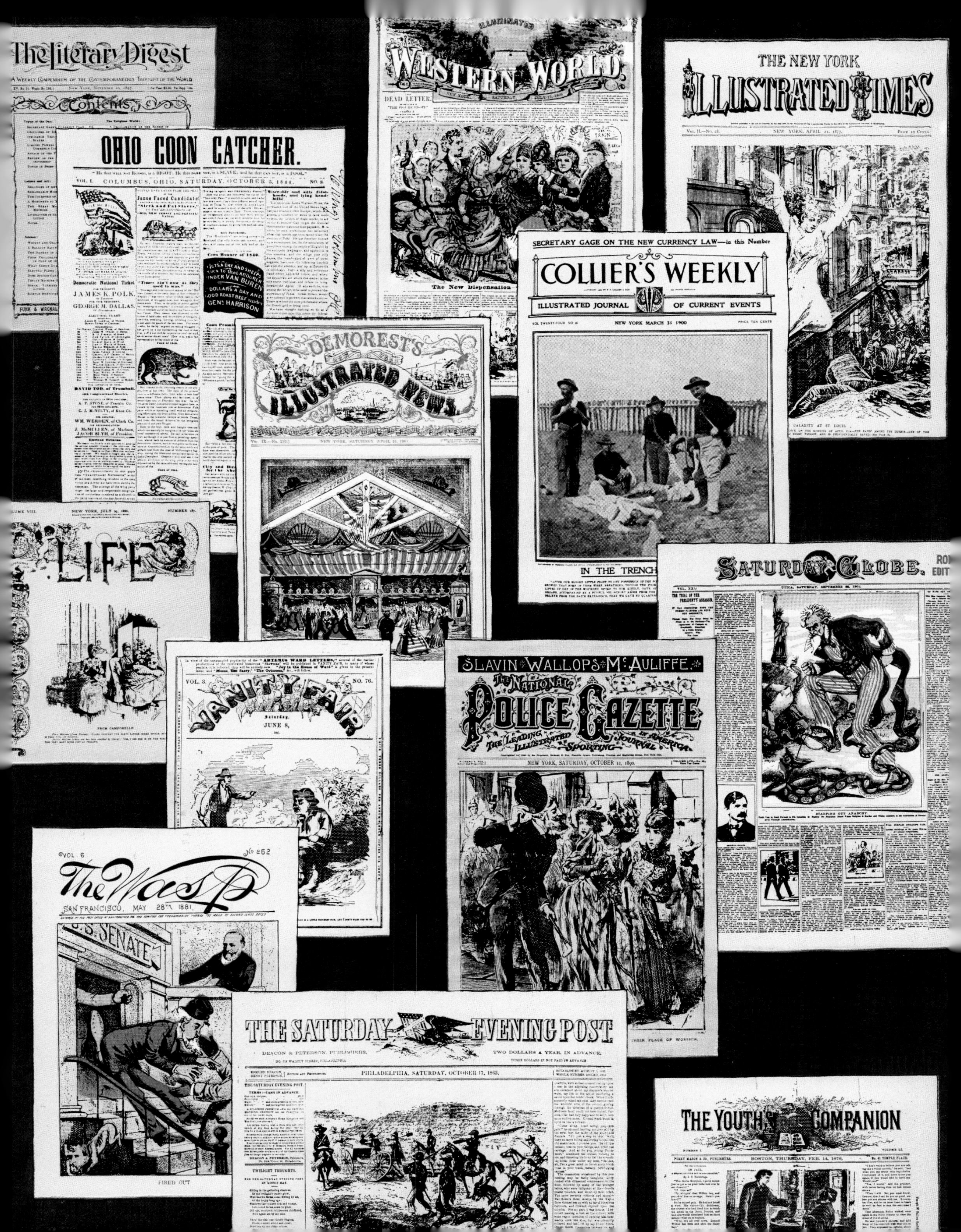
The Literary Digest
A Weekly Compendium of the Contemporaneous Thought of the World
Contents

OHIO COON CATCHER.
"He that will not Reason, is a BIGOT; He that dare not, is a SLAVE; and he that can not, is a FOOL."
VOL. I. COLUMBUS, OHIO, SATURDAY, OCTOBER 5, 1844. NO. 8.
Democratic National Ticket.
JAMES K. POLK,
GEORGE M. DALLAS,
Janus Faced Candidate!
Coon Hunter of 1840.
"Times ain't now as they used to was."
DAVID TOD, of Trumbull.
WM. WERDEN, of Clark Co.
FUNK & WAGNALLS

ILLUSTRATED WESTERN WORLD
DEAD LETTER.
The New Dispensation

THE NEW YORK ILLUSTRATED TIMES
Vol. II.—No. 28. NEW YORK, APRIL 21, 1877. Price 10 Cents.
CALAMITY AT ST. LOUIS.

SECRETARY GAGE ON THE NEW CURRENCY LAW—in this Number
COLLIER'S WEEKLY
ILLUSTRATED JOURNAL OF CURRENT EVENTS
VOL. TWENTY-FOUR NO. 26 NEW YORK MARCH 31 1900 PRICE TEN CENTS
IN THE TRENCH

DEMOREST'S ILLUSTRATED NEWS.
NEW YORK, SATURDAY, APRIL 16, 1864.

LIFE
NEW YORK, JULY 1886. NUMBER 187.
FROM CAMPOBELLO.

VANITY FAIR
VOL. 3. NO. 76.
Saturday, JUNE 8, 1861.

SATURDAY GLOBE.
UTICA, SATURDAY, SEPTEMBER 1901.
THE TRIAL OF THE PRESIDENT'S ASSASSIN.
STAMPING OUT ANARCHY.

SLAVIN WALLOPS MC AULIFFE.
The National POLICE GAZETTE
THE LEADING ILLUSTRATED SPORTING JOURNAL IN AMERICA.
NEW YORK, SATURDAY, OCTOBER 11, 1890.
THEIR PLACE OF WORSHIP.

VOL. 6 No 252
The Wasp
SAN FRANCISCO, MAY 28TH 1881.
FIRED OUT

THE SATURDAY EVENING POST.
DEACON & PETERSON, PUBLISHERS. TWO DOLLARS A YEAR, IN ADVANCE.
PHILADELPHIA, SATURDAY, OCTOBER 17, 1863.
TWILIGHT THOUGHTS.

THE YOUTH'S COMPANION
PERRY MASON & CO., PUBLISHERS. BOSTON, THURSDAY, FEB. 14, 1878.

but for the enduring and resuscitating powers of art. . . Could the days of Elizabeth or others as bright and earlier still be unfolded to us through such a mirror what a mint of wisdom might we gather. . . !

Of just as much captivating value then is such a book to the future. It will pour the lore of the Antiquarian into the scholar's yearning soul, and teach him truth about those who have gone before him. . . This volume is a work that history *must* keep.

So far as the *Illustrated London News* is concerned, these words are lastingly true. Its bound volumes are a matchless treasury of the whole world's history, as seen through English eyes. From the start it put special emphasis on the speedy gathering and dramatic picturing of news. Since nobody had done this before, it had to invent its own techniques.

All of its early pictures were woodcuts, drawn on the wood by artists and then engraved by craftsmen who were often artists too. But it began making use of photography before the end of its first year. It commissioned one M. Claudet, a manipulator of the newly invented Daguerrean apparatus, to build a stand on the Duke of York's column, 120 feet high, and take the first photographic portrait of the city of London. The resulting print, distributed with the issue for January 7, 1843, was almost four feet wide and three feet deep, consisting of two engraved panoramas, looking north and south from the column. It is still the biggest pictorial bonus ever issued to subscribers of any magazine or newspaper.

As the earliest specimen of photojournalism, the London print was a historic achievement. But in terms of technical enterprise, it was simply astounding. The picture began with "a very great many" small silver daguerreotype plates which were copied in pencil by an artist working on top of the column alongside M. Claudet. (Thus he could, as the paper explained, fill in "small deficiencies . . . from nature.") After being fitted together, the whole picture was copied again on a prodigious block of Turkish boxwood, which all engravers preferred to use because of its special hardness. This block, however, was not a single piece of wood; the engraving was done across the grain, and even the best boxwood timber did not provide cross-section slices more than six or seven inches wide. It was for the *Illustrated London News*—and in part for this very picture—that Charles Wells of Lambeth perfected a method of fastening boxwood sections together with bolts inserted through channels in the back, to form a single smooth surface of very large size. This was far superior to gluing or cementing, and it made possible the printing of full-page and double-page pictures on the presses used by newspapers.

In the case of the great London print, the drawing was done on the full-sized block, which was then unbolted in the back, and the sixty separate sections of boxwood were distributed among nineteen engravers for cutting. Already these quick-fingered experts were doing their job in assembly-line fashion—certain specialists engraved only architecture, others did trees and foliage, and others shaded in the "tints," which was the term used for light and shadow effects. We are told that this one engraving took two months to complete, "the work never stopping night or day." Finally, because the outsized block was much too valuable to risk in a steam press, where heat and moisture might warp the wood, it was pressed into soft clay, and a solid metal stereotype was cast and used for the actual printing.

On May 28, 1842, in its third issue, the *Illustrated London News* published its first "candid" picture—"A SCENE IN THE NURSERY AT CLAREMONT"—showing the young Queen Victoria holding the Prince of Wales on her lap. Some Britishers thought that this invasion of privacy was unpatriotic and probably illegal, but the Queen didn't seem to mind. The editors, as usual, fended off criticism with a bouquet of graceful prose:

Our Artist has chosen for illustration one of those happy moments of maternal life when the magnificence and etiquette of the Queen is put aside by womanly tenderness for the expression of a mother's love. . . But far be it from us to intrude further upon the secresy of such domestic scenes, although the feelings of all fathers and mothers amongst her Majesty's most loving and loyal of all subjects, cannot be prevented following her in thought and with heart. . .

A few months later the *Illustrated London News* published the first double spread of pictures ever to appear in a magazine or newspaper, thus opening up the layout techniques that are still standard in pictorial journalism. The subject of this *coup d'oeil,* as the caption writer called it, was a tour of Scotland by the Queen and her handsome Consort, Prince Albert. The paper boasted that its "distinguished artist" had secured "a position near the immediate escort of our Sovereign during the whole progress of her journey." This was the first time an artist-reporter was assigned to cover a running story at any great distance from home.

By the time of the Crimean War in 1854, the *Illustrated London News* had developed all the basic techniques for reporting great events in pictures. Beautifully executed views of fortifications, harbors, and camps—often much more revealing than photographs—were rushed from the battlefront into print, along with pictures of violent combat for which the "special artists" endangered their lives. One artist sketched the

TEXT CONTINUED ON PAGE 96
ILLUSTRATIONS CONTINUE ON THE FOLLOWING PAGES

THE PICTORIAL PRESS IN THE
NINETEENTH CENTURY

AN AFFECTIONATE PORTFOLIO

In the pages that follow are some of the actual news pictures and cartoons and historic front pages that marked the rise of pictorial journalism up to the year 1900. All of these are from the collection assembled by Roger Butterfield, author of the accompanying article, and recently acquired by the New York State Historical Association at Cooperstown. With its 200,000 items —books and pamphlets, broadsides and catalogues, newspapers and magazines—it has long been recognized as one of the finest private collections of Americana in this country. The editors of AMERICAN HERITAGE—a more recent arrival among pictorial magazines—are pleased to present this visual salute to the pioneers of a great profession.

THE ILLUSTRATED LONDON NEWS

No. 4.]　　　FOR THE WEEK ENDING SATURDAY, JUNE 4, 1842.　　　[SIXPENCE.

ATTEMPTED ASSASSINATION OF THE QUEEN.

LOUD and loyally as the universal voice of England has outspoken its affection for our Sovereign from the first happy omen of her accession to the throne of her ancestors, through all the events and influences of her interesting career, it would still seem that national love is insufficient to guard against the insidious approaches of isolated crime, and that the person held most sacred, and deemed most dear by all the good and virtuous who dwell in the land she governs, may have to brook the hazard of individual treason, and dare the peril of madness or murder in the bosom of her people and at the threshold of her throne. Our dear and noble Queen has been once more exposed to the danger of assassination, and once more protected by the providence of God. The passions of the million are indignant in the conviction of her peril, but anon, the heart of the empire is electric with the joy of her escape.

Our readers will find elsewhere a detail of all the features and circumstances of this new atrocity, but we shall presently show that it is a theme for reflection in a broader social sense than that in which it is first taken under the delirium of popular excitement, and the warm impulses and agitation of a loyal love. It is an event that should run into the deeper channels of thought, and be regarded with other aspects than that which it presents in the first blush of its dire enormity. Morality and philosophy should combine to defend themselves against the growing up of that morbid and insane species of wickedness of which this is only the last and most execrated example.

Let us describe the crime—the second (and therefore the more serious) that has directed its malignity against her Majesty's life.

We are supposed to dwell in a well-ordered country—a land wherein social virtue has been more studied, and social decorum more firmly maintained, than in any other within the pale of civilization. A land where peace is the result of prowess—wealth the land-mark of order—manliness the symbol of the people and their institutions, and loyalty the motto engraved upon the national heart. Religion, too, holds a strong and temperate sway over all—none despise it—none dare outrage it. Society has undergone none of the disorganizing influences that have made a wreck of the morality of France. There is no *public* infidelity, and revolution is a word hated by all but those whom all men ought to hate. Political excitements have gathered upon us; but we are still far from having allowed these to stir one brick in the beautiful social fabric which enshrines the love, the religion, and the happiness of the empire.

Well, in such a condition of national existence, a Sovereign and a woman—young, beautiful, and virtuous—sways our destinies and commands our respect. She sits like the spirit of goodness and purity—the grace of England's throne. As a queen, she wears the lofty aspect and the proud bearing of one in whom dignity and decision are inborn. As a woman, she tempers her queendom with the mild and winning gentleness of her sex. As a wife, she is exemplary; and has the happiness, so rarely awarded to those who have in marriage to consult expediency more than affection, of loving and being loved. As the mother of her children, she is (the best virtue we can give her) what *her* mother was to *her*; and, lastly, as the mother of her people, she has blessed the common family with benignant sway—she has promoted their interests—partaken of their diversions—sympathized with their depressions—listened to their grievances, and participated in all their joys. She is, in a word, at once the focus and embodiment of the people's affections. What then? Why, in the pleasurable exercise of a daily familiarity with her subjects—in the very disporting of her beautiful confidence in the loyalty she has earned—in the strength of her own virtue as a queen—in the companionship of her husband—and under the shield of a popularity, as universal as it is intense, the arm of the assassin is raised to take her life; and the unconscious young one, who, in the happiness of her cheerful spirit,

believed that all was love around her, might, in another second, have winged her soul to Heaven; to leave behind her, along with a blessed memory, a husband widowed—children orphaned—and a whole nation weeping, and darkened with the mourning garments of grief!

What human motive could point to such a result—what passion could be gratified—what accountable design achieved? There are but two clues to the commission of such a crime, and they are either treason and conspiracy of the blackest dye, and couched in the most inconceivable spirit;—or madness, engendered by an imaginative gloating over similar works of evil that have made loud notoriety, and registered their hideous example for the dangerous contemplation of wild and morbid minds. This last is what we fear; and in the instance before us, both fear and hope. It seems impossible to find the impulse in mere treason; for had the Queen been shot, no proximate aim of treason could have been attained. There is a future king training for the succession; and were revolution the aim, there is nothing in the Sovereign's death that could revolutionize the empire. The King of Hanover does not now stand next the throne; and were her Majesty to be hurried into immortality by any sudden event, there is not manifest one single element of unpopularity that she could leave behind her. No commotion save that of sorrow could be stirred—no ambition of party could be forwarded—no malice could be gratified —there would be nothing to triumph over, and no one to rejoice. No! it should seem that madness—madness only—is the incitement to the crime.

The wretched being who has attempted an act for which no punishment could be too dreadful, no retribution too severe, if sense were linked with sin—seems, with the singular mental sympathies of criminals of his morbid class, to have followed precisely in the wake of his predecessor, Oxford—he is equally without a motive, he takes the same weapon, he repairs to the same spot, he seeks to work out his wanton mischief with total absence of contrivance, as if he knew no responsibility but the goading impulse of a resistless infatuation.

We are of those who believe that the spirit in which this would-be regicide went to his deadly purpose, is a spirit engendered by the notoriety of crime. We apply the remark not less to the fearful act before us, than to some of the remarkable suicides, and still more atrocious murders, of recent date.

In the celebrity of a most paramount wickedness, with men of morbid imagination, consists its charm. It fixes them with the eye of a basilisk, it haunts their visions, it colours their waking fancies, it lures them into the circle of monstrosity, it plunges the mind into delusion, and steeps the eye in blood. A bad example is ever more contagious than a good one; but there is nothing to equal the contagion of any glaring and outrageous enormity to the hopeless, idle, ever-dreaming wretch, who gazes upon its notoriety with envy, and with the wild ambition of a fanatic, resolves to build up the shrine of a bad eminence in the blackest corner of the temple of crime.

It is against the "growing up of this insane species of wickedness" as a wondrous social evil, that we would enlist "philosophy and morality," in the spirit of one of the earlier sentences of this article—the first of several which we purpose writing on the subject,—and, to the end of our future arguments, as well as of our present hope, we predict that in this morbid madness lies the secret of the attempted assassination of our beloved Queen; should it prove otherwise, we are of those who would rush into the very heart and vortex of that mighty flood of popular passion which is everywhere raging for punishment upon one who is only not a monster and a miscreant unless he be horribly and hopelessly mad. We would not fly in the face of an affliction from Heaven—but we would visit upon the sane assassin the most woeful of the retributions of earth.

Now, however, let us leave alike the speculation of philosophy, or the cry of vengeance, to swell the torrent of loyal and exhilarating congratulation which crowns the preservation of our Sovereign —which strengthens the love of her people, by bringing full upon their hearts and before their glance the priceless value of the treasure that has been risked—which is glistening in the eyes of every gathered multitude of Englishmen, and fluttering with wild and tremulous happiness the beating bosom of the land.

PARTICULARS OF THE COWARDLY AND DISGRACEFUL ATTEMPT ON THE LIFE OF HER MAJESTY.

Shortly after the return of Prince Albert to Buckingham Palace on Monday afternoon, her Majesty, accompanied by his Royal Highness, proceeded in an open carriage and four horses, preceded by outriders, for her accustomed drive in Hyde Park, &c., the royal equerries, as usual, accompanying the *cortège* on horseback. On her Majesty's return about ten minutes or a quarter past six o'clock down Constitution-hill, when within a few yards of the spot at which the former attempt at her assassination was made by the boy Oxford, a young man, who had previously been noticed standing with his back against the brick wall skirting the garden of Buckingham Palace, was observed to advance towards the road along which the royal *cortège* was passing, and upon the carriage approaching the spot at which he stood, he was seen by police-constable Tounce, A 53, to advance within three yards of it, and at the same instant take from his waist-coat pocket a pistol. Tounce instantly rushed towards him for the purpose of knocking it out of his hand, seeing that it was aimed at her Majesty, but at the moment he seized him the pistol went off

While shepherds watched their flocks by night, — All seated on the ground

Our two opening pages are devoted to the world's first picture newspaper, which has appeared each week for 120 years under its familiar heading of the Thames water front and St. Paul's dome. The parade of top-hatted placard men shown in the woodcut below promoted the sale of the first issue of the *Illustrated London News,* for May 14, 1842. The first authentic spot-news picture in history appeared on page one of its fourth issue, reproduced on the opposite page; this was in the hands of readers only five days after the "disgraceful attempt" to assassinate the Queen. Color printing was inaugurated in the Christmas supplement for 1855, above. The "house ad" at the right describes its reporting triumphs during the Crimean War.

DECEMBER 23, 1854

THE
ILLUSTRATED LONDON NEWS.
TO THE
1,000,000
READERS!

THE means by which the Gallery of Pictures in the ILLUSTRATED LONDON NEWS is produced, present striking instances of rapidity, skill, and truthful representation, such as can only be ensured in an age whose scientific triumphs, it has been said, bid fair "to annihilate time and space." The Steamboat, the Railway, and the Daguerréotype have greatly aided the genius of Art in the execution of the enterprise which first projected the ILLUSTRATED LONDON NEWS, in which the Pictures and Letterpress possess the same living interest. It has been well remarked, what valuable records would have been similar journals of ancient nations; and which would have exceeded in interest even the sculptures which, in our time, have been excavated from the sand of ages.

The production of a Picture in the ILLUSTRATED LONDON NEWS is briefly told. The locality, event, or incident, is sketched by an eye-witness, one of the professional artists of the Journal, or one of the contributors at home or abroad. Perchance it is a piece of artistic news from the seat of war, sketched in the "tented field," in the fleet, or before the fortress walls; and is forthwith dispatched by post. In many cases the photographic process is employed, as in details of the wonders of the Great Exhibition of 1851; and the same process is employed for portraits of distinguished personages, pictures, works of art, &c.

To individualize all the eventful scenes represented in the ILLUSTRATED LONDON NEWS, since its commencement, would far exceed the present limit. Among the memorable events, her Majesty's visit to various portions of her own dominions, and the Continent, have yielded many scenes of loyal welcome and picturesque festivity; the wars of Kaffraria and Hindostan, many important incidents of conquest and defeat. The French Revolution; the Great Exhibition of 1851; and the Gold Discoveries in California and Australia, have presented a succession of scenes of varied interest. The death and funeral of the great Duke of Wellington are recorded in this pictorial chronicle; and some of the numbers illustrating these events, attained the unprecedented sale of Two Hundred and Fifty Thousand Copies in one week! The war with Russia has greatly extended the fame of this Journal, whilst it has tested its success in the Illustration of great events of the time, by means of Artists, despatched to the several localities of the War. By such aids and appliances, the ILLUSTRATED LONDON NEWS has attained the weekly circulation of upwards of One Hundred and Thirty Thousand copies! Occasionally, large Pictures of the most stirring events are presented gratuitously to Subscribers with supplementary Numbers. The Journal has also been permanently enlarged to allow a fuller account of the News of the Week to be given; thus rendering it in every way worthy of becoming

THE FAMILY NEWSPAPER.

Give an order for six months, to ensure all the gratuitous Prints and Supplements. Supplied by all Booksellers and Newsmen.

OFFICE, 198, STRAND, LONDON.

THE "ILLUSTRATED LONDON NEWS," PUBLISHED EVERY SATURDAY. THIRTY ENGRAVINGS. PRICE SIXPENCE.
The above Engraving represents the public announcement of this Paper on Friday last. Two hundred men paraded the streets of London to proclaim the advent of this important publication.

PRINCETON.　　　　VERMONT.　　ALLEGHANY.　　　ST. MARY'S.　　　　MACEDONIAN　　　VANDALIA.　　　PLYMOUTH.　　SARATOGA.

A SUPERB VIEW OF THE UNITED STATES JAPANESE SQUADRON,

UNDER COMMAND OF COMMO

A PICTORIAL PIONEER IN BOSTON

The first American picture weekly imitated the *Illustrated London News* even in its engraved heading, which was an obvious attempt to make Boston's harbor and State House look like the English magazine's view of the Thames. *Gleason's* began on May 3, 1851, changed its name to *Ballou's* in 1855, and died in 1859. Although it was printed in Boston, some of its best engravings were created elsewhere, like the splendid double-page spread, below, of Commodore Matthew Perry being rowed out to his flagship off Norfolk, at the start of his voyage to Japan. This was drawn and engraved by New York artists who probably did not see the fleet depart but followed existing pictures of the ships, and their imagination. Such double-page layouts were pioneered by the *Illustrated London News*, which developed a method of joining small wood blocks into a large engraving surface. In the cuts below, the fine white lines of separation are barely visible.

RETURNED CALIFORNIANS WAITING AT THE MINT.

One day in 1851 a free-lance artist named Devereux happened to pass the Philadelphia Mint while a group of California miners were waiting to have their gold dust weighed. He made a sketch without disturbing his subjects, who are strewn across the hard stone steps in various natural attitudes. The resulting woodcut was a genuine triumph of "candid" pictorial reporting. *Gleason's* gave it added importance by naming the artist—the first time this was done in a U.S. picture weekly.

'PI, (FLAG SHIP.)   SUSQUEHANNA.   POWHATAN.

Y, BOUND FOR THE EAST.

FEBRUARY 12, 1853

THE WEEKLY HERALD.

Vol. X., No. 26.

NEW YORK, SATURDAY, JUNE 28, 1845.

Whole No. 404.

GRAND FUNERAL PROCESSION

IN MEMORY OF

Officiating Clergymen—Orator of the Day—Ex-President Van Buren—His Excellency Governor Wright.—The Court for Correction of Errors—State Officers—Ex-Governors—Clergy and other Invited Guests of the Corporation—in Carriages

Preceded by the Light Guard, and Independence Guard—Scotch Company of Artillery, &c. General Scott Commanding the Army of United States.—The Commanding Officer of the United States Military Districts and Aids—Colonel Bankhead

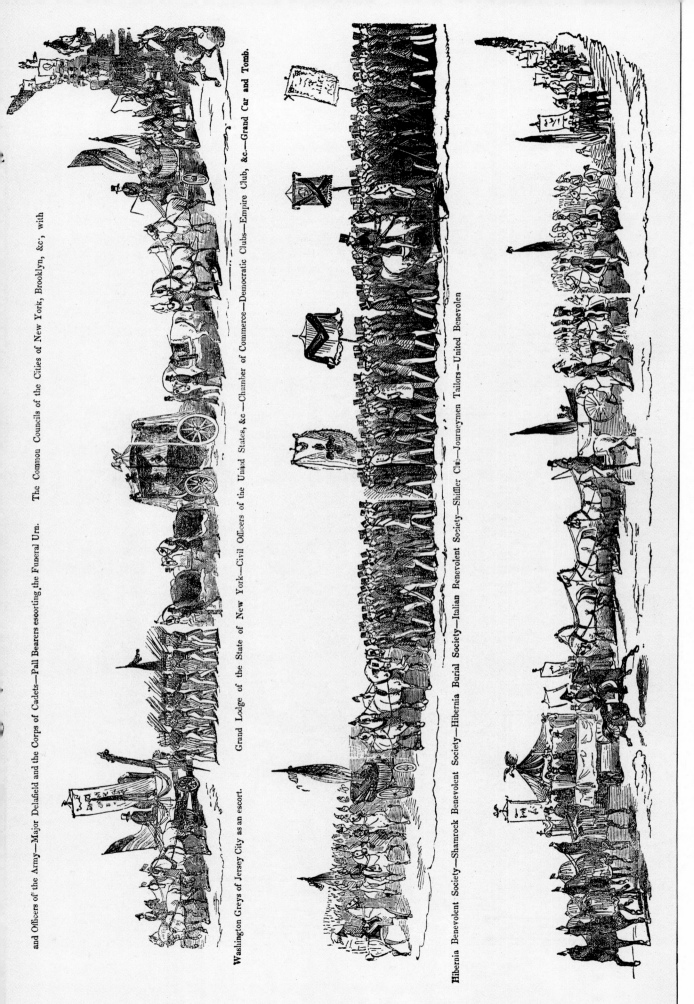

and Officers of the Army—Major Delafield and the Corps of Cadets—Pall Bearers escorting the Funeral Urn. The Common Councils of the Cities of New York, Brooklyn, &c., with

Washington Greys of Jersey City as an escort. Grand Lodge of the State of New York—Civil Officers of the United States, &c.—Chamber of Commerce—Democratic Clubs—Empire Club, &c.—Grand Car and Tomb.

Hibernia Benevolent Society—Shamrock Benevolent Society—Hibernia Burial Society—Italian Benevolent Society—Shiffler Club—Journeymen Tailors—United Benevolen

This first full page of pictures ever published in an American newspaper shows how New York City mourned the death of ex-President Jackson. The engravings appeared first in the daily *Herald*; in transferring them to the weekly edition, the printers lost some of the caption type. Bennett's penny daily *Herald* began printing occasional news pictures in 1835 but was never strictly an illustrated paper. After 1850 the *Herald* and most other American dailies gave up pictures entirely, thus leaving pictorial journalism to the weeklies.

FRANK LESLIE'S
ILLUSTRATED

NEWSPAPER

Entered according to Act of Congress in the year 1857, by FRANK LESLIE, in the Clerk's Office of the District Court for the Southern District of New York. (Copyrighted May 10, 1858.)

No. 128—Vol. V.]   NEW YORK, SATURDAY, MAY 15, 1858.   [PRICE 6 CENTS.

OUR EXPOSURE OF THE MILK TRADE OF NEW YORK AND BROOKLYN.

FROM a hundred sources we are receiving, day by day, thanks for our public spirit and fearless exposure of a nefarious and revolting trade, and good wishes and prayers for the ultimate and speedy success of our undertaking.

We feel sincerely gratified and deeply grateful for the outside encouragement we receive; it will move us to new exertions, for we feel that we have obtained the ear of the public; that its sympathies and hopes are with us, and armed with this assurance we feel our power equal to the emergency. That our blows have been dealt strongly and truly we have ample evidence. Our exposure has not only broken up all the milk routes we have published, but one whose name we were fortunately enabled to give, is selling off his swill milk cows. His stable is broken up, his swill trade, gone, and mark the consequence—he has contracted with the country dairies for the milk he requires for his customers. Is not the good work begun? May we not hope for the future?

EXPOSURE OF THE MILK TRADE.—MILKING THE DYING COW. WHEN THE ANIMAL, FROM DISEASE AND ULCERATION, CAN NO LONGER STAND, MECHANICAL MEANS ARE USED TO SUPPORT IT WHILE UNDER MILKING, AND THE PROCESS IS CONTINUED UNTIL THE COW DIES. THE MILK IS USED WITH THE REST. SEE PAGE 380.

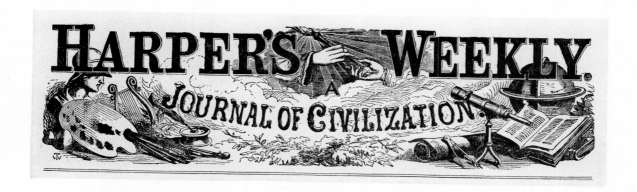

PICTURE REPORTING, AMERICAN STYLE

In the United States the best picture weeklies were *Frank Leslie's* and *Harper's*, which began in 1855 and 1857 respectively. Both were directly inspired by the success of the *Illustrated London News* but quickly developed styles of their own. *Leslie's* featured hairsbreadth thrills and sensational crusades; the dying cow on the opposite page was one of the many harrowing scenes it printed while battling to clean up the milk supply of New York. *Harper's* was more sedate—as befitted "A Journal of Civilization"—but it pulled ahead in circulation by means of its magnificent reporting of the Civil War and by publishing powerful cartoons and editorials. The Union sharpshooter by Winslow Homer, at right, and *The Tammany Tiger Loose!* by Thomas Nast, below, were perhaps the most famous pictures that *Harper's* ever printed. But there were hundreds of others—battle scenes and Lincoln cartoons, Nast's Republican elephant and Democratic donkey, and his lanky, beaver-hatted Uncle Sam—which entered into the national consciousness and were fixed in history by *Harper's*. It was a Nast cartoon that followed the runaway Boss Tweed to Spain and led to his identification and arrest in 1876. Tweed himself blamed his downfall on the cartoons. Even though the voters couldn't read, he remarked, they could "look at the damned pictures."

NOVEMBER 15, 1862

NOVEMBER 11, 1871

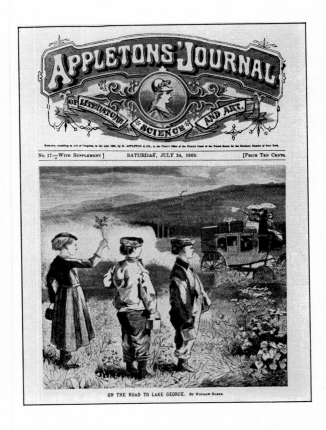

ON THE ROAD TO LAKE GEORGE. By WINSLOW HOMER.

HEAD OF BARON OF OXFORD.—DRAWN FROM LIFE BY EDWIN FORBES FOR THE AMERICAN AGRICULTURIST.

Minnie applied the current, and with a howl of pain Claude twisted himself up.

SOMETHING SHOCKING;

A TERRIBLE REVENGE.

A handful of specialized pictorials are grouped on these two pages. The juvenile at the upper left was one of the first in America to print color. *Appletons'* catered to culture buffs with French fiction and superior engravings that could be framed. *American Agriculturist* was the farmer's favorite from 1842; *The New Sensation* specialized in lurid revelations of sin. *Scientific American,* founded in 1845, was the nation's leading pictorial register of new scientific developments, including the discovery—made by the high-speed cameras of Eadweard Muybridge—that a running horse sometimes lifts all four feet off the ground. This set of photographs led to the earliest motion pictures.

SCIENTIFIC AMERICAN

A WEEKLY JOURNAL OF PRACTICAL INFORMATION, ART, SCIENCE, MECHANICS, CHEMISTRY, AND MANUFACTURES.

Vol. XXXIX.—No. 16.
[NEW SERIES.]

NEW YORK, OCTOBER 19, 1878.

[$3.20 per Annum.
[POSTAGE PREPAID.]

THE SCIENCE OF THE HORSE'S MOTIONS.—[See page 241].

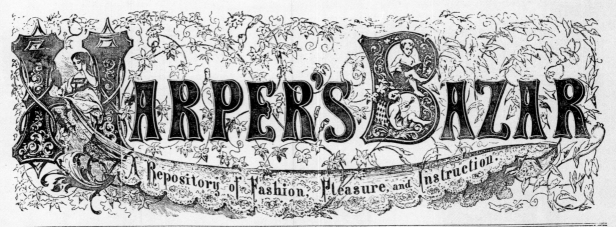

HARPER'S BAZAR

A Repository of Fashion, Pleasure, and Instruction.

VOL. I.—No. 49.]   NEW YORK, SATURDAY, OCTOBER 3, 1868.   [SINGLE COPIES TEN CENTS.
[$4.00 PER YEAR IN ADVANCE.

Entered according to Act of Congress, in the Year 1868, by Harper & Brothers, in the Clerk's Office of the District Court of the United States, for the Southern District of New York.

Fig. 9.—Manner of using Crimping Pin.

Fig. 3.—Fleur de Lis Coiffure. Front.

Fig. 1.—Coiffure for Girl from 12 to 14 Years old.—Front.

Fig. 6.—Negritine Coiffure.—Back.

Fig. 4.—Fleur de Lis Coiffure.—Back.

Fig. 12.—Chignon of Curls.

Fig. 11.—Marguerite Knot.

Fig. 8.—Coiffure of Curls.

Fig. 10.—Diadem of Curls.

Fig. 13.—Fleur de Lis Coiffure of Braids.

Fig. 14.—Braid Chignon fastened to Comb.

Fig. 5.—Negritine Coiffure.—Front.   Fig. 7.—Manner of Making Negritine Coiffure.

Fig. 2.—Coiffure for Girl from 12 to 14 Years old.—Back.

Fig. 15.—Chignon of Long Curls.

FALL STYLES OF HAIR DRESSING.—[See next Page.]

NOVEMBER, 1868

American women acquired a pictorial weekly of their own when *Harper's Bazar* was launched in 1867 by the same firm which issued *Harper's Weekly* and *Harper's New Monthly Magazine*. The *Bazar* was especially attractive during the Empress Eugenie period, when it provided detailed reports from Paris of the newest hairdos and bustle-propped styles. It also printed serialized fiction by such writers as Thomas Hardy. Its occasional colored supplements (above) were fine steel engravings colored by hand in the old tradition established by *Godey's Lady's Book*.

THE HOLOCAUST ON THE SOUND.
DESTRUCTION OF THE SEAWANHAKA BY FIRE LAST MONDAY.

A SCENE IN SHANTYTOWN, NEW YORK.
REPRODUCTION DIRECT FROM NATURE.

MARCH 4, 1880

PICTURES IN THE DAILY PRESS

The world's first pictorial daily (upper left) is almost entirely forgotten today. But during its career of sixteen years it had a tremendous influence in directing American journalism toward providing more news in pictures. In spite of its name this original New York *Graphic* had no connection whatever with the raucous Macfadden tabloid of the 1920's. It was started in 1873 by two Canadians, William Leggo and Joseph Desbarets, who had already patented a method for reproducing photographs through a primitive halftone screen. In 1880 the *Graphic* published a famous pioneer halftone (center left) which was prepared "directly from nature"—that is, without being copied by hand—by means of a single-line screen. Although it produced a much coarser picture than the finer screens of the 1890's, this marked the practical beginning of photojournalism in the United States. Since most *Graphic* pictures were drawings and paintings superbly printed on coated stock by lithography, the result often looked more like a work of art than a hustling newspaper.

At this time the regular dailies were much too fat and contented to go to the trouble of printing news pictures. But they were shocked into action after Joseph Pulitzer bought the New York *World* in 1883. Pulitzer assigned artists to work alongside reporters and sprinkled their overnight "spots" through his news columns. The *World's* circulation shot up to the highest in America; when it omitted the pictures, for a few weeks only, circulation dropped almost as fast. Rival papers, like brother Albert Pulitzer's *Journal,* followed the *World's* example; below is its extra on the great blizzard of '88. William Randolph Hearst, after he was expelled from Harvard, worked for the *World* as a cub reporter, and noted in a letter home that "illustrations embellish a page . . . and stimulate the imagination of the masses." When Hearst got a newspaper of his own (opposite) he embellished its clamorous pages with colored halftones and stimulated the masses with his chauvinistic personal reporting of the Spanish-American War.

The Examiner.

VOL. LXVI.   SAN FRANCISCO: WEDNESDAY MORNING, JUNE 29, 1898.   NO. 180

SHAFTER'S HOST READY TO SPRING ON THE COWED ENEMY AT SANTIAGO.

PEACEFULLY--- IF POSSIBLE.

How General Merritt Will Enter Manila.

CONCILIATORY PROCLAMATION

Major-General Wesley Merritt, recently apppointed Military Governor of the Philippine Islands, will sail to-day for Manila on the steamer Newport. Yesterday he consented to talk about his plans for the future.

"If I can make a peaceful entry into Manila, all right," he said. "If I can't enter the city peaceably I will be obliged to force my way in. I am not a glutton for military glory. I instructed General Greene, who went here with the second expedition, to consult on his arrival at the harbor of Manila with Admiral Dewey as to the advisability of their making a joint attack on the city and forcing an entrance. They will do the proper thing, beyond question. Both men have great ability. They can cope with any emergency.

"I will go on board the steamer Newport at 9 o'clock to-morrow morning, and sail promptly at 10 o'clock. The Newport should reach Manila by July 25th, or by August 1st at the very latest. I ordered the transports which left here on Monday last to make all possible speed to Honolulu and finish coaling at that port by the time the Newport gets there. The Newport will accompany the transports to Manila.

"Once I have established an official residence in Manila I will issue a proclamation in the name of the President of the United States, in which I will announce my appointment as Military Governor of the Philippines, and declare the islands subject to the authority of the United States. The proclamation will be issued in both English and Spanish. The proclamation has been prepared. It will inform the inhabitants of the islands that the United States will not interfere with their forms of religious worship, will not destroy their churches, will not confiscate their property, will not imperil their lives or happiness, and will not inflict upon them an arbitrary and unreasonable form of government and system of laws.

"Information of this character will be set forth in the proclamation in order to offset representations to the contrary that have been made to the people of the Philippines by Spanish priests, politicians and military authorities.

"Let me say a few words about the ceremony of installation at Military Governor. I have seen newspaper statements that it will be elaborate. There will be nothing elaborate about it. There is every reason why it should be a simple ceremony, one that will in no way be inconsistent with the democratic sentiment of our country.

"The Philippine Expeditionary Force is made up of soldiers who will give a good account of themselves. Officers and men are of the right stuff. The soldiers are well equipped. Those that have come from the national guards of the several States need a little more drilling, but they are fit to make good fighters at this moment.

"I shall never forget San Francisco's cordial treatment of the soldiers, and myself as their commander. I have been shown every courtesy and the kindest treatment. The loyal spirit, the strong patriotic impulse, the unselfish kindness, the hospitality without end of the citizens of San Francisco, are indelibly stamped upon my mind. I say, God bless the ladies of the Red Cross and the other societies of this State who have done so much for the soldiers."

General Merritt was asked if it were true that he had requested the Secretary of War to appoint Major J. L. Rathbone as a volunteer officer, in order that the Major may become his personal representative in San Francisco.

"Yes," replied General Merritt, "I want the War Department to make Major Rathbone a volunteer appointment and assign him to duty in San Francisco as my personal representative after all the troops are

(Continued on Page Two.)

MAJOR-GENERAL MERRITT, MILITARY GOVERNOR OF THE PHILIPPINES.
In an interesting interview General Merritt gave yesterday an outline of his course in the Philippines. He says the installation ceremony will be simple. His proclamation will be issued in both Spanish and English, and will be such as cannot fail to impress all with the safety and beneficence of American rule if they will submit to it.

AUGUSTI WILL NOT YIELD.

MADRID, June 28.—The Government has received the following despatch from Captain-General Augusti, dated from Manila on June 23d:

"The situation is still as grave as ever. I continue to maintain my position inside the line of blockhouses, but the enemy is increasing in numbers, as the rebels occupy the provinces which are surrendering. Torrential rains are inundating the intrenchments, rendering the work of defense difficult. The numbers of sick among the troops are increasing, making the situation very distressing and causing increased desertions of the native soldiers.

"It is estimated that the insurgents number thirty thousand, armed with rifles, and one hundred thousand armed with swords, etc. Aguinaldo has summoned me to surrender, but I have treated his proposals with disdain, for I am resolved to maintain the sovereignty of Spain and the honor of the flag to the last extremity. I have over one thousand sick and two hundred wounded.

"The citidel has been invaded by the suburban inhabitants, who have abandoned their homes, owing to the barbarity of the rebels. These inhabitants constitute an embarrassment, aggravating the situation, in view of the bombardment, which, however, is not seriously apprehended for the moment.

"The Governor of the Viscayas and Mindano islands cables that he has defeated the insurgents in an engagement, during which Chief Arco, Aguinaldo's representative, was killed. He adds that tranquility now prevails throughout these islands, and he further asserts that the principal Malay chiefs of the Mindano group declare they desire to fight on the side of the Spaniards against the invaders.

"According to our advices, the emissaries sent out to seek General Monet's column of one thousand men returned after a fruitless search.

Captain-General Augusti's family is still in the hands of the insurgents. General Pena, with one thousand soldiers, has surrendered. His soldiers, most of whom are natives, joined the insurgents.

YANKEE TROOPS HIGH IN SPIRIT.

Drawing the Lines Closer About the Spanish.

COUNTING THE DAYS TO GLORY

By William R. Hearst.

GENERAL SHAFTER'S CAMP, SIBONEY, Cuba, via Port Antonio, June 28.---It is satisfactory to be an American and here on the soil of Cuba, at the very threshold of what may prove to be the decisive battle of the war. The struggle for the possession of Santiago and the capture of Cervera's fleet seems to be only a few hours away, and from the top of the rough, green ridge where I write this, we can dimly see on the sea the monstrous forms of Sampson's fleet lying in a semicircle in front of the entrance to Santiago harbor, while here at our feet masses of American soldiery are pouring from the beach into the scorching valley, where the smells of stagnant and fermented vegetation, ground under the feet of thousands of fighting men, rise in swooning hot mists through which vultures that have already fed on the corpses of slain Spaniards wheel lazily above the thorny, poisonous jungle.

SANTIAGO IS OURS.

Santiago and the flower of the Spanish fleet are ours, although hundreds of men may have to die on the field before we take possession of them. Neither Cervera's crews nor General Linares' battalions or squadrons can escape, for the American fleet bars the way by sea and our infantry and dismounted cavalry are gradually encircling the city, driving the Spanish pickets backward toward the tiers of trenches in which the defenders of Spanish oppression must make their last stand.

There are three commanders who will direct the fight against Santiago: Sampson

VOL. VIII.–No. 207.   Price, 10 Cents.

"What fools these Mortals be!"
MIDSUMMER NIGHTS DREAM

Puck

PUBLISHED BY   NEW YORK   OFFICE No. 21-23 WARREN ST
KEPPLER & SCHWARZMANN.   TRADE MARK REGISTERED 1878.

PETER COOPER,
NEW YORK'S PET PHILANTHROPIST.

JUNE 15, 1881

The last thirty years of the century were the golden age of political caricature in America, when the cartoonist's work was more eagerly discussed, more vividly drawn, and more fearlessly published—and more savage—than ever before or since. Many brilliantly colored cartoons appeared in a group of pictorial weeklies whose "humor" was often far from funny to their victims. The most famous of these was *Puck*, started by Joseph Keppler in 1876 in German, and in 1877 in English; it was long edited by Henry Cuyler Bunner. *Puck* was uproariously Democratic in national politics, but it attacked Tammany Hall, the labor bosses, prohibitionists, and even the Pope with equal gusto. At the left is one of its milder caricatures, drawn by Keppler himself, of old philanthropist Peter Cooper, winner of so many honorary degrees that he carries a cushion with him to the platform.

Earlier American magazines had been satisfied with one big cartoon in each issue. Keppler published three each week—a full-page front cover, a double-page center spread, and a full-page back cover. His cartoons were exuberant and even gaudy when compared with the fine pen-and-ink work of Thomas Nast in *Harper's*. The fact that they were drawn with crayon directly on the lithographic stone gave them a freehand feeling that appealed to artists and brought Keppler some able assistants, as well as some formidable competitors.

Eventually *Puck* lost ground to its Republican rival, *Judge,* represented in this portfolio by a double-spread on the next two pages. In 1898 some Democrats financed the short-lived *Verdict* to attack the Vanderbilt interests and beat McKinley and Hanna in the 1900 presidential campaign. They failed in this but they did produce some amazing pictorial libels, including the vulture Hanna pinning down American labor, at right.

Overleaf: The Republicans did not cower in silence under the lashings of *Puck* and *The Verdict.* They had their own weekly, *Judge,* which pictured Bryan and Cleveland as smirking clowns, and Lincoln and Grant as noble statesmen, in Gillam's cartoon *The Sliding Scale*

ALFRED HENRY LEWIS, Editor.

THE VERDICT

VERDICT PUBLISHING COMPANY, BY O. H. P. BELMONT, President.

CAPITAL HAND IN HAND WITH LABOR!

"IF THERE IS ANYTHING THE MATTER WITH TRUSTS THE REPUBLICAN PARTY CAN BE RELIED UPON TO FIX IT." HANNA.

Judge

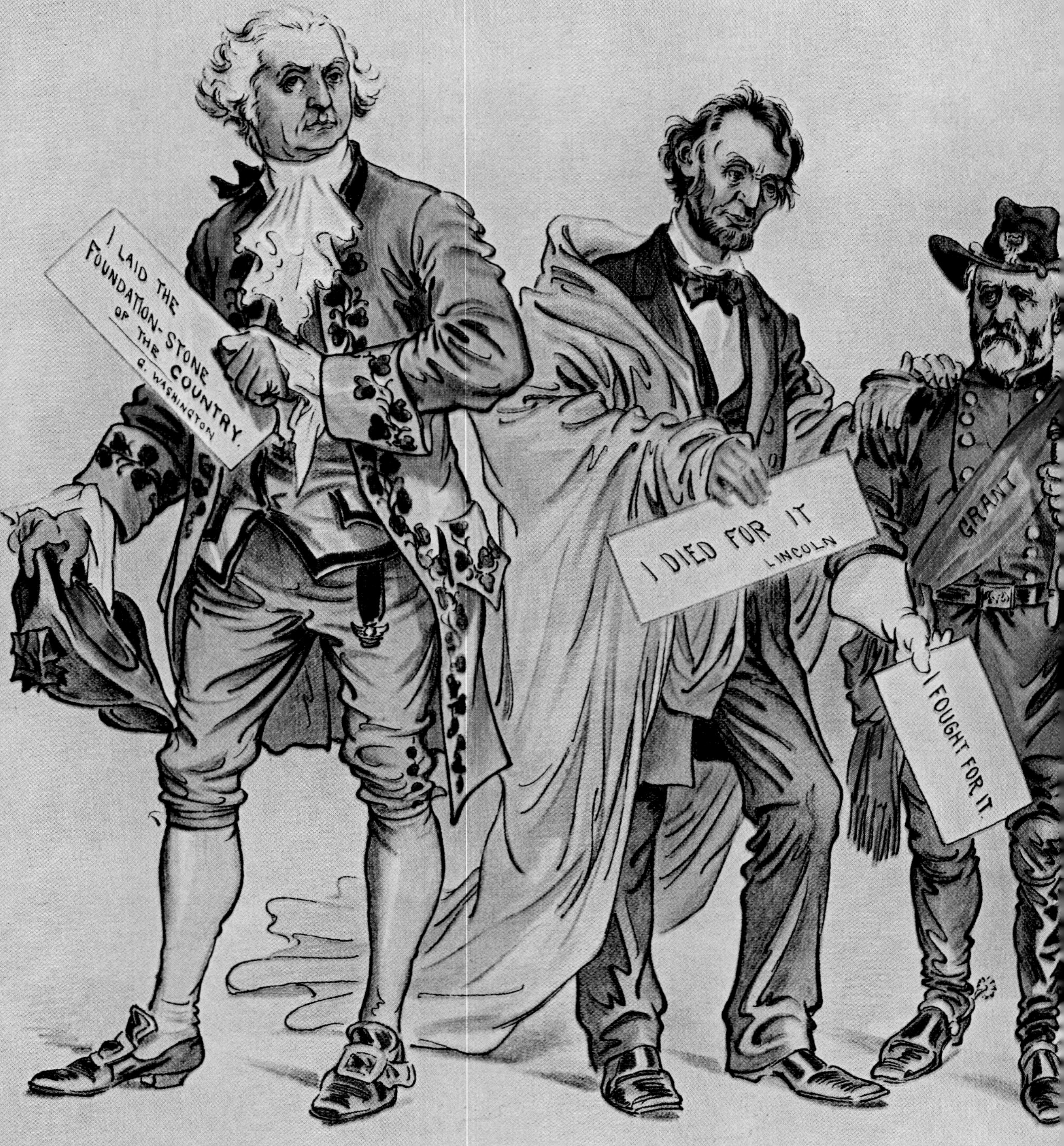
I LAID THE FOUNDATION-STONE OF THE COUNTRY.
G. WASHINGTON
I DIED FOR IT
LINCOLN
GRANT
I FOUGHT FOR IT.

THE SLIDIN

SCALE.

(CITIZENS TAKE NOTICE.)

Born (as Gleason's) May, 1851; died of editorial anemia December, 1859.

Born a "naughty picture mag" 1896; died a respectable lady, 1936.

Founded (not by Franklin!) in 1821 Revamped by Lorimer, 1899-1936.

Born January 13, 1857. Died after facelift May 13, 1916.

Born 1890; bet on Landon, 1936; merged into Time, '38.

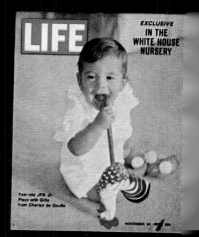

Born 1883 as cartoon weekly; reborn, with photos, November, 1936.

First issue December, 1855. Merged to death June, 1922.

Born October, 1881. Faded to monthly 1932. Obiit 1947.

Puck, born March 14, 1877, lives on only as heading for "comics."

Born April, 1888. Killed January 4, 1957, despite 3,732,304 circulation.

Born April 16, 1827; lived to ripe old age of 102. Died as monthly in 1929.

Born (as Bazar) 1867, sold 1913 to Hearst, extra "a" added 1929.

World's best weekly; little change since 1842; same editor since 1900.

Born 1845; monthly in 1921. Strong new editing since 1948.

The great-grandpa of scandal sheets was born a picture weekly in 1845.

Farmers' favorite, born 1842, still features bovine beauty on page one.

HOW HAVE THEY FARED?

The years have been kind to only a few of the publications that rose and flourished during the first sixty years of pictorial journalism. Some, like *Gleason-Ballou's,* died young and with very few mourners. Others, like *Harper's Weekly* and *Leslie's,* lingered on into the twentieth century, long after the editorial spark that had made them great was gone. *Judge* abandoned politics early, about 1910; but its japes and jazzy cartoons were never very popular after the 1920's. In its enfeebled pages, the two-line joke made its last stand. One of the last to die, *Collier's,* was mercifully bashed in the head after falling victim to a modern disease—advertising deficiency. This ailment occurs when a magazine's mass circulation swells to expensive dimensions but is not sufficiently large to take away enough soup, soap, and underwear advertising from its rivals.

Among the survivors of the nineteenth-century weeklies it is impossible to chart any definite trend. The *Saturday Evening Post,* the oldest of all, was never really picture-minded until its great editor, George Horace Lorimer, began running two-color covers in 1899. Last year it experienced the latest of innumerable face-liftings during its 140-year career. *Life,* the giant of photojournalism, took nothing but its name from the famous old humor weekly which Time Inc. bought and laid to rest in 1936. Almost alone among the old-timers, the *Illustrated London News,* with its dispassionate pictorial record of world events, its gentlemanly essays, and its absence of blatant advertising, still maintains the *ton* of the earlier journalism. It no longer has an American counterpart. *Scientific American* ended its course as a picture weekly back in 1921, and it has now had a complete rebirth as a high-level monthly of modern science.

The biggest change of all has come from high-speed photography, which transformed picture reporting from an art to a push-button science, and from the perfection of halftone engraving, which substituted a mechanical process for the craftsman's fingers and gravers. News pictures in our own time are far more precise, real, and immediate than the woodcuts of the nineteenth century. But in this inevitable progression some things that only the artist could add—perspective, imagination, and charm—have often been deadened or lost.

He was born in 1868; when he died he was ninety-two. He was the eighteenth and final child of his father, an Episcopal bishop who had already lost two wives before marrying his third.

It was hard for his parents to pick a name for the baby. All the ancestral ones, and most of the biblical, had already been divided among his seventeen elders. The Bishop finally named him for a long-dead youth with whom, in the 1820's, he had studied theology.

The boy grew up in a household of sanctity, but neither his righteous father nor his gentle mother could protect him from his mischievous older brothers. To teach him to swim, they threw him off a dock into the deep waters of Narragansett Bay. Behind the family farmhouse in Rhode Island was a raspberry patch. When there were not enough berries for all, the other boys would call out, "Watch out for the weasel!" to frighten him, and he would run out of the patch, himself no higher than the bushes, as fast as his spindly legs could carry him.

He was left-handed by nature, and stammered throughout his life. He claimed that one handicap caused the other, for the Bishop forced him to eat with his right hand. A misplaced elbow at mealtime could throw the whole circle of feeders into chaos. It was a rule of the Bishop's board that if any of the children failed to eat all his food, the remainder was brought back, meal after meal, until he did. As an old man, No. 18 remembered, with disgust, finally downing a four-day-old spoonful of oatmeal. By another rule, the children took turns at saying grace before meals. The elder ones were adept at the conventional blessings, but when No. 18's turn came—he was five years old then—he said simply, "O Lord, make us g-graceful."

That was the first utterance he remembered making. His first composition dates from 1880, when he was twelve. In that year his native town became two centuries old. The Bishop had been named Poet of the Day. He sat on the piazza with a ream of foolscap and half a dozen quills, constructing one of those ponderous Odes, in several cantos, for which, in that tolerant decade, he was a little more than locally famous.

No. 18 sat behind him—out of sight, I am sure, of his groaning father—and saw no reason why he couldn't write a poem too. Here it is:

> It is morning; I am sitting by the door,
> And I listen to the humming-birds
> And watch to see them soar.
> And I think of Little Rhody,
> The place where I was born,
> And the fishhawks slowly circling
> In the cool September morn,
> And the sand so whitely glistening,
> And the shells along the shore,
> And the bay so blue and sparkling
> Which I shall see once more.
> For I dream it in my dreams,
> And fancy them I see,
> And wish that it might come to pass
> That thither I might flee.

In this age of the small, temporary family, when rootless organization-couples roam from one bedroom suburb to another, ending up in a Florida trailer, our readers may enjoy a reminder of what we used to regard as the Good Life. This gentle and appealing trib-

The fact that he was right *in* Little Rhody at the moment never struck him until years later, and never struck the Bishop at all.

Not that the Bishop was without humor. His see was Central Pennsylvania, and his Palace, as he liked to call it, stood in Reading. He loved to tell his children about the Pan-Anglican Convention at Lambeth, somewhere in the 1870's, when Queen Victoria received the American bishops along with her own. As he and his wife entered the door—he in shovel hat and black apron and she in bombazine—the major-domo bellowed down the hall, " 'IS GRICE THE LORD BISHOP OF CENTRAL PENNSYLVAN-*EYE*-A and mrs. 'owe."

The boy went to college at Lehigh in Bethlehem, not far from the cathedral. By the time he had finished, and was ready for a profession, the Bishop faced the same dilemma as at his christening: all the careers were pre-empted by the older sons and sons-in-law. There was a doctor, two ministers—and even another bishop—and a naval officer, a stockbroker, a fledgling author, and two brothers in coal and iron. There seemed nothing left for No. 18.

The Bishop, in conclave with the elders, decreed architecture for No. 18, in the belief that neither stammering nor left-handedness would impede a boy who was to spend his days over a drawing-board. He had chosen literature for No. 17, who stammered too, and whose eyes were weak;

ute by a son to his father was written by George Howe for a few friends, but we think other people will be moved by it. "Number 18" was Wallis Eastburn Howe, 1868–1960, an old-fashioned gentleman, an architect, and a lifelong resident of old Bristol, Rhode Island.

neither an architect nor a poet needs the same vision or fluency as a coal and iron man. Through the rest of their long lives, these youngest two, No. 17 and No. 18, were to remain closer comrades than any other pair in the Bishop's brood.

From Lehigh, No. 18 went to Massachusetts Tech, and No. 17 to the Harvard Graduate School. They roomed together on Mt. Vernon Street in Boston. Their landlady seated the two stammerers apart, to spare them the titters of the table d'hôte. One day she led a new boarder over to their corner. The brothers scrambled to their feet, and stammered their how-do-you-do's. The newcomer held up three fingers, said simply, "th-th-three," and sat down beside them.

When No. 18 was graduated from architectural school, a classmate proposed a partnership in New York. But No. 18 told him, "I'd rather be a big frog in a small puddle than a small frog in a big one."

"Well," said his friend, "why not be a big frog in a big puddle, as I shall be?"

And he was; but No. 18 chose to stay in his birthplace. He started as a draughtsman for three dollars a week, at an office in Providence, eighteen miles away. He commuted by electric train, and continued the same routine for fifty years, until automobiles put the trains out of business. By the time he was twenty-nine he had saved enough to be married. He fell in love with the prettiest girl in town. The girls wore

corsets then; he used to boast that he could—and often did—encircle her waist with his two hands. She was the only child of the Episcopal minister. Since her mother had died when she was only six, she depended on her widowed father, and he on her. She was a popular girl at clambakes and Germans—so popular that her father feared he would lose her and be left alone in the rectory. He was glad when she chose the young architect; and the Bishop, who was twice a widower himself, was glad too.

They were married in 1897 by her father in his own church, when she was twenty-one. No. 17, the favorite brother, was best man. The groom fainted at the rail, somehow without the knowledge of anyone but No. 17. When the Rector put the question, "Wilt thou have this Woman to thy wedded wife . . ." and when the answer came back, "I w-w-will," he never noticed that it was the best man, not the groom, who had answered—or if he did, he never let on.

Married life began in the rectory. When the first child was born, the young father was so fretful at the childbed that the mother shooed him away. When the second child came, he lolled at the window with pipe and novel. "Brute!" his wife gasped, "what are you reading?"

"The Iron Woman," said No. 18, "by Margaret Deland."

Neither his left-handedness nor his stammering did impede his work or his happiness. Once he fell down the empty hoistway of an elevator, breaking his left wrist.

"Damned fool that I am," he scolded himself. "I just didn't look."

But he learned to draw with his right hand, and was ambidextrous thereafter. At the age of eighty-seven he drew, at 1/16" to the foot, a sheet of the ancient buildings in his beloved home town. It was a present for her 275th birthday, and it would honor a draughtsman of any age. He loved his trade.

His humor! Once he was visited by a client who proved to be stone deaf. When he had left, one of his draughtsmen asked him how the interview had gone.

"W-w-well," he stammered. "a team can get along with a no-good catcher *or* a no-good pitcher. Not with both. Now *he* can't catch and *I* can't pitch. But we got the job anyway."

When he sang, he ceased to stammer—whether it was Mandalay at the piano, or the Offertory with the choir, or just a hymn with his morning shower. There, his favorite was:

> *New every morning is the love*
> *Our wakening and uprising prove;*
> *Through sleep and darkness safely brought,*
> *Restored to life, and power, and thought.*

In the bathroom was a framed certificate that the Bishop "Having Contributed to the Pennsylvania Training School for Feeble-Minded Children the Amount Required by Law," was a "Member of said Corporation for Life." The family used to ask No. 18 whether the certificate meant an amount of money or an amount of feeble-minded children; he would laugh and say that he wasn't sure himself.

Again, a client was describing to him a color she wanted: "gray and pink, but not really either, because it must have *light* in it."

"I know exactly," he told her. "The color of the inside of an elephant's ear by moonlight."

There was a builder in town whose initials were C. I. The trade always nicknamed him Cast Iron. His son's initials were E. H. "They," said No. 18, "stand for Even Harder."

But none of his children remembers seeing him angry with anyone but himself, for even the best of reasons. If they disappointed him, his sorrow was punishment enough. He was president of the town council during a strike at the town's big factory. A striker, in the crowd at the gates, threw a stone which caught his temple.

"It was quite a *hard* stone too," he said rubbing the bruise, "but I don't believe it was meant for me. There isn't such a good shot in town."

When his father-in-law had to give up the rectory because of his age, No. 18 built a house of his own and took him along to it. There the venerable clergyman died at eighty-three. Those of his grandchildren who are old enough still remember his daily cold plunge, and the smell of tobacco and theologies in his room, and the photostat of Shakespeare's epitaph over the door, whereby he warned broom-wielders to keep out:

Good Friend, for Jesus' sake forbear
To dig the dust enclosed here.

The couple had six children, spaced over twenty-three years. Every Christmas No. 18's present to his wife was sweetened by a poem or a drawing, or both. When the first grandchild appeared, for instance, he made up a necklace of artificial pearls, strung among six wooden beads. The beads stood for the children. A red wooden heart—the grandson—closed the necklace at the bottom, and there hung from it a single pearl—a real one. In his beautiful calligraphy he illuminated this parody on a sheet of cardboard, and sang Nevin's famous melody to her, with gestures, before the Christmas tree:

The bairns you've borne to me, Dear Heart,
Are as a string of pearls to me;
I count them over, every one apart,
My Rosary.
Each boy a pearl, each daughter fair,
To cheer my heart, expand my lung;
I tell each bead unto the end, and there
A grandson's hung.
Oh Memories that bless, not burn!
Oh boundless gain, though fiscal loss!
I kiss each bairn and grandson in his turn
Though old and cross,
Sweetheart,
Though old and cross.

In that same year a friend of his marvelled, "How you can carry on your profession, and Mary can run a taxi service and an antique shop, and the two of you run the Library and almost run the church, and still look after six children, from a grown man down to a baby, *I don't* know."

"I d-d-do have a varied life," he conceded. "Before I go to bed I've got to see that my youngest son gets his bot-tle, and my oldest d-d-doesn't get his."

His youthfulness! He ate lunch at a businessmen's club in the city. His tablemates looked on him as a firebrand radical, more dangerous with each passing year, though he was senior to them all. He believed in the goodness, and the irresponsibility, and the immortality of the common man.

As the years glided past, his descendants multiplied. He could hardly remember the names of all, still less their birthdays. On his own, then, he would send each of his six children a check. The amounts were for the number of *their* children and grandchildren—that figure he proudly kept track of—multiplied by two dollars.

His self-sufficiency was part of his happiness. When his wife died, a few years after their golden wedding anniversary, his oldest son stayed a week with him in the empty house. Mostly he stared out at the harbor, saying little, but when he drove his son to the train, and kissed him good-bye, he blurted out, scolding himself again, "D-d-damn it, I don't miss your mother yet."

He designed a double gravestone, such as you sometimes see in ancient cemeteries, with his wife's dates, and the day of their marriage, and the names of both sets of parents all cut on it, and the date of his own birth on his side.

"We hope you don't feel gloomy," his children told him, "to see the stone waiting for one more date."

"On the contrary," he answered, "it gives me a sense of S-s-social Security."

He addressed his last parody to his own photograph (and it is rare to see two, nine decades apart, of the same face):

Speak, speak, thou fearful pest,
In rumpled bathrobe dressed,
Who, with thy shrunken breast,
Comest to daunt me:
Under the old pajams
Nestle thy withered palms,
Stretched as if asking alms:
Why dost thou haunt me?

He died surrounded by his children. A tempest roared over the harbor, but applewood glowed in his fireplace. When the next breath failed him, there was a flutter in the room as if a bird had flown, or as he would have said himself, had h-h-hatched.

Man's monuments prolong him briefly; his children, who are another word for his love, may extend him forever. No. 18 leaves five hundred buildings as a reminder, and a round fifty descendants. None, in the sixty-three years since he fainted at the altar, had preceded him, and there are more to follow. They cannot repine.

George Howe is a Washington architect and the author of Call It Treason *and* Mount Hope. *His article in our October, 1961, issue, "The Minister and the Mill Girl," included two drawings of buildings by his father, No. 18. The father of No. 18, the Bishop, was the Right Reverend Mark Anthony DeWolfe Howe; No. 17, who bore the Bishop's name and covered it with literary distinction, died last year at ninety-six.*

"BULL RUN" RUSSELL

LLOYD OSTENDORF

The first modern war correspondent won a nickname, much Northern ill will, and a lasting reputation out of his account of a famous battle

By JOSEPH L. GARDNER

Shortly after dawn on a pleasant midsummer morning just a century ago, a two-horse gig drew up in front of private lodgings on Pennsylvania Avenue, in Washington. Inside the house a stout, middle-aged gentleman finished his cup of tea, put more tea in a container, picked up a paper of sandwiches and a bottle of light Bordeaux, and then thoughtfully stopped to fill his brandy flask. A moment later, clad in a khaki "Himalayan" suit, a brown felt hat, and an old pair of boots, the man appeared on the street to inspect the vehicle. The date was July 21, 1861; and *The Times* of London, in the person of William Howard Russell, was off to cover what turned out to be the First Battle of Bull Run.

Russell was easily the most celebrated newspaper correspondent of his day. Irish-born, he had joined *The Times* in 1842 as a press gallery reporter in the House of Commons. Subsequently, he had covered the potato famine and the O'Connell sedition trial in Ireland, the Schleswig-Holstein rebellion on the Continent, and the Sepoy Mutiny in India. He had won a world-wide reputation by his reports from the front during the Crimean War in 1854–55. His revelations of military incompetence at the highest level had toppled a British government; his descriptions of inadequate hospital facilities in the field had been indirectly responsible for Florence Nightingale's famous mission of mercy; and his stirring account of the Battle of Balaclava may well have inspired a stay-at-home, Alfred, Lord Tennyson, to compose "The Charge of the Light Brigade."

Yet, in February, 1861, Russell had been reluctant to go to America to cover the impending hostilities for *The Times*. "I felt I had few qualifications for the post," he later admitted. "I was almost entirely ignorant of the nature of the crisis or the issue at stake, though I had read *Uncle Tom's Cabin*. . . ." Urged by his friend William Makepeace Thackeray, he nonetheless accepted.

At the outset, Russell found it difficult to suppress a certain sympathy for the Union cause. "Nothing could grieve my heart . . . more than to admit the fact that the great experiment of self-government had reached its end in dissolution, smoke and ashes," he stated in an address at a New York St. Patrick's Day dinner. "I cannot and will not believe that the people of the United States are about to whistle down, a prey to fortune, the greatest legacy a nation ever received. . ." These sentiments brought a stiff reprimand from his superiors in London, for in its editorial policy *The Times* was espousing the Southern cause. Warned by the home office, Russell quickly trimmed his sails and thereafter maintained a detached and lofty objectivity.

He reached Washington on March 27 and the following day was presented to Lincoln, who remarked: "The London *Times* is one of the greatest powers in the world—in fact, I don't know anything which has much more power—except the Mississippi. I am glad to know you as its minister." The next day Russell dined at the White House, and two days after that he received a bouquet of flowers from Mary Todd Lincoln. He was received by Winfield Scott, the dropsical septuagenarian who headed the Union Army, interviewed Senator Stephen A. Douglas, and played whist with Secretary of State William H. Seward. Despite this congenial atmosphere, Russell did not linger in Washington but determined, rather, to journey south so as to familiarize himself with both sides of the great political controversy.

He was in Charleston two days after the formal surrender of Fort Sumter on April 14. In Montgomery, he interviewed the new Confederate President, Jefferson Davis, and members of his Cabinet. He observed much and noted well everything he saw. For William Howard Russell this was an all-important period of self-education. Apart from the usual mild British disdain for American institutions and mores, his reports

Brigadier General Irvin McDowell was dignified, portly, and above all else, very unlucky.

to *The Times* were reasoned, objective, and amazingly perceptive. A swing through the Cotton South and a journey up the Mississippi brought him back to Union territory at Cairo, Illinois, by late June. Hearing that a major offensive was to be launched against the secessionists in Virginia, Russell hastened back to Washington.

On the evening of July 16, the British journalist reached Washington, where he met Brigadier General Irvin McDowell at the railway station. McDowell, a studious forty-three-year-old staff officer who had never led men in the field, had been promoted from major in May and put in command of Union forces concentrating on Washington. Lincoln had called 75,000 state militia into service for ninety days. It was McDowell's thankless task to mold them into an army. As he worked, pressure built up in the North for a decisive advance into Virginia. Horace Greeley's influential New York *Tribune* led the press in a shrill cry of "Forward to Richmond!" By the end of July, the term of service of most of the Union's three-month soldiers would expire, and immediate action was imperative if this force was to be utilized.

On June 24, McDowell had presented a plan of attack. In it he proposed moving a force of some 30,000 men from Washington to Manassas Junction, Virginia, twenty-five miles away, where General P. G. T. Beauregard had encamped his Rebel army, 25,000 strong. Beauregard, a Louisiana Creole, was just then the South's most popular hero—perhaps as much for his dark handsomeness as for the part he had played in the capture of Fort Sumter. He and McDowell had been classmates at West Point, Beauregard finishing second of forty-five in the class of 1838; McDowell, twenty-third. Success of the Union movement against Beauregard would hinge, McDowell foresaw, on the ability of a Union army at Harpers Ferry, some fifty miles up the Potomac River from Washington, to prevent General Joe Johnston's 12,000 Confederates in the Shenandoah Valley from reinforcing Beauregard.

Lincoln's Cabinet approved the plan on June 29, and the advance was scheduled for July 8. One frustrating delay after another, however, forced McDowell to postpone the movement. Now, on the evening of July 16—the day the advance actually got under way—McDowell himself was reduced to inquiring at the railway station for two missing batteries of artillery. His staff, he ruefully explained to Russell, was too busy to attend to such details. Russell accepted from McDowell a lift to his lodgings, and on the way the harried general told him that he had made plans for correspondents to accompany the Union Army to Manassas. But, he suggested, all newspapermen should wear white uniforms "to indicate the purity of their character."

On the afternoon of July 16, the Union Army had marched out of its camps near Alexandria—bands blaring martial music, unsullied banners fluttering gaily in the breeze. Standardization of uniforms had yet to be applied; and the uniforms of different outfits, reflecting individual taste and local pride rather than national identification, provided brilliant blocks of color. The men knew little enough about marching. Their officers, almost to a man, knew nothing about moving such a large body of troops from one place to another. Lines stretched out and closed up in convulsive, accordion-like twitches. Often men in the front were halted endlessly in the sun, while those in the rear jogged up at double-time to close lengthening gaps.

The exuberant spirits of these farmers and mechanics of the North—citizens all, sovereigns in uniform—simply could not be curbed. They broke ranks on the slightest pretext, stopping to drink from an inviting brook, pick blackberries along the roadside, or merely lounge in the shade. Impromptu foraging parties were launched against nearby chicken coops; and any Virginia farmer wavering between union and secession must have found the decision made easier by the unbridled antics of these invaders from the North. One captain in kilts was wildly hailed by his men for leading a squad in a breathless chase after a pig that left him hung up and somewhat exposed on a fence.

Two and one-half days after starting, the Union Army reached Centreville. It had covered a little more than twenty miles.

Bisecting the six-mile distance between Centreville and Manassas Junction was Bull Run, a small, sluggish stream with steep and rocky banks, easily fordable at several points. The broken, thickly wooded terrain rose on either side of the stream into open, gently rolling countryside. Beauregard had deployed his forces on the southern bank, along some ten miles of Bull Run's serpentine loops—from Union Mills on the right, past Blackburn's and Mitchell's fords at the center, to the stone bridge—where the Warrenton Turnpike from Centreville crossed the stream—on the left. The Confederate commander was about to sit down to dinner on July 18 when a stray Federal shell dropped unceremoniously into the fireplace of his headquarters farmhouse near Blackburn's Ford to announce the arrival on his front of his West Point classmate.*

*The owner of the house, Wilmer McLean, subsequently sold his property to move to a safer locality, some seventy miles southwest of Richmond. Nearly four years later the war would once more surge up to his doorstep. It was in the parlor of McLean's second house, at Appomattox Court House, that Robert E. Lee surrendered to Ulysses S. Grant.

McDowell quickly broke off the initial demonstration at Blackburn's Ford and concentrated his entire force at Centreville. The Confederates dignified this indecisive skirmish on July 18 by calling it the Battle of Bull Run. The principal clash, three days later, was always to be known in the South as the Battle of Manassas, and only in the North as Bull Run.

Beauregard had already asked Richmond for reinforcements, and his plea had been relayed to Joe Johnston in the Shenandoah Valley on July 18. Leaving 1,700 invalids at Winchester, Virginia, Johnston got 9,000 of his men through Ashby's Gap and onto trains for Manassas. It was the first demonstration, in this or any war, of the importance of a troop movement

CONTINUED ON PAGE 78

OVERLEAF: *About all that can be said for sure concerning the fancy cartoon that appears on the next two pages is that the artist had scant sympathy for the Union. His identity is unknown, his spelling (where it can be read) is sadly defective, and all that can be deduced from the sketch is that he was deriding the beaten Federals. Unhappy General McDowell rides to the rear, the "Fire Zouaves" are in full retreat, and here and there are glimpses of congressmen picking themselves up to join in the mad rush for safety.*

NATIONAL ARCHIVES

P. G. T. Beauregard made a battle plan which vanished in the mist, but found himself a hero.

THE BATTLE

1
2
3
4
ASSES YOU WOULD GIVE OUR
LIBERTY, GO HOME AND REMEMBER
WHITE SHOEMAKER
SLAVES AT SYNN
MASS.
OUR BROTHERS YOU TAKE THE ARMS,
DON'T RUN AWAY, WE GIVE YOU THE CARTRIDGE
NEW YORK
12
9
8
GEN:
DRIVING THE BULL, THAT THE ENEMY
WAS TAKEN BY
6
US
If we had known, we
would not be so Fulisch

ULL'S RUN.

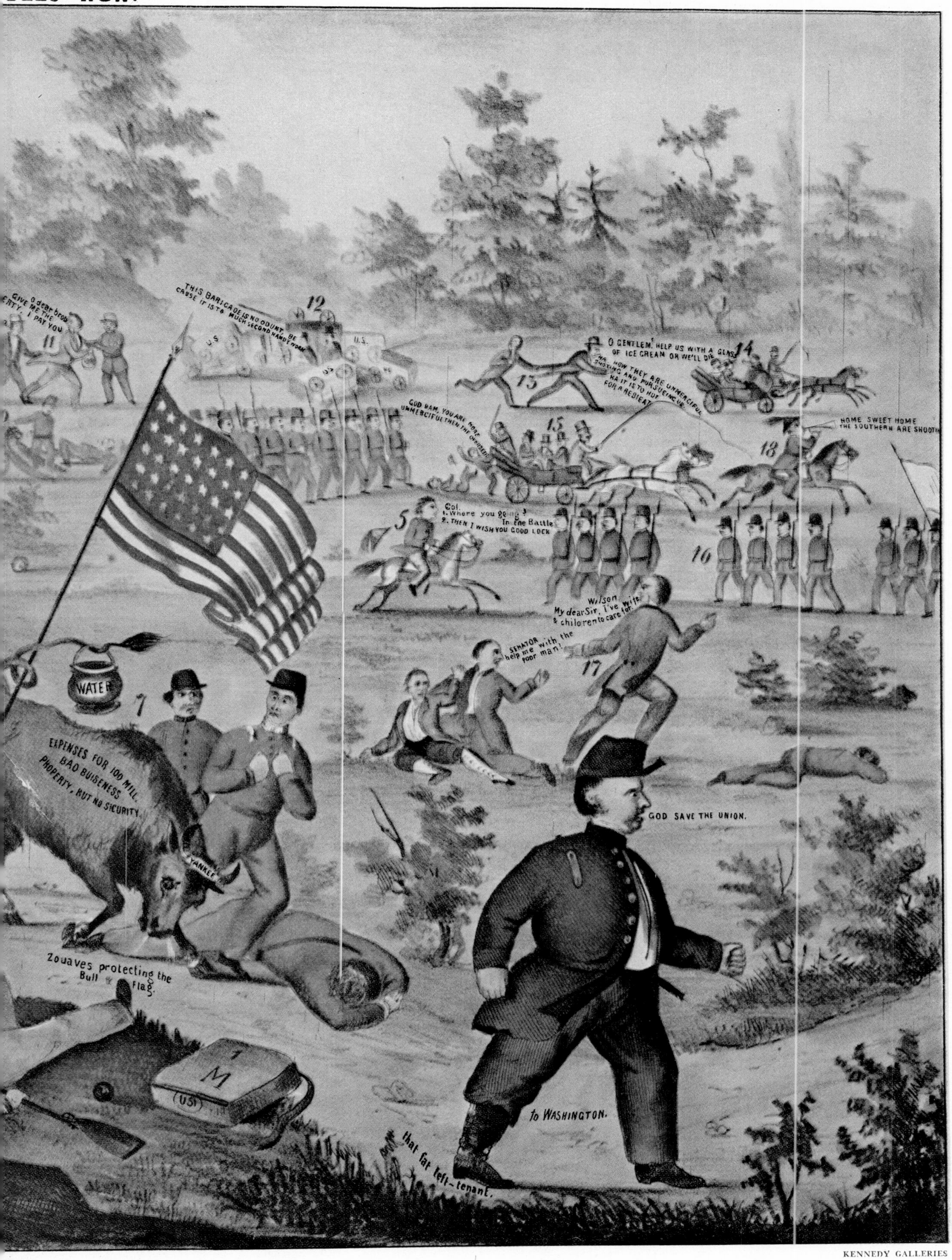
O dear brob
GIVE ME THE
ERTY, I PAY YOU
11
THIS BARICADE IS NO ODUNT, BE
CAUSE IT IS TO MUCH SECOND HANDY WORK
12
U.S
U.S.
O GENTLEM! HELP US WITH A GLASS
OF ICE CREAM OR WE'LL DIE
14
13
HA HOW THEY ARE UNMERCIFUL
SHOTING AND PURSUEING US.
HA IT IS TO HOT
FOR A REBEAT
GOD DAM, YOU ARE MORE
UNMERCIFUL THEN THE OVERSEER
15
HOME SWEET HOME
THE SOUTHERN ARE SHOOTI
18
Col.
1. Where you going?
In the Battle
2. THEN I WISH YOU GOOD LOCK
5
16
Wilson
My dear Sir, I've wife
& chiloren to care for.
SENATOR
help me with the
poor man!
17
WATER
7
EXPENSES FOR 100 MILL.
BAD BUISENESS
PROPERTY, BUT NO SICURITY
YANKEE
GOD SAVE THE UNION.
Zouaves protecting the
Bull & Flag.
1
M
(US)
to WASHINGTON.
that fat left-tenant.

KENNEDY GALLERIES

Copyright 1876 by Currier & Ives N.Y.

GEORGE WASHINGTON. GENL HENRY KNOX, Secy of War. ALEXANDER HAMILTON, Secy of the Treasury. THOMAS JEFFERSON, Secy of State. EDMUND RANDOLPH, Attorney General.

WASHINGTON AND HIS CABINET.

Some faces in a formal portrait

The Wartime Cabinet

Cordell Hull's feud with a brilliant subordinate; a trick cigar for General de Gaulle; how a Supreme Court justice is chosen; the silencing of Father Coughlin; the rage of Harold Ickes—in his autobiography, the former Attorney General describes calm and crisis among F.D.R.'s lieutenants

By FRANCIS BIDDLE

There hangs in my study a photograph of the Second World War Cabinet, signed by each of the eleven members, plus the President. Next to it is an engraving by Currier & Ives published in 1876, slightly larger than the photograph, portraying President Washington's Cabinet of four, in which Jefferson and Hamilton had been so hostile, and Edmund Randolph so discouraged because his associates were not able, as Washington had fondly hoped, to form a privy council of advisers, patterned on the British model, who would be *au dessus de la mêlée.* President Washington sits next to his Secretary of War, General Henry Knox, who looks not unlike his namesake at our table. Secretary of the Treasury Alexander Hamilton is standing, a hand on Knox's chair, the other tucked in his waistcoat below his ruffled shirt, concentrated and determined, his look suggesting irritation below the slight frown. At Hamilton's left sits Thomas Jefferson, the Secretary of State, holding a piece of paper, his stock very simple and without frills, as became a Republican, his unpowdered hair curly, a line of worry between the eyes. At the other end of the little table is Edmund Randolph, the first Attorney General, my mother's great-grandfather, his right hand separating the pages of a book, his hair brushed away from his forehead and caught in a "horse's tail" back of his neck; a serious young man.

In the photograph of the War Cabinet, Frank Knox, Secretary of the Navy, is at the corner of the long table next to me—short, stocky, straightforward, more prepared to be friendly than hostile. He had been a Rough Rider during the Spanish-American War, and followed his colonel, Theodore Roosevelt, into the Bull Moose Party in 1912. Nineteen years later as owner of the Chicago *Daily News,* he became one of the leading critics of the New Deal, and was the Republican vice presidential candidate in 1936, when Alfred Landon was so disastrously beaten for the Presidency. Knox and Landon were much alike—amiable, middle-class, friendly, with a sort of sturdy averageness about them. When his appointment to the Cabinet was announced, Frank repeated a cliché that every one could understand: "I am an American first, and a Republican afterward!" He was the kind of person on whom you could count for that sort of sound, safe platitude. He died before the war was over, on April 28, 1944. I liked Frank Knox. He was not subtle, but he was healthy and decent to the core.

The two pictures mentioned in the text are shown at left. F.D.R. and his Cabinet, counterclockwise from right: Frank Knox, Secretary of the Navy; Francis Biddle; Henry Morgenthau, Jr., Secretary of the Treasury; the President; Cordell Hull, Secretary of State; Henry L. Stimson, Secretary of War; Frank Walker, Postmaster General; Harold Ickes, Secretary of the Interior; Jesse Jones, Secretary of Commerce; Vice President Henry Wallace; Frances Perkins, Secretary of Labor; Claude Wickard, Secretary of Agriculture.

President Roosevelt

This excerpt is taken from Mr. Biddle's account of his long and varied career in public service, *In Brief Authority,* to be published late this fall by Doubleday. It begins where the first volume of his autobiography, *A Casual Past,* left off, and covers his activities in Washington as Chairman of the National Labor Relations Board (1934–35), Solicitor General (1940), Attorney General (1941–45), and finally, as the U.S. member of the Nuremberg war crimes tribunal (1945–46). This is a book that may prove to be one of the most distinguished accounts of the Roosevelt era yet written.

Francis Biddle

I sat on Knox's right; and Henry Morgenthau, Jr., the Secretary of the Treasury, was on my other side—we took our places in the order in which our Cabinet positions had been created. Henry had been a gentleman-farmer neighbor of Roosevelt's in Dutchess County, and had served under him in various state and federal positions. I never could feel close to Morgenthau, although I respected his courage, singleness of purpose, and devotion to the President—a bit doglike at times. The President was fond of Henry, patted him when he looked hurt, teased him in public without striking a spark of humor—humor there was none—and protected him as far as possible against the annoyance which his missionary zeal in fields not the Treasury's occasionally caused the rest of us. He had a tendency to send memoranda to F.D.R. about the work of others—which doubtless touched his own, for almost everything was related by the war effort—instead of first discussing it with them.

I hasten to add that his sights were high, his probity impeccable, and the efficiency of his department well above the average, for on the whole he chose good men to serve under him and leaned over backward, sometimes unnecessarily far, it seemed to me, to keep away from politicians. We shared the same aims, even if the means chosen to accomplish them, or, more precisely, the method of going about the choice, did not on all occasions lead to a warm sense of team play. One could trust him, except where consideration for the feelings of others entered the picture. How could one be at ease with a man who, suspicious of the present and concerned with the future, recorded your telephone talk with him—"Wait a minute, Francis, I would like to put on my secretary to make a record of what you are saying"—to be collected for eternity in those endless volumes of the diary that chronicled the minutiae of his daily career?

To Henry Morgenthau's right, at the center of the table, sat the President; then came Secretary of State

Hull and Secretary of War Henry L. Stimson. Beyond Stimson was Frank Walker, the Postmaster General, and next to him Harold Ickes, Secretary of the Interior, looking belligerently at the photographer.

By tradition, the Postmaster General was the political representative in the Cabinet of the party in power and usually chairman of the National Committee at the same time. Although Frank Walker became Postmaster General in 1940, he was not chairman of the National Committee until 1943, and served for a year only. He disliked his political job, but always did what the President wanted him to do, and just then the President wanted the politicians off his back so that he could get on with the war. Frank was never a professional politician in the sense that Jim Farley was, or Ed Flynn (who succeeded Jim as chairman) or Bob Hannegan, who followed Walker. Frank was too mild, too decent, too gentle, to fill that toughest of all political jobs. But he could and did protect his friend, the President.

Harold Le Claire Ickes was a very different type. If Frank Walker was not a professional politician by temperament, there was nothing amateurish about him. People instinctively understood and liked him. Harold Ickes, on the contrary, was the opposite of the politician—a reformer, a liberal (few politicians on either side are liberal by conviction), and an independent (witness his activity as a Progressive from 1912 to 1916). A good cabinet minister should be a competent administrator, and there was none better than Ickes, who sat all through the Roosevelt Cabinet and for a year under President Truman, until he resigned in 1946 with a clarion blast against that President—who was no unworthy opponent himself. He spent another six years wasting his talents on a syndicated newspaper column that gave him narrow scope for his fierce invective and occasionally lending his now-mild influence to some liberal measure. Harold Ickes was not a man who, having tasted the satisfactions of public office on a high level, could bear the narrower existence of a critic and gadfly.

I had not fully realized what a suspicious and thwarted human being he was until his secret diaries were published after his death. He had no heroes, and his friends—Tom Corcoran, Ben Cohen, and I were among the closest—remained so only as long as they did not oppose him. Obversely, his enemies were those who stood against his strong urges toward increased official dominion.

In spite of his faults I liked Ickes. Occasionally I lunched with him in his office in the Interior Department, where, looking like an angry and belligerent Donald Duck, he would let go as much at the Democrats as at the Republicans. I can still see him on a particular occasion when he was wartime petroleum and solid-fuels administrator. Striding up and down, his hands clasped behind his back, his lower lip protruding, he announced that he had won a terrific victory over some oil barons whom he had persuaded to cooperate with him, and that under such circumstances one must either kiss a woman or have a drink: would I join him in a Martini? . . .

I had first come into personal contact with him in 1938, when I was counsel for the committee investigating the Tennessee Valley Authority. He called me in Knoxville to ask if I would give him professional advice about whether a political speech he was going to make in Philadelphia was libelous. I flew from Knoxville to Washington—I had some T.V.A. business in the capital—and read the speech, the Secretary's gimlet eyes watching me from behind his desk. The speech was libelous, and I told him so. "Very well, then," he quacked, "I'll make it." I remember his last sentence. After denouncing two Republican stalwarts in the city, Moe Annenberg, the owner of the Philadelphia *Inquirer,* and one of the Pews, he ended: "Pew! Annenberg! Annenberg, phew!"

A striking characteristic of Harold's was his ability to fire a subordinate without the slightest qualm or hesitation if he thought him disloyal or incompetent—there was no beating around the bush or trying to place the man elsewhere. Once, after a row in which an undersecretary of the Interior was involved, the Secretary had decided to get rid of him promptly; Ickes gave instructions that after the incumbent had left for the day, the lock on his office door was to be changed—he was not to be admitted to his office or given access to his personal files.

Ickes was combative, shrewd, belligerent. He was a very effective radio speaker—he did not ad lib—and he had a genius for what Justice Holmes called hitting the jugular. He was disliked by many of his subordinates, feared by members of Congress, and highly respected by the public, who regarded him with a mixture of amusement and admiration. He could not have been a happy man. He took too much and gave too little to have understood what love or friendship could mean. Yet the grains of suspicion and malice in his nature, mixed with fearlessness, gave him a sharpness of character which was a relief after so much that was soft and sentimental floating on the placid surface of American life. Harold was never a bore.

Jesse Jones, Secretary of Commerce, sat between Harold Ickes and Henry A. Wallace, Vice President from 1941 to 1945. They were three men as unlike as it is possible to imagine. Jones, publisher and owner of the Houston *Chronicle,* was Texas in the *Giant* sense, conscious of his power, proud of his wealth, a pioneer who found the acquisition of material possessions no limit to his spirit; hard, shrewd, ruthless, strong, conservative. He seemed a huge man. One had the impression that his mind never stopped circulating, never relaxed.

Wallace, on the other hand, was a type—mystical, humorless, profoundly earnest, indubitably American —and the President liked types, up to a point.

The Secretary of Labor, Frances Perkins, in her invariable dark dress and pearls with a three-cornered felt hat planted firmly and low over her forehead, came next at the table; and finally Claude Wickard of Indiana, successor to Wallace as Secretary of Agriculture, who reflected in his amiable person all the sunny, smiling, and friendly, if sometimes tasteless, qualities of the great corn and wheat states.

The Cabinet was not a group of outstanding men. But they were competent and offered an experience that reflected the diversity and range of America. Cordell Hull—he was then seventy-one but seemed older—had been in politics for forty years. He had fought in the Spanish War, practiced law, served in the Tennessee legislature, and been a judge, a representative, and a senator before appointment to the Cabinet. As the terrible strain of war built up, he tired easily and had to leave Washington for increasingly longer rests, while Sumner Welles, the Undersecretary, ran things.

Welles was Hull's opposite in every way. A career man, he had been admirably trained in the old school of diplomacy. He spoke French and Spanish fluently, had some Italian and German, and knew thoroughly the intricacies of Latin American politics and our relations to them. When a foreign diplomat came to Washington, he made a formal call on the Secretary and then spent two hours with the Undersecretary, who was usually at home in the visitor's tongue. Welles was under fifty, robust, a tireless worker, with correct and formal manners, intelligent rather than imaginative, instinctively "liberal" in a department where that quality was not often apparent. He never walked from the State Department to the Metropolitan Club without his Malacca cane, and in summer wore an impeccable Panama.

Although as a rule a member of the Cabinet consulted only his opposite number in another department when a problem arose, it was accepted that one did not disturb Mr. Hull, but called Welles, who was quick to understand and to act. The Secretary disliked administration and turned it over to others. This choice left him free for the planning of policy. Yet it involved a weakness inherent in our system: no permanent civil servant, even at the highest level below the head of the particular government unit, can altogether relieve his principal of the ceaseless grind of administrative decision. Mr. Hull suffered from a partial abdication of power.

Secretary Hull stood in high repute throughout the country for his rugged honesty and independence, and was looked upon by members of the Congress with something approaching veneration. He was not very intelligent or original. The President counted on him to be his chief liaison with Congress when the time came to sell the United Nations to the Hill. President Roosevelt was determined not to make the same mistakes that President Wilson's idealistic and obstinate temperament had invited after the First World War.

I saw very little of Secretary Hull outside Cabinet meetings. We almost never met socially, and then usually for a meaningless exchange of amenities at one of the formal and solemn dinners that the Secretary gave for visiting potentates when the President had completed the first gesture or the visitor did not rank a reception at the top. These dinners took place at the Carlton Hotel—it was before the government had purchased Blair House—and they were not gay. The Secretary was usually tired and worried, but he would not forego what he considered his duty, impelled perhaps by his dislike of his Undersecretary—he did not enjoy Welles' stepping into his shoes even on the social side.

I particularly remember a dinner given for General de Gaulle. The President had disliked the General since their first meeting at Casablanca, felt that his bosom harbored the ambition to be a Man on Horseback, and was insistent that we should never "recognize," however indirectly, anyone whom the French people had not themselves freely chosen. We should wait for the time when they could make the choice. Eisenhower was ordered not to sign any agreement with de Gaulle from which a suggestion of "recognition" might be squeezed, nothing formal to which he could later point as conferring authority. De Gaulle,

the President said, thought of himself sometimes as Marshal Foch, sometimes as Jeanne d'Arc, the Maid in shining armor. He was a bore. . . .

At this dinner for the French general the American Secretary had little opportunity to judge, for he spoke no word of French and his guest was totally deficient in English. No interpreter was present—I suspect that the Chief of Protocol, George Thomas Summerlin, affectionately known as "little Summy," thought that an interpreter would have introduced an undesirable note of formality. So the Secretary and the General sat stiffly in informal silence, the American drooping a little, the Frenchman solemnly and forbiddingly erect, all six feet six of him, balancing a chip like an epaulet on each martial shoulder—he had not had his twenty-one guns on arrival.

After dinner Bill Bullitt, the ex-Ambassador to France, who spoke the language fluently and had known the General there, brought up several of us to be introduced to him as he sat in isolated dignity, unsmiling and showing no interest in our tentative remarks. Sol Bloom, chairman of the House Committee on Foreign Affairs, was among the first. Bill must have murmured in his ear a word or two about the desirability of breaking the ice, an exercise for which Mr. Bloom was eminently qualified, having, in his career as professional entertainer, introduced the lovely Fatima as a belly dancer to the American public.

Bill stated the Congressman's name very clearly to the guest of honor and indicated his importance. Mr. Bloom, bent at all costs on a *rapprochement*, produced a trick cigar from some inner recess, and offered it to the General, who for a moment hesitated. "Take it, take it," the New Yorker insisted. But when General de Gaulle put out his hand the cigar disappeared up Sol's sleeve, withdrawn by some invisible elastic mechanism. Puzzled, suspecting that he was being laughed at, the General turned to his aide: "What does the American statesman wish?" he inquired. The other did not seem to know, and no one dared to laugh. It was not a successful evening.

It was inevitable that Hull and Welles should drift apart. When the Secretary was resting at Hot Springs in Virginia, the President would send for the Undersecretary, who admirably supplemented Mr. Roosevelt's imaginative and creative impulses. The President rarely remembered that he was not his own Secretary of State. As a foreign diplomat put it, together they would mix an international salad, F.D.R. adding the garlic as he rubbed his hands and tasted the dressing.

Hull came to distrust Welles and finally to hate him. The President knew this long before the Secretary came to him with the final ultimatum—one of them must go. Yet before that, the President did little to better their relationship, often bypassing Hull by taking up a matter directly with Welles, and even communicating with him by code outside the regular State Department channels when Welles went to Africa as the President's special representative.

The President cared little for administrative niceties. If someone had remonstrated with him—and I suspect that Mr. Hull frequently did—he would look a little sheepish, apologize, murmur that he had not wanted to "trouble" you with it, and repeat his conduct after a decent interval.

The President had a way of building you up after knocking you down, particularly in the case of Mr. Hull, who under the circumstances that I have related was "touchy," as the President well knew. The building up took the form of an emphatic compliment at a Cabinet meeting for the way Mr. Hull had handled something, a day or two after the Secretary of State had lost in one of those incessant jurisdictional disputes that infringed so on the President's time.

I think President Roosevelt hated to make the choice between the two men, but it was clear that Welles would have to go. Welles resigned on September 30, 1943; and Mr. Hull, under pressure of ill health, was forced hardly more than a year later to give up the work to which he was completely dedicated. Welles was succeeded by Edward R. Stettinius, Jr., who then took Mr. Hull's place in 1944.

Stettinius was young—forty-four—for such an important position. Yet he seemed much younger: he seemed like a rosy and friendly sophomore, he wanted to be liked, and one could not help liking him. That he had had an enviable career in private business was accounted for by the fact that his father was a partner in J. P. Morgan and Company when Ed was growing up. At twenty-six the son was made assistant to the vice president of General Motors; at thirty-one, vice president in charge of industrial and public relations; and at thirty-five, chairman of the board of U.S. Steel. But one can be a board chairman and remain innocent.

He joined the government in 1939. The job he did best was lend-lease, probably because his contribution to it—an important one—was the establishing of smooth public relations. Ed Stettinius was essentially a public relations man.

But his appointment to head the State Department was a weak one. The President wanted to act as his own Secretary of State, and Ed was there to take orders and not to reason why—the war was nearing an end. His first act after his appointment (in December, 1944) was to send autographed photographs of himself to the newsmen who went to his press conferences, wishing them a most hearty Merry Christmas. They all

N.Y. Times

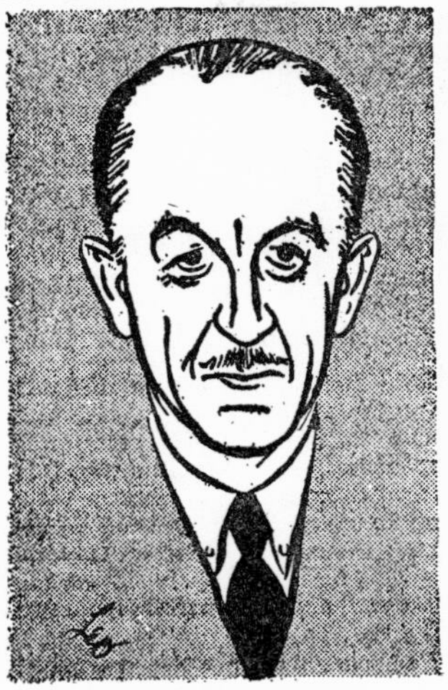

Sumner Welles

N.Y. Times

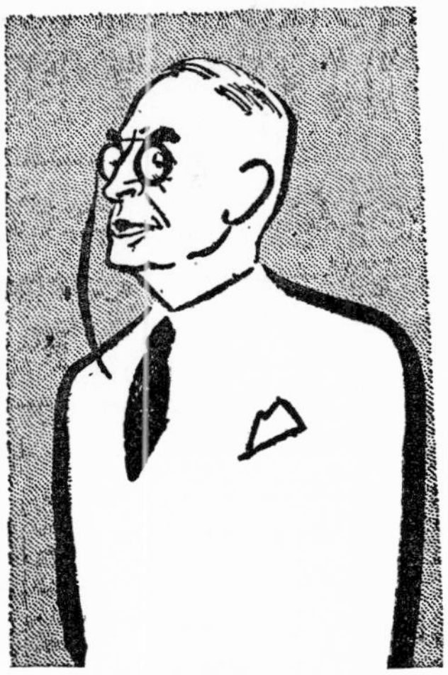

Cordell Hull

liked him and laughed at such displays of well-disposed artlessness. Washington newspapermen are highly intelligent and seldom naïve. I never heard Ed express a judgment; occasionally he would echo one he had heard, handing the words along to us as if he were cautiously reciting from a textbook. We all liked him—and disregarded him.

Although I rarely came in contact with him except at Cabinet meetings, the member of the Cabinet I most admired was Henry Stimson. He was in his seventies, his "tough and tranquil old age." He was as loyal to the President as Morgenthau, but stood up to him, which Morgenthau did not. He tired easily under the new strain of war and left the office early each day to keep fit, but he always looked ruddy and clear-eyed. If you had to see him, it was wise to go in the morning —by five o'clock he was weary and peevish. He had no small talk. On those few occasions when we did not talk shop—once or twice, for instance, when I went to see him and stayed for lunch at the Pentagon to finish a discussion—I found him difficult and rather shy.

I never thought of calling Stimson by his first name, as did Morgenthau, a familiarity which I felt he resented. I suppose he was old-fashioned. He did not particularly welcome the views of others on matters in his field. He had the Elizabethan sense of humor of a sturdy man; though not often revealed, it was like a gust of wind when stirred. I remember his telling a story about General George Patton when our troops were in Europe. Patton detested rules and regulations, army forms, and army reports. After General Eisenhower had warned him that he should pull himself together and follow the fitting formulas, the first of Patton's reports showed that he had taken the suggestion to heart; it was impeccable--succinct, objective, impersonal, strictly according to army Hoyle—until the last sentence: *P.S. I have just pissed in the Rhine. . . .*

Mr. Stimson used strong language with the men he was fond of, an intimation that to them he could let go. In Washington he was closer to Jack McCloy, who was his Assistant Secretary throughout the war, than to anyone. Once, when Mrs. Stimson had not been feeling well, Jack and his wife went over to spend the night with them. The next morning Mrs. Stimson, entirely recovered, was having breakfast with the Mc-Cloys. The Secretary's voice, suddenly rising from an adjoining room, broke into the peaceful meal: "I'll be damned if I will," he shouted, "I'll be God-damned if I'll do anything of the sort." "It's nothing," said Mrs. Stimson. "Mr. Stimson likes to dictate his journal in the morning, and he often gets rather excited." They could hear him striding up and down the room, as the expletives burst on the air. Then he came in for his soft-boiled egg, relaxed and smiling. . . . To me he was a heroic figure of sincerity and strength.

It has been customary for critics and historians to discount the changing roles of the Cabinet as it developed with the times, charging it with ineffectiveness because it had not fulfilled the original function for which it was intended. But what of that? The Cabinet was thought of by the first President as an advisory and authoritative body, an American Privy Council, to form policy and decide major questions as they arose. Today it is composed of a dozen administrators heading vast departments, who generally meet once a week to discuss their problems and report to the President what they are doing. Though the members are not primarily there to shape policy, their decisions often do. For policy can never be wholly separated from operation and often is developed and defined by the cumulation of action rather than by a reasoned decision taken before the event. Operation down the line, sometimes far down the line among the N.C.O.'s of government, can change and modify the original plan or even create a new one which is hardly recognizable. The American Cabinet gives some unity to this vast, sprawling, poorly co-ordinated system and keeps the President informed of what his chief administrators are doing. During my three-and-a-half years there was of course a single overriding consideration which created a sense of unity: the successful prosecution of the war.

President Roosevelt liked to use memoranda—the telephone was more for immediacy. Looking over some of his brief and pungent messages, I am again amazed at the number of matters on which he kept a hand. It has often been repeated that he was not a good administrator; but it may be questioned whether administrative ability is an attribute that is necessary or altogether desirable in a President of the United States. He practiced the far more difficult art of driving a score of subordinate princelings, few of whom could be described as tame, and of keeping their actions in perspective with the needs and the will of the country, settling their disputes, stroking their ruffled feathers, and nicely balancing the need for competent appointments with the political demands of the party system. He had the country to lead at the same time and, finally, the war to direct. I do not think that his success would have been as great if he had neglected one function in favor of the others.

As the war went on and absorbed more and more of his time, Roosevelt tended to concentrate on his job as Commander in Chief, but never to the exclusion of everything else. Toward the end he became weary

THE PERILS OF AN ATTORNEY GENERAL:

I. The Radio Priest from Royal Oak

The handling of wartime seditionists was at all times a thorny problem, and especially in the case of Father Charles E. Coughlin, the famous "radio priest" of Royal Oak, Michigan. Coughlin had become prominent through his anti-Semitic and anti-New Deal tirades on the air and in his weekly newspaper, Social Justice. *According to Biddle, Father Coughlin's opposition to the war effort and his predictions of defeat posed a very real danger, for even after Pearl Harbor the priest still commanded a huge following. Ordinarily, Biddle would have instituted legal action, but he feared that a sedition indictment against Coughlin would stir widespread resentment among the Catholic population and from the powerful isolationist press at a time when national unity had to be preserved at all costs. Another means of quieting the troublesome priest had to be found.*

I asked Leo T. Crowley, a prominent Catholic layman and a close friend of the President whom I knew well and trusted, to lunch with me. He was then chairman of the board of the Federal Deposit Insurance Corporation. He was very skillful at settling rows and cleaning up messes. I went over the priest's past activities—and his future—in some detail. If the grand jury indicted Coughlin, I told Crowley, the resulting controversy might do infinite harm to the war effort. Why could we not appeal to the Church hierarchy to silence Coughlin? Surely the Church did not want that kind of a fight—and we would have to go through with it if we started. The point was to win the war—not to indict a priest for sedition. Who was the man, I asked him, to whom we could appeal, a man of real power, who could and would act? The grand jury might indict Father Coughlin at any moment.

Archbishop Edward Mooney of Detroit, he answered at once, was the only prelate who had authority and would

of the constant details of politics, particularly the endless appointments. I have before me a touching plea: could I not persuade Congress, he wrote me, to get rid of the law requiring him to sign the appointments of notaries public? He was patient until he died, and I sometimes think the little dull burdens were more responsible for his death than the weight of the great decisions.

He grew infinitely tired of the continual bickering between department heads, which went on as if there had been no war; this noisy friction gave the country a sense of disunity and a feeling that the administration did not know where it was going. Differences of opinion were healthy, but the jurisdictional fights for power between the departments and the new war agencies, avidly seized on and dramatically exaggerated by a press eager to exploit struggles among the temporarily great to achieve power, created public confusion and blurred the vision of the war effort. Heads of departments "planted" stories that would present their position, particularly when there was a dispute, or arrange for a subordinate to do so. The subordinate who disagreed with his superior might give his side of the picture to a newspaper friend, whose code forbade him to reveal the source of his information. One hardly dared to share a confidence lest it turn up in a column. There was no domestic censorship, and the use of information was largely left to the patriotism of the reporters. The military found it easier to clamp down on everything than to exercise the difficult practice of judgment, and the military point of view was continually in conflict with the civilian. I remember soon after war had been declared one of my friends' saying to me that to a great extent my part in the war effort would be fighting the Army. . . .

Every now and then the President would lecture the Cabinet on the unseemliness of washing our dirty clothes in public, or write a letter to the department and agency heads. In the middle of that hot and depressing summer of 1942 he sent out such a communication suggesting that we desist from arguing controversial questions in public. Elmer Davis, Director of the Office of War Information, had told him that satisfactory progress had been made toward eliminating much of the conflict and confusion among the departments and agencies so far as their press releases and speeches were concerned. But remarks at press conferences and elsewhere often did not contribute either to the accuracy or the consistency of public information. "If the agencies," the President concluded, "would refrain from resorting to public debate of this kind they would have a good deal more time to attend to their business, and the nation would have a good deal more assurance that the business was being done right."

The language of Roosevelt's memoranda was fresh, informal, and often amusing. "For preparation of a reply"—he wrote once—"with the thought that an offensive's always better than a defensive." He saw that criticisms of my decisions were relayed quickly to me if they touched some essential matter: "There is a good deal of a howl because the Department of Justice has refused to participate as *amicus* in the Texas Primary case. How about it?" I told him that the "howl" came from Walter White of the National Association for the Advancement of Colored People—the President remembered people, not organizations; that we had established the right to vote in primaries as a right enforceable in the federal courts in the Classic case; and that if we intervened here again the South would not understand why we were continually taking sides. I attached a three-page memorandum from the Solicitor General discussing the legal aspects of the case—the

Father Coughlin

exercise it. Father Coughlin was directly under him. "Do you know him?" "Well," he said. "Will you see him *at once*?" He agreed; he was certain he could persuade the Archbishop. He would fly out to Detroit the next day. Should we talk to the President first? On the contrary, Leo said, that would embarrass both of them—"I'll bring it back tied up—then we can tell the President."

In three days he was again in my office, smiling and rubbing his hands at the success of his mission. The Archbishop had agreed at once, without any stipulation or condition. He had sent for Father Coughlin and told him that he must stop all his propaganda, on the air or by pen, for the duration. *Social Justice* should not be published again. The Archbishop wanted his word. The alternative was being unfrocked. The priest agreed, and the Archbishop confirmed his understanding of the arrangement in a brief letter to the President. F.D.R. was delighted with the outcome. That was the end of Father Coughlin.

President liked to read that sort of thing. If it bored him or if it was too long, he put it on a pile of papers to be read, and when the pile got too high would tell his personal secretary, "Missy" LeHand, to take it away.

But usually the President did not want a balanced report; he wanted to be told what should be done, and how to do it. As late as January 10, 1944, he wrote me: "Your memo of January sixth is very interesting but it does not tell me what to do. Do please suggest an *out*, a *modus vivendi*, something really brilliant which will go down into history as a judgment of Solomon!" He could be very terse, exact, and firm. Whenever Congress tried to get hold of correspondence of the Chief Executive or his subordinates that for any reason he did not wish released, he was, in accordance with the tradition of his great office, adamant.

One of the most knowledgeable and pungent messages that I received from him concerned the conditions in Hawaii, where martial law had been declared immediately after Pearl Harbor.

Harold Ickes and I had sent out our representatives, with the President's approval, to investigate what was going on. The Army ran everything—food supply and distribution, communications, traffic, hospitals and health, price control, civilian defense, liquor distribution, gasoline rationing, fiscal matters—even to a large extent the courts. General Delos Carleton Emmons, who was in command of the Hawaiian Department, styling himself "Military Governor," established and enforced the law by issuing military orders. The resulting administration appeared to be autocratic, wasteful, and unjust. A confidential report from the FBI stated that it was common knowledge that blackout regulations were flagrantly violated by officer personnel and that cocktail hours lasted far beyond blackout hours—Pearl Harbor conditions again after a brief year! Emmons got most of his knowledge of local affairs from a small handful of powerful pineapple planters—the Big Five, as they were known. Among the populace there was deep resentment that did not come to the surface, since criticism of the local administration was suppressed by the military.

By the end of 1942 it seemed desirable that the civilian government should be reinstated. After discussing the matter with Ingram Macklin Stainbeck, Governor of the Territory, we took it up with the President, who approved our recommendation to end martial law and told us to prepare a proclamation for his signature and clear it with the Army. The Army in this case meant Assistant Secretary of War John J. McCloy, General Emmons, and another general, Emmons' executive officer, a stuffy, overzealous, unyielding type who had prepared an elaborate and complicated chart

Henry Stimson

showing the setup. I sent it along with a confidential report to the President, as it told the story with laborious eloquence. I ended by saying that the situation had the makings of a lurid congressional investigation and enclosed a note to Grace Tully (who became the President's secretary after "Missy" LeHand's death), asking her to give it to him at once.

The President responded promptly and vigorously. I should talk the matter over with Secretary Stimson *in person*, and tell him from the President that the situation was bad and that he knew from many sources that Emmons got most of his knowledge of conditions from the Big Five. There must be a special Army and Navy investigation into violations of blackout regulations. Hawaii was a thoroughly insidious place for officers stationed there. "That statement needs no argument. There should be a constant rotation of officers and men."

Before Pearl Harbor the President was much concerned with the activities of America First, which he thought of as substantially treasonable. "Will you speak to me about the possibility of a Grand Jury investigation of the America First Committee? It certainly ought to be looked into and I cannot get any action out of Congress." There were too many isolationists in Congress for any such investigation, and there were no grounds to warrant a grand jury investigation—which, the President believed, would show that much of America First's money came from Germany.

There had been a good deal of German propaganda before Pearl Harbor, but there was not much pro-German response, not nearly as much as in the First World War. In the twenty-five years between the two wars there was little German immigration; a large number of the older immigrants had died, and their sons had been quickly absorbed. But the Irish-American population, unified by Catholicism, held its immense identity. Almost all of them were Americans by naturalization or by birth, but they retained the ancient grudge against England. Their isolationism was calculated to prevent linking our fate with that of Great Britain. There it stopped.

Isolationism, as a way of American life, had deep if sometimes irrational roots, going far back into what had been a simpler but not too-distant past. What gave the word a reproachful connotation, often unjustifiably, was that many isolationists shared some of the same views as those who cherished and thrived on hatred: the Jew-baiters, the anti-English, the pro-Germans, and others of that ilk who at heart despised American democracy.

The extravagant abuse of prosecutions for sedition had been the most serious example of hysteria in the First World War. The chief element in the crime of sedition, loosely defined, is incitement by action or language against the government. During a war any criticism of the government is too often construed to be incitement, and severely punished. When, therefore, early in 1942 there were several arrests for "seditious" utterances palpably innocuous, I ordered that the men be released and the prosecutions dropped. One man had expressed the opinion, in a letter to a congressman, that "the Administration of Roosevelt would prove to be as unpopular as the Popular Front government of Daladier and Blum, that undermined the morale of France." Another had told a small group of listeners that the President should be impeached for asking Congress to declare war. A third, a Danish seaman, had started a barroom brawl by proclaiming that Roosevelt was no good and that he himself was for Hitler. Half a dozen isolationists were held in $25,000 bail each. The journalist Jonathan Worth Daniels noted a few other foolish acts that had followed the declaration of war: a man who booed the President's picture in a Chicago theater got thoroughly pommeled by his neighbors—he explained that he was a Republican who had contracted the habit of booing Roosevelt on all occasions and had not had time to readjust himself to new conditions of national unity. He was fined $200 by a magistrate—on Bill of Rights Day.

I directed that thereafter no United States attorney should institute any prosecution based on sedition without my personal written authority and that information about arrests already made should be at once reported to me. I announced that freedom of speech should be curtailed only when public safety was directly imperiled. The majority of the press supported this restraint.

Harold Ickes

Unfortunately, the fifth columnists and their dupes on the lunatic fringe, some of them shrewd enough to find a not-unprofitable way of life in organizing movements based on racial prejudices, took heart at what they considered an official pledge on my part to protect them and allow them to say anything they wanted. A pamphlet, distributed at a West Coast rally, boasted: *"Remember: the United States says we have a perfect right to talk—and we will! . . ."*

The attacks on our allies—without foundation of fact and pandering to hatreds of every possible class and race—increased after war had been declared. These were no longer the voices of isolationists concerned lest we should be dragged into a war that was not our business, but the cries of defeatists welcoming a program of domestic fascism calculated to demoralize the war effort. The movement grew; it was apparently well organized and centrally directed. Nor was it a matter of a handful of scattered publications—the *Christian Science Monitor* estimated that there were nearly a hundred of them.

The "line" in all was about the same and was taken directly from or closely related to official German propaganda: America, not Japan, was guilty of starting the war in the Pacific; American aid to Britain was a Jewish plot, and Roosevelt ("Rosenfeld") was a Jew; American boys were being killed to support a tottering British and French imperialism; the secret manipulations of the new money power and the munitions makers had brought about the war; fighting was useless against the New Order, and we should retire from the war.

The President began to send me brief memoranda to which were attached some of the scurrilous attacks on his leadership, with a notation: *What about this?* or *What are you doing to stop this?* I explained to him my view that it was unwise to bring indictments for sedition—although considering the temper of the times it would be easy to obtain true bills and to convict—except where there was evidence that military recruitment was being substantially interfered with, or where the attacks had some connection with propaganda centers in Germany. I reported that we were in the midst of a study of the material—we must have had a ton of it in the Department—and might ask for some indictments if we could tie up these strident voices with the enemy. Roosevelt was not much interested in the theory of sedition or in the constitutional right to criticize the government in wartime. He wanted this antiwar talk stopped.

The President was getting a good deal of mail complaining about the "softness" of his Attorney General. After two weeks during which F.D.R.'s manner when

I saw him said as plainly as words that he considered me out of step, he began to go for me in Cabinet. His technique was always the same. When my turn came, as he went around the table, his habitual affability dropped. He did not ask me as usual if I had anything to report. He looked at me, his face pulled tightly together: "When are you going to indict the seditionists?" he would ask; and the next week, and every week after that, until an indictment was found, he would repeat the same question. Of course I felt uncomfortable. I told him when we were alone that there was an immense amount of evidence; that I wanted the indictment to stick when it was challenged; and that we could not indict these men for their naked writings and spoken words without showing what effect they had on the war effort. His way of listening made my explanation sound unreal. At the Cabinet meeting a day or two after the return of an indictment * he said, now in his most conciliatory manner: "I was glad to

see, Francis, that the grand jury returned a true bill." I cannot remember any other instance of his putting pressure on me. He never tried to interfere with any decision I made, even if he thought it might have serious political repercussions.

There were a great number of memoranda about appointments. "Tom Connally wants Keating for Judge. Has been Attorney General of Texas—just over age. Can we do?" The age limit for federal judges, to which the President referred, was sixty—an arbitrary measure he had fixed on when he was trying to enlarge the Supreme Court, and which he disregarded when it suited him. Or again in longhand: "F. Biddle: Bill Cole of Md. for Customs Ct. in N.Y. Speaker [Sam Rayburn] and John [McCormack, Democratic majority leader of the House] say O.K.???" Sometimes, if the suggestion seemed without enthusiasm and the candidate unpromising, I would table it, and often the President would not mention it again—he had done his bit, and could say to Tom or Sam or John that he had taken it up with the Attorney General.

Now and then I would send him something that I thought might amuse him. When his old friend Ed Flynn, chairman of the Democratic National Commit-

---

* On July 29, 1942, twenty-six native Fascists were indicted under the Espionage Act of 1917 and the Criminal Conspiracy Act of 1940. It was a case beset with difficulties, not the least of which was the violent conduct in court of the defendants. Their trial dragged on for more than a year, and was eventually dropped after the death of the judge. Though none of the accused was ever convicted, their seditionist activities had been throttled.

THE PERILS OF AN ATTORNEY GENERAL:

II. The Intractable Mr. Avery

"No act of mine as Attorney General," Francis Biddle writes, "caused more sharp resentment and blame than the part I played in connection with the seizure by the government of the Chicago plant of Montgomery Ward & Co. The criticism came chiefly from those who were opposed to President Roosevelt and the New Deal. . . But the seizure was, I regret to say, unnecessarily melodramatic, and had the quality of opéra bouffe, for which I must share the blame. Yet it was essential for the war effort that the step be taken.'

The dispute revolved around the intransigence of the chairman of the board and president of Montgomery Ward, Sewell Avery, "a shrewd and thoroughly reactionary individualist," in Mr. Biddle's phrase, "who fought organized labor all his life." For years he had successfully barred unions from his company. Then, in the early days of 1942, a C.I.O. local won an election in his Chicago plant. Avery refused to recognize it as a bargaining agent, and repeatedly defied the efforts of the War Labor Board to mediate. Since the resistance of such a large corporation could affect the precarious stability of wartime labor-management relations, thereby jeopardizing war production, the President ordered the Secretary of Commerce to seize the Chicago plant. Avery still balked, and as the situation deteriorated, Attorney General Biddle, the nation's highest-ranking legal officer, was brought into the fray. Flying to Chicago, he confronted the government's powerful adversary:

Mr. Avery walked into his office at five minutes before ten. He had evidently got wind of our arrival—there was a reporter at the airport when we got there. I told him that we were extremely sorry to interfere with his business, that we

tee, was accused of using WPA work in connection with a private road that he was building at about the same time Errol Flynn of movie fame was engaged in more romantic adventures at sea, a little verse by Thomas Hornsby Ferril appeared in the *Rocky Mountain Herald*. I sent it to the President:

> *Flynns Errol and Ed confuse my head—*
> *I'm daft with yachts and paving blocks;*
> *I'm all mixed up with right behaving,*
> *(Who's without Flynn can throw the first paving)*
> *I'm all mixed up on women and wine*
> *(To Errol's human, but to Flynn divine).*

F.D.R. didn't like it—he was a little hurt or angry or indignant when his professional friends were under attack; after all, he was the most professional of all of them. He rejoined curtly—"You must think you're quite a poet."

But if he did not like this verse about the Flynns, he unreservedly enjoyed a book I sent him, not long before he went to the fateful conferences at Yalta. It was Mark Twain's famous *1601; or Conversation at the social fireside as it was in the time of the Tudors*. It was hard to get, too ribald to send through the mails, and my copy from some anonymous publisher

in Canada had been sent years before by express. Roosevelt once told me that when he was librarian of the Fly Club at Harvard he had tried unsuccessfully to obtain a copy of this description of Sir Walter Raleigh's unseemly behavior at Queen Elizabeth's court.

Finally a friend of mine secured one for me. I took it over to Cabinet and gave it to him after the meeting —everyone had gone except Jesse Jones, who seemed determined to be the last and evidently had something of importance to take up that he did not wish anyone else to hear. The President picked up the book eagerly, began to thumb through it, and called to Secretary Jones: "Come here, Jesse, and listen to this—how little Willie wet the bed": and in his strong resonant voice he began to read to us Eugene Field's poem, which was included in the book, while Jesse, who did not like anything, particularly humor, to come between him and the President, listened with a dark, patient look to a man who at times could be so inappropriately boyish.

After the President had died I asked Grace Tully if she had ever heard him speak of the book. She remembered that he had given it to her and told her she must put it away carefully in his library where no one would find it, and she was not to look at it, it was

were obeying orders, acting under the President's direction issued under the law. I asked him to co-operate. Avery bluntly refused to do so. I suggested he direct that the company's books be turned over to the government bookkeepers, so that a new set of books could be opened. This, too, he declined to do. He said that he was the boss, and would do things his own way. Wayne Taylor [the Undersecretary of Commerce, who had been directing the operation up to that point] suggested Avery call a meeting of his staff and ask them to co-operate with us. Avery said he would do just the opposite—"To hell with the government." There was a pause. I was deeply shocked. This reckless old man was paralyzing the national war effort that had been built up with such infinite pains. Turning to Taylor I said: "Take him out!" Avery looked at me venomously, summoning the most contemptuous words he could think of; and finally—*"You New Dealer!"* he managed to say. Taylor suggested to the officer in command of the half dozen soldiers who were waiting that, "on advice of counsel," he should remove Mr. Avery. Under the directions of the officer, who kept apologizing to Avery, two soldiers gingerly picked him up and put him on a "hand-seat," crossing their hands and gripping each other's wrists under him, while he sat, comfortably relaxed, and as dignified as the circumstances of his ride permitted, his hands crossed benignly over his stomach. They put him on an elevator which bore him to the ground floor, and finally deposited him near a "no parking" sign where his car and chauffeur were waiting. He bowed to the crowd, smiled frostily, and stepped into his car. One photographer who somehow had been locked out of the building when the government took over was

RETURN OF THE VICTORIOUS GENERAL BIDDLE

there when this solemn and absurd little group arrived, and managed to get an excellent photograph of Avery (at left) carried by the soldiers, before he got into his car—an exhibition that was destined to flame with accompanying headlines in every paper across the country: U.S. TROOPS EJECT AVERY . . . The picture did more to rouse the country to Avery's defense than any argument on the merits of the controversy. Jesse Jones called me from Washington: "I hear you've been wrapping packages all day," he said. "Only one," I told him.

very naughty, and now and then she might remind him where it was—Jesse Jones had given it to him after a Cabinet meeting. Thus is history written! I hope the book is preserved in the Hyde Park library. . . .

I tried never to bother the President with anything that was not essential, and to wait until a substantial number of problems—many of them appointments—had accumulated. I would call "Pa" Watson, the President's appointment secretary, and was often summoned for lunch with the President in his study, where we had solid food—an omelette or fish or chops, with plenty of coffee. When he would lean back in his chair and take the first long, deeply inhaled pull at his cigarette, I would get down to business, sometimes submitting a brief memorandum or directive for initialing. In this way I could get in a comfortable hour, except during the last year of his life, when he began to resent such accumulating burdens, and to postpone them.

His training had made him cautious; he knew that everyone who saw him was in a hurry to get quick approval; he had come to practice the procrastination that brought him a sense of relief. Yet when he wanted to act, particularly where the war called for speed—and war decisions almost invariably did—he would hound the responsible official, often calling him more than once personally.

Henry Morgenthau, Jr.

He rarely queried me about department problems, but frequently asked what I thought of so-and-so. He liked to relax in reminiscence, and I would ply him with questions about his own life, about Cousin Theodore, or about the war. Once I remember suggesting that there were those—I was not one of them—who thought him too pro-British, too much led by Churchill, who had recently been staying at the White House. I hoped he fought back now and then; the British understood that, and always respected a show of opposition. He agreed, nodding his head. He told me of a proposal—half serious, half jocular—that he had made recently to "Winnie," one of several "after-the-war" arrangements, like the internationalization of Hong Kong, about which his lively imagination used to play without coming to rest on them. Why not, when the war was over, F.D.R. had said to his guest as they relaxed together over brandy after dinner, why not give the Elgin marbles back to Greece? It would be a wonderful gesture of international friendship; the whole Near East would applaud at the sight of the British lion disgorging. "You know you stole them and you ought to give them back. You could announce that you had been cleaning them and putting them in proper shape." "How did he take it?" I asked. "Take it!" he answered. "He almost went through the roof."

F.D.R. took his time about appointing judges and never considered there was any particular hurry about filling a vacancy. While I was in office there was only one on the Supreme Court, caused when James Francis Byrnes resigned on October 3, 1942, to become Director of Economic Stabilization. For ten months Byrnes had been on leave of absence from the Court, working with the President in the war effort.

Several times I suggested to F.D.R. that the Court was shorthanded, that Byrnes ought to resign, and that the President should appoint a successor; but he waved me aside a little impatiently, saying, "Let's keep it open for Jimmy, they can get along." But when the 1943 term of Court opened, there were several mildly critical editorials. For nearly two years the Court had felt the burden of the extra work, a load which is always great and which at times, when each member is not pulling his weight, may become intolerable. Chief Justice Harlan Fiske Stone asked me if I would speak to the President, and I took it up with him again, urging him to make the appointment as soon as he could find the right man. He nodded an unwilling assent—he supposed I was right, he would think it over.

Eventually I convinced him that we could not keep the position open for Jimmy Byrnes any longer. Well then, he asked, could we not appoint some old boy for two or three years who would agree to retire when he had reached seventy, so that Jimmy could be brought back? I replied that this would not quite fit in with his often avowed intention to put younger men on the high tribunal. I suppose not, he acquiesced without enthusiasm. I suggested that I might talk to Chief Justice Stone again, and he assented. "See if you can't get me a nice, solid Republican," he said as I left, "to balance things a bit, preferably someone west of the Mississippi, and not a professor."

When I saw Stone early in November, he said at once that he wanted someone who would "stick." He wanted a man of broad legal training and experience—a judge from one of the Circuit Courts would fit in admirably. I said I thought the Circuits had little material of first-rate caliber. "Nonsense, Biddle!" he said, and pulled out a volume of the Circuit Court reports containing a list of the judges. This he read carefully; then looked up. "By gum," he said, "you're about right."

But there were a few: Learned Hand, head and

Henry Wallace

shoulders above any others; John J. Parker, Sam Bratton, who had been on the Tenth Circuit since 1933 (a good Democrat, he had been Senator from New Mexico); Orie Phillips, if you wanted a Republican, also from the Tenth; and Wiley Rutledge, who had been on the U.S. Court of Appeals for the District of Columbia for four years after teaching law for fifteen —Rutledge was a good man and young, a little pedestrian but sound. And Charley Fahy, the Solicitor General, I asked him. He considered, his chin in his hand. They had all liked the way Fahy presented his cases— he was objective, clear, scrupulous. But if we put another Catholic on the Court in addition to Frank Murphy, he suggested, the Church might feel it was always regularly entitled to two. I mentioned Dean Acheson, but it was clear that Stone preferred one of the federal judges.

Outside of Hand, who was far more distinguished than any of the others, Rutledge seemed to me the most promising. His views were sound, carefully reasoned, and lawyerlike. He was apt to be long-winded, probably because he suffered from a sense of obligation to answer everything in the case. He was a liberal who would stand up for human rights, particularly during a war when they were apt to be forgotten. But there was nothing extreme or messianic about his approach. He was certainly not a nice solid Republican.

All of which I reported to the President. Where did Rutledge come from, he asked me. He was born in Kentucky, had taught high school in Indiana, New Mexico, and Colorado and law in Colorado and Iowa. "He'll do," said the President, and then, "What do you think about Hand?" I repeated what the Chief Justice had said—head and shoulders above the others. The President told me that he had had a great many letters from men whose opinion he valued, favoring Hand. When I saw him again, he was much cooler when I spoke of Hand; and I heard later that he resented what he called the "organized pressure" in Hand's behalf. The President told me that he had determined to appoint Rutledge, and that I should get the papers ready and send them to Grace Tully.

Rutledge was a modest man and was amazed when I told him—he really believed he was not up to it. Ten years later, when a chance ocean-crossing threw Hand and me together, and I got to know him and to admire his really first-rate qualities of heart and mind, I came to believe that his appointment would have been more suitable and that I should have urged the President to appoint him in spite of his age. He had the "fire in his belly" that old Holmes used to talk about.

During the many discussions and speculations about Byrnes' successor, it was natural that I should have been mentioned. My two predecessors, Frank Murphy and Robert Jackson, had gone from the Attorney Generalship to the Court; the precedent seemed to have been established. I was determined, however, not to accept the appointment even if the President wished me to do so. My brief experience on the Circuit bench had not been satisfactory, and I did not wish to renew the mild level of judicial life, on which I had felt cut off from the world and out of things. The members of the Court in Washington seemed to me terribly overworked. I had immensely enjoyed arguing cases as Solicitor General, but that was different—I was doing the arguing, not listening to it.

I dreaded the quiet, plodding, uninterrupted work of a judge. And I did not want to leave the heart of things while war was on. I was always more interested in the vivid present than the future. I was afraid that the President might send down my name without speaking to me first, and it would be embarrassing then to say no. I said a word to Lewis Wood of the *New York Times,* whom I knew well, as he was assigned to cover the Justice Department and the Court, and in a story he reflected the "impression" that I did not want to be appointed. Soon after, I went over to see the President.

I told him I had come to talk about the vacancy on the Court. Did I want it, he asked. No, I said, I did not wish to leave him during the war, I was happy where I was, I had not liked being a judge. I reminded him of the time he had asked me three years before to go on the Circuit Court, and I had said that being a judge was like being a priest. The President was listening, enjoying the recollection. I added that on that occasion I had asked for an hour or two to think it over; and he had said he was going to a movie and to call him back; and that I had replied that I would call his assistant, Marvin McIntyre. "No," he had said, *"don't call Mac, call me."* He laughed again—he was in a good humor that day —and took my arm: "You are quite right, Francis," he said, now gravely. "You and I are too young to go on courts; we've got our careers ahead of us"—he was sixty, I fifty-six. I believe I never liked him more than at that moment.

N.Y. Times

Frances Perkins

"Bull Run" Russell CONTINUED FROM PAGE 61

by rail. Effectively screening Johnston's movement from the Union commander who was supposed to detain him in the Valley was the cavalry of Colonel J. E. B. Stuart. In the vanguard of Johnston's force was a Virginia brigade commanded by a stern, God-fearing former instructor at the Virginia Military Institute—Thomas J. Jackson.

The Union attack, scheduled for Sunday morning, July 21, called for an initial feint at Blackburn's Ford, toward Beauregard's right, followed immediately by a second diversionary effort at the stone bridge by 8,000 men of Brigadier General Daniel Tyler's First Division. While the enemy's attention was riveted on these actions, McDowell proposed to take the 12,000 men of the Second and Third Divisions, led by Colonels David Hunter and Samuel P. Heintzelman, on a circuitous route to Sudley Springs Ford, about three miles above the bridge. This force was to cross Bull Run and fall upon the unprotected Confederate left flank. As the attack swept down the Southern-held bank of Bull Run, the enemy was expected to roll back, opening the way for Tyler's men to cross all along the line. More than 10,000 troops, almost a third of McDowell's army, were to be kept in reserve in and around Centreville.

McDowell's plan was, essentially, a good one. But for an amateur army, led by inexperienced officers, it was plainly too elaborate and involved too many risks. It called for clock-like co-ordination of widely separated units, and McDowell's staff organization was virtually nonexistent. Also, it did not take into account the possible reinforcement of Beauregard on the eve of the battle.

Joe Johnston and the first contingent of his men from the Shenandoah Valley reached Beauregard at Manassas about noon on Saturday, July 20. Growing restless over McDowell's failure to attack, Beauregard formulated an offensive plan of his own—and this he presented to Johnston, who quickly approved it. Though senior in rank, Johnston agreed to give field command to Beauregard because of the latter's familiarity with the terrain, but he retained over-all command of the army for himself. The Confederate battle plan was curiously similar to McDowell's in that it hinged on a thrust against the enemy's left. Had both plans been put into operation successfully, the armies might well have swung completely around in the manner of a revolving door. As it came about, success was to fall to the commander who failed to execute his plan.

Back in Washington, excitement over the impending clash was mounting. Russell, determined not to miss the fight, was combing Washington livery stables for horses and a rig to take him to Virginia, but prices rose with each new report from the front. The reporter was outraged when one man asked $1,000 for a spavined bay. "Take it or leave it," the man told Russell. "If you want to see this fight a thousand dollars is cheap. I guess there were chaps paid more than that to see Jenny Lind on her first night, and this battle is not going to be repeated, I can tell you." Reluctantly, Russell paid an exorbitant price for a two-horse gig and prepared to set out at dawn for Bull Run.

Shortly after two o'clock on that Sunday morning, July 21, McDowell had his sleepy men roused and formed for the movement into battle. Once again this force demonstrated its seemingly limitless incapacity for organized movement. Colonel Heintzelman never found the road he was to take and was forced to follow blindly in Hunter's path. Not until after 9 A.M. did the first Union brigade, commanded by Colonel Ambrose E. Burnside, reach Sudley Springs Ford.

At that hour William Howard Russell had just crossed the Potomac and was beginning to enjoy this early morning spin through the pleasant Virginia countryside. "The promise of a lovely day, given by the dawn, was likely to be realised to the fullest," he later recalled of that moment, "and the placid beauty of the scenery . . . breathed of peace." His reverie, however, was shortly interrupted by the sound of firing. "They are at it," he shouted to his driver. "We shall be late! Drive on as fast as you can."

Soon after, Russell stopped at a farmhouse to gather information and inquire for directions. His attention was suddenly directed to a cloud of dust on the road in front of him. Out of it slowly materialized a large body of laughing, chattering men, moving in twos and threes down the road away from the sound of firing. It was the 4th Pennsylvania Regiment. The correspondent stopped one of its officers. "May I beg to know, sir, where your regiment is going to? . . . I should think there is severe fighting going on behind you, judging from the firing. . . ."

"Well, I reckon there is," the officer replied. Then, after a long pause, he added by way of explanation: "We are going home because, as you see, the men's time's up, sir. We have had three months of this sort of work, and that's quite enough of it."

McDowell himself had pleaded with this regiment to stay on for the battle, but, its ninety-day term of service expiring on July 20, the 4th Pennsylvania had simply walked away. This was Russell's first experience with the volunteer soldier on the field, and he was frankly horrified.

The firing had been going on since early morning. Tyler opened his showy feint at the stone bridge at 5:15 A.M., but the Confederates across the bridge, under the calm and efficient command of Colonel Nathan G. Evans, correctly interpreted this for the diversionary effort it was. Meanwhile, Evans was watching the suspicious clouds of dust rising far to his left. About 8 A.M. he realized that a major effort would shortly be made to turn his left flank. Precisely according to the regulations of the book, he notified the commander to his immediate right that he was abandoning his position and within an hour had about half his men concealed in the woods facing Sudley Springs Ford.

The first Union troops across Bull Run, Burnside's Rhode Islanders, debouched out into the open, where they were easy targets for Evans' waiting Rebels. The division commander, David Hunter, was almost immediately felled by a sharpshooter's bullet. McDowell was present, but he was being forced to spend more time than he should have in attending to petty details. In addition, a digestive complaint this morning made it impossible for him to mount a horse. And so he careened about the battlefield executing the functions of an aide-de-camp from the seat of a carriage. It was a distinctly uninspiring sight to his men.

The Confederate commanders, Johnston and Beau-regard, had more correctly selected an observation post, one overlooking Mitchell's Ford, where they hopefully expected the development of the battle they had planned. Not until nearly 11 A.M. did they realize that the battle on their right was never going to proceed according to plan. Johnston quickly made some final disposition for reinforcements and set off for the scene of developing action beyond the Warrenton Turnpike. Mounting the first of four horses he was to exhaust that day, Beauregard joined him without a word. After they had surveyed the situation, Johnston agreed to return to the rear to send reinforcements, and Beauregard took up front-line command.

McDowell, his flanking movement no longer a surprise, had wisely doubled up his troops to get Heintzelman's division on the field alongside that of the fallen Hunter and thus overlap the Southern defensive line. It was one of the last clear command decisions of the day. Henceforth the men would be fighting almost as individuals. The battle drill by which a regiment of ten companies moved from column to line was complicated enough when practiced on the drill field in camp. On the field, with woods and gullies separating these units, with shouted orders lost in the din of gunfire, such intricate movements were all but impossible for poorly trained men. The commander of a Vermont regiment saw his force disintegrate when he attempted to move them from one

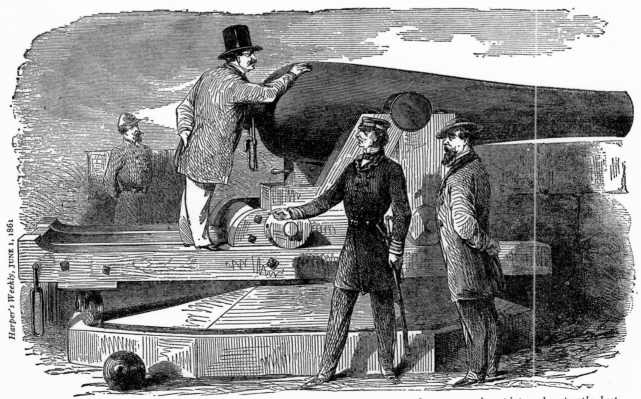

Harper's Weekly, JUNE 1, 1861

Before Bull Run, while Russell was still lionized by both sides, a northern magazine pictured a portly but distinguished gentleman inspecting a ten-incher at the Confederate-held Fort Pulaski near Savannah, Georgia.

place to another. To get them off the field, he ordered a right-face past enemy artillery and another right-face to go to the rear. Apparently, the command of about-face had slipped his mind.

Two competent U.S. Regulars, Captains Charles Griffin and J. B. Ricketts, whipped their batteries of artillery onto the scene and, supported by a regiment of zouaves, took up an advanced position near the Warrenton Turnpike. Their advance was largely responsible for the initial success of McDowell's flanking movement. The Confederates reeled back across the Turnpike to take up an uneasy defensive position on Henry House Hill.

Evans' makeshift defense against McDowell's attack had been strengthened by the Confederate brigades of Bernard Bee, F. S. Bartow, T. J. Jackson, and the 600 men of Hampton's Legion, privately recruited and outfitted by South Carolina's immensely wealthy Wade Hampton. Pushed back across the Turnpike, these intermingled units had hastily formed an uneven defensive line about the Henry house. Bee, realizing that his men were on the verge of retreat, pointed to the hill where Jackson's brigade was stoutly resisting the Federal sweep. "There stands Jackson, like a stone wall," he was later reported as crying. "Rally on the Virginians." And a name and a tradition were born. Yet it seemed at that hour that the Southern cause was irretrievably lost.

Russell had reached Fairfax Court House by 11 A.M. En route to Centreville, six miles further on toward the front, he experienced a little of the frustration that had earlier plagued McDowell in finding his way about this section of tangled Virginia countryside. The fields and forests of the region were interlaced with a network of narrow country lanes, all appearing identical to the British journalist. But somehow, by 1 P.M., he managed to reach his destination.

The Russell carriage pulled up alongside a crowd of eager spectators on a hill near Centreville overlooking the valley of Bull Run. This was a holiday outing for senators, congressmen, and their ladies, who had brought picnic lunches.

Below the hill stretched a densely wooded vista of some five or six miles. The woods echoed with cannon fire, and tatters of blue smoke drifted lazily over the trees. Through them, Russell detected the twinkle of sun striking bayonets. He joined the group of spectators. A lady with opera glasses shouted loudly at each discharge of cannon: "That is splendid. Oh, my! Is not that first rate? I guess we will be in Richmond this time tomorrow." Another bystander asked Russell's professional opinion: "Are we really seeing a battle now? Are they supposed to be fighting where

N.Y. Illustrated News, sept. 2, 1861

After the Union disaster, a cartoonist caricatured the English correspondent as a swinish boozer who viewed the battle from a safe remove through bleary eyes and a spyglass.

all that smoke is going on? This is rather interesting, you know." A soldier borrowed Russell's flask and took "a startling pull, which left little between the bottom and utter vacuity." *The Times* of London was not amused.

After lunch an officer rode up to tell them that the Federals were sweeping the field. This brought a series of cheers; and the politicians shook hands around, exclaiming, "Bully for us. Bravo, didn't I tell you so." Russell's practiced eye was not satisfied with the distant view from the hilltop, however, and secondhand reports were of little value to him. Mounting the saddle horse he had brought for this occasion, he jogged down the hill for a closer look.

Russell, of course, was still far to the rear, completely ignorant of the action raging in the early afternoon around Henry House Hill. Colonel William Tecumseh Sherman, commanding a brigade of Tyler's division, had been posted above the stone bridge since early in the morning and had finally got his men across a previously undetected ford to add new muscle to the Federal attack on the hill. Here the Union batteries of Griffin and Ricketts seemed to have command of the situation. The Rebel defenders hung on desperately; but McDowell's army was on the brink of success. Then, in a moment of confusion, the Union's hope of ending the rebellion with one quick stroke was shattered forever.

Out of the woods in front of the Union artillery appeared a blue-clad regiment, its battle flag hanging limply in the still air of this oppressively hot day. There was no clear battle line in this fight, and the Federals held their fire for fear of killing their own men.

The unit—it was the 33rd Virginia Regiment of Jackson's brigade—advanced to within seventy yards and then calmly let loose a deadly volley that destroyed the Union position. Ricketts was wounded and captured; Griffin was forced to abandon his guns and retreat. The ground he left behind, a Confederate artillery officer noted after the battle, "looked as though it had been rooted up by hogs."

This was not the only case of mistaken identity on the field that day. At about this hour, Jeb Stuart's cavalry was coming to the aid of the nearly overwhelmed Confederate defenders of Henry House Hill. Seeing a dispersed group of men, he called out: "Don't run, boys; we are here." A vagrant wind stirred their lifeless banner; it was the United States flag, and Stuart hastily ordered a charge that sent these men flying and checked the Union advance on Jackson's hard-pressed men. (Earlier in the day, Sherman had sent forward the 2nd Wisconsin, proudly outfitted in natty gray uniforms. The men soon came scurrying back: they were being fired on by other Union troops.)

The overthrow of their batteries on Henry House Hill was the beginning of the end for the Union that day. Fresh Confederate soldiers under Jubal Early and Kirby Smith—the latter being the final detachment of Johnston's men from the Shenandoah Valley—reached the field about 3:30 P.M. to pound in the sagging Union right. Burnside's Rhode Islanders, having engaged in the initial skirmish at Sudley Springs that morning, had been out of action for six hours, lounging in the shade and waiting for orders that would send them back into the fight. When the order came, about 4 P.M., the Union line had disintegrated. There was no battle to which they could return.

This was no rout. Men on both sides, exhausted by the long and arduous struggle, were simply leaving the field by twos and threes, discussing among themselves the fortunes of the day. Jefferson Davis, arriving very late in the afternoon, was appalled at the number of Southern stragglers coming to the rear. But the men paid no attention whatsoever to the tall civilian on horseback who attempted to rally them. There was little chance of pursuing the Federal army. His Confederate force, Joe Johnston would one day sadly recall, "was more disorganized by victory than that of the United States by defeat."

McDowell's order to withdraw, when it came, was utterly superfluous. The decision, he noted in his official report of the battle, "had been anticipated by the troops." Back they came, splashing across the now uncontested fords of Bull Run and crowding onto the Warrenton Turnpike that led to Centreville. In the process, unit organization broke down completely; and McDowell's army became just so many individ-

uals scrambling to save themselves. A New York boy complained of the sporadic Southern artillery that harassed the retrograde movement: "Captain," he asked, "why do the rebels keep shelling us when we're doing our best to leave them alone?"

The correspondent of the London *Times* had meanwhile traveled on horseback some distance beyond the hill at Centreville and toward the fighting at Bull Run. Suddenly he perceived several wagons coming toward him at a reckless speed. At first he thought they must be returning from the field for fresh supplies of ammunition. But, as the traffic grew thicker, he began to realize that something was wrong.

"What is all this about?" Russell politely inquired of an officer. "Why it means we are pretty badly whipped, that's the truth," the man gasped before rushing off. Displaying righteous indignation, Russell attempted to interfere with a driver going so fast that he was losing all his baggage. A loaded musket was pointed at his head, and the Britisher gracefully withdrew his protest. "My attempts to save Uncle Sam's property were then and there discontinued," he later wrote.

The road now was choked with carts, wagons, straggling foot soldiers, and mounted officers. Those returning from the field had pushed up against those still en route to the battle, and there was a hopeless, inextricable snarl. A stray burst of Rebel artillery upset a wagon on the Cub Run bridge between Bull Run and Centreville, and the traffic jam became complete.

To men who repeatedly asked him where the army would halt, Russell calmly replied "Centreville"—it seemed a logical rallying point to this veteran observer, as long as anyone was interested in his opinion. Although his personal sympathies were undoubtedly with the Union, the correspondent was here motivated by a dislike of military incompetence and a very strong conviction that the mounting panic was completely uncalled for. His military judgment was quite correct at Centreville; it would have been possible for him to at Centreville; it would have been possible for him to hold this place and regroup his forces but for the senseless panic that swept through his retreating army.

Contributing greatly to this panic was the fear among the Union stragglers that they were about to be charged by the enemy's Black Horse Cavalry, a Rebel bogeyman that had received a good deal of publicity. Russell pooh-poohed the notion of cavalry operating in this broken and crowded terrain. "There's no enemy to pursue you," he told a frightened group. "All the cavalry in the world could not get at you." But there was little room for logic in this confusing situation. Seeing that he could accomplish nothing, Russell finally joined the irresistible tide flowing back to Centreville.

As yet, the epic proportions of the retreat were not apparent to him, and, beyond Centreville, he was thoroughly surprised to see the movement continuing unabated. Again assuming a knowledgeable air, he approached an officer. "I venture to suggest that these men should be stopped, sir," he said. "If not, they will alarm the whole of the post and pickets on to Washington. They will fly next, and the consequences will be most disastrous." The officer dashed forward to act on Russell's proposal. Satisfied that a rout had been avoided, the reporter continued on to Washington. To a road companion ready to acknowledge defeat, he sharply retorted: "Oh, don't say that . . . it's not quite so bad, it's only a drawn battle and the troops will occupy Centreville."

Still exuding confidence, Russell passed over the Long Bridge and entered Washington by moonlight at 11 P.M.

Toward evening Lincoln had returned from his carriage ride to learn the bad news. At the War Department telegraph office he read the latest dispatch: "The day is lost. Save Washington and the remnants of this army. The routed troops will not re-form." The President spent a sleepless night on a sofa in the White House Cabinet room. "If there were nothing else of Abraham Lincoln for history to stamp him with," Walt Whitman later wrote, "it is enough . . . that he endured that hour, that day, bitterer than gall—indeed a crucifixion day—that it did not conquer him—that he unflinchingly stemm'd it, and resolv'd to lift himself and the Union out of it."

Russell, that night, attempted to record his impressions of the day's events. But his head drooped, and at last he fell sound asleep at his desk. At six the following morning he was awakened by the steady tattoo of rain on his window. A different sound, that of tramping feet, brought him out to the street. To his immense surprise, he saw a steady stream of mud-spattered men, many without weapons, coats, or knapsacks, pouring up Pennsylvania Avenue to the Capitol. He asked a passing officer where these men were coming from and what was their destination.

"Well, sir," the man replied, "I guess we're all coming out of Verginny as far as we can and pretty well whipped too." "What! the whole army, sir?" inquired the incredulous reporter. "That's more than I know," came the answer. "They may stay like that. I know I'm going home. I've had enough of fighting to last my lifetime."

Stunned, Russell returned to his room. He had two alternatives: spend the day gathering more detailed information on the magnitude of the disaster, or immediately record his impressions of the previous day while they were still fresh in his memory. He chose the latter course and remained closeted the entire day, only occasionally glancing up from his desk to watch the dismal procession outside his window.

A great many preposterous claims would be made about this battle. Johnston, for instance, reported that 8,000 Rebels had defeated 35,000 Federals; Beauregard hinted that the Union force numbered 55,000. McDowell contented himself with saying that the enemy "brought up all he could . . ." Actually, the forces had been amazingly well matched. Each side managed to engage about 18,000 of its 30,000 available men. The official casualty lists also reflected a strange similarity. The Union lost 470 men killed to the Confederacy's 387; 1,124 Northern soldiers were wounded to the 1,582 for the South. But 1,312 Federals were reported missing and presumed captured to the Rebels' 13. More importantly, the Southerners picked up 28 fieldpieces, including eight badly needed rifled guns; 500 muskets with 500,000 rounds of ammunition; and scores of horses, wagons, and caissons abandoned by the fleeing Northerners. The casualty figures were modest in comparison with the bloody toll of later Civil War battles, but at the time they were sobering enough.

The South, of course, was exultant over its victory and confident that independence had been won. Johnston and Beauregard issued a high-blown congratulatory proclamation: "You have created an epoch in the history of liberty," their men were told, "and unborn nations will call you blessed."

The Northern press was forced to admit a defeat. But out of the ignominy of Bull Run came a new resolve to preserve the Union and a gradual realization that the struggle would be a long one. On July 23, Lincoln outlined a new program: The blockade of the Confederacy would be tightened; Maryland would be kept in the Union at all costs so as to prevent the isolation of Washington; and three-month militia would be replaced with long-term volunteers.

The excitement generated by Bull Run was slow in dying. Once the initial shock was over, press and public became anxious for the views of *The Times'* famous correspondent. "We scarcely exaggerate the fact," commented the *New York Times*, "when we say the first and foremost thought in the minds of a very large portion of our people after the repulse of Bull Run was, What will Russell say?" They had a month to wait; for Russell's story, published in London on August 6, did not reach America until August 20.

The report began with the frank admission that it was not an account of the action itself but merely the story of the retreat as Russell had observed it. This did not lessen the impact of one of the opening paragraphs, which read:

. . . the repulse of the Federalists, decided as it was, might have had no serious effects whatsoever beyond mere failure . . . but for the disgraceful conduct of the troops. The retreat on their lines at Centreville seems to have ended in a cowardly route [*sic*]—a miserable, causeless panic. Such scandalous behaviour on the part of soldiers I should not have considered possible, as with some experience of camps and armies I have never even in alarms among camp followers seen the like of it.

In six and one-half columns Russell went on to tell of men "whom it were a disgrace to the profession of arms to call soldiers" running wild-eyed and frightened from battle. He criticized the baggage-wagon drivers as ignorant, declared inadequate the system of guards and pickets, and took a passing pot shot or two at the never-ending political interference in military affairs.

The reaction in the North to this frank dispatch was immediate and stormy. Friends warned Russell not to stray outside unarmed; one said he would not take a million dollars to be in his place. His mail was flooded with anonymous letters threatening him with tarring and feathering or death by revolver or bowie knife.

William Tecumseh Sherman, however, endorsed Russell's report; the photographer Mathew Brady told him that his description of the retreat fell far short of the actual disgrace. And Irvin McDowell confided that "Bull Run was an unfortunate affair for both of us, for had I won it you would have had to describe the pursuit of the flying enemy and then you would have been the most popular writer in America and I should have been lauded as the greatest of generals."

The press, on the other hand, was relentless in its condemnation of Russell. The Chicago *Tribune* flatly stated that he had not even seen the rout he described. The New York *Herald* accused him of being a Confederate agent who led the retreat. He became the subject of many spiteful cartoons that caricatured his tendency to plumpness and hinted that the entire story had been conjured up out of a bottle of London stout (see page 80).

But cruelest of all was the epithet of "Bull Run" Russell which someone, he never knew who, pinned on him. This crude attempt to equate the unfortunate name of the battlefield with Russell's imaginary flight from the scene of the action puzzled him as much as it hurt him. "The Americans," he wrote, "seem to think that a disgrace to their arms becomes diminished by fixing the name of the scene as a *sobriquet* on me who described it."

Russell's position in Washington became increasingly untenable. He thought he detected a snub on the part of Lincoln early in September. *The Times* continued its strongly pro-Southern editorial policy. Russell's frankness in reporting Bull Run cast doubt on his objectivity as a reporter. That fall the Trent affair, growing out of the seizure by a Federal officer of Southern emissaries to Europe aboard a British mail steamer, raised the threat of war between the North and Great Britain.

The following spring, at the invitation of Major General George B. McClellan, Russell applied for permission to accompany the Army of the Potomac down to Fortress Monroe at the outset of the Peninsular Campaign. At the last minute Secretary of War Edwin Stanton had him pulled off the steamer. It was the last straw. Two days later, on April 4, 1862, Russell engaged a berth on the very next ship leaving New York for England.

A year later, in 1863, Russell published his intimate reminiscences of what he had seen of the Civil War in a two-volume book called *My Diary, North and South*. It went virtually unnoticed in America, where once everything Russell wrote had been a national topic of conversation. This was a crucial year in the war— and people just then were talking about the Vicksburg campaign of Major General Ulysses S. Grant and the bitter three-day clash of arms at a Pennsylvania crossroads village named Gettysburg.

Joseph L. Gardner is assistant editor of the American Heritage Book Division.

First Things First

Please send me by the Rock Creek stage 100 pounds salt, ½ barrel brown sugar; 100 45-calibre Winchester cartridges, 10 gallons best sour mash whiskey—like the first sent. Also send me two woolen undershirts for a lady quite thick, two hoopskirts for a lady of some em bom point, and a corset for a girl of 15. P.S. Send 50 pounds of coffee, a few late copies of the Weekly Boomerang, a copy of the New Testament and Psalms bound together, large print, and be very particular about the quality of the sour mash whiskey.

—A letter from a Wyoming ranchman of the 80's to his merchant in town, from the Laramie Daily Boomerang, *February 12, 1884; contributed by Helena Huntington Smith.*

READING, WRITING, AND HISTORY

By ALBERT E. STONE, JR.

Best Novel of the Civil War

Shortly before Christmas in 1864 a captain of the Twelfth Connecticut Volunteers came home to New Haven from the Shenandoah. His appearance was hardly that of the returning hero. He was thirty-eight. His coarse blue fatigue uniform was threadbare and begrimed with vestiges of Virginia mud and the dust of two days' travel on the railroad. His face, thin and sallow from the effects of malaria and dysentery, was all but hidden behind an enormous ragged brown mustache and three weeks' growth of beard. His body was emaciated to a wolfish thinness. He had served honorably for over two years in the South and had been slightly wounded at the siege of Port Hudson, and he was returning with the same captain's bars on his shoulder straps he had carried away in 1862. By all accounts, John William De Forest's military career was closing on a note grim and unsuccessful enough to match the mood of the nation.

Both the Union and the Connecticut captain survived that terrible winter of '64–65. When spring came, in fact, De Forest had so far regained his health that he was permitted to re-enlist in the Invalid Corps, a special cadre for incapacitated veterans, and was assigned a desk job in the Provost Marshal General's office in Washington. Moreover, during these months of convalescence and the unexpected return to duty he was occupied with another task. Now, while memories were fresh and the inspiration strong, he was writing a book. It began as thinly veiled autobiog-raphy, a novel of his own experiences. But in the writing it outgrew the bounds of mere personal adventure to become a panorama of the war.

So powerful were the thoughts and emotions working within him that the whole story, which in characteristic nineteenth-century fashion ran to thirty-seven chapters and five hundred pages, was completed in ten months; by December, 1865, it was in the publisher's hands. De Forest called it *Miss Ravenel's Conversion from Secession to Loyalty*. In spite of the clumsy title, which will never fit the marquee of a movie theater, no better novel of the Civil War has ever been written.

It might be hard to believe such a major work could have been composed so swiftly and under such circumstances if another and greater writer had not accomplished a similar feat at almost the same time. While De Forest labored in Washington's summertime heat to finish *Miss Ravenel's Conversion*, a second-class clerk in the Bureau of Indian Affairs was putting the last touches on a slender pamphlet of poems. One of these verses was "When Lilacs Last in the Dooryard Bloom'd." Thus in that short season when victory was won, the Union saved, and Lincoln lost, the events were simultaneously memorialized by a great poem and a fine novel.

Whitman's elegy has become perhaps the single most famous poem in our literature. It is one of history's minor ironies that John De Forest's achievement has had to wait almost a century for recognition. If the Civil War Centennial helps to rescue *Miss Ravenel's Conversion* from oblivion, it will be a case of long-deferred justice.

Both Whitman and De Forest wrote under the pressure of vivid, intimate, and recent memories. Whitman's soul-wrenching months in the hospitals of Washington and Virginia issued almost at once in *Drum Taps*. But Whitman's knowledge of war and battle was marginal when compared with De Forest's. The Connecticut veteran had a matchless advantage over the poet and indeed over nearly every other writer of his day—he *really* had fought in the war. "Served two years in Louisiana under Butler and Banks," runs the laconic letter he later sent Harper's as a publicity release, "& one campaign under Sheridan in Virginia. Was in the battles of Georgia Landing, Pattersonville, the Opequan, Fisher's Hill, & Cedar Creek, also two grand assaults & a night attack on Port Hudson. Including battles, assaults, skirmishes, & trench duty, saw forty-six days under fire. Served as Inspector General of division, Aid on staff of 19th Army Corps, Adjutant General of Veterans Reserve Corps, & commandant of a Freedman's Bureau District."

This was indeed a comprehensive and respectable record. If, as Robert Penn Warren has recently reminded us, the Civil War is "the great single event of our history," it remains a commonplace but immensely significant fact that virtually all the finest writers of the emerging generation did not fully participate in the crucial event. James, Howells, Twain, Adams, were passed by or escaped direct involvement. John De Forest, together with Lanier, Bierce, Whitman, and a few others, knew the glory and the horror at first hand. They were there in the field.

Within a literary tradition that could be characterized by Hemingway's dictum, "Never write about anything you don't know everything about," this situation had far-reaching effects, both for De Forest and for younger writers. *Miss Ravenel's Conversion* rests firmly on a basis of the intimate, first-hand knowledge of its creator. On the other hand, Stephen Crane's *The Red Badge of Courage*, which most readers consider our best Civil War novel, depends for its veracity upon the skillful way Crane confines himself to the mind of his schoolboy-soldier. Both books respect the rule of experience.

Besides this fund of first-hand military experience De Forest had little to recommend him in 1865 as the potential author of a major novel. Before the war, it is true, he had published five books—two novels, two travel books, and a history of the Indians of Connecticut—but none of these had caught the popular fancy. His personal experience had perhaps been wider than that of other Connecticut Yankees; he had lived in Syria and in Europe and read widely in French, Italian, Russian, and English literature. Tolstoy's *War and Peace*, which was begun a short time before *Miss Rav-*

enel's Conversion, was not available to De Forest until some years later; it is clear, however, that the Russian and his provincial American contemporary were both attempting the same feat: to write a national prose epic on the theme of war.

Miss Ravenel's Conversion, then, grew out of De Forest's European experience as well as his American, and is distinctly European in scope and tone. Like Thackeray and George Eliot, De Forest is not concerned with unusual individuals isolated from society, but rather with normal people in constant and concrete relationship with their world. In other words, De Forest is a social realist; in fact, he is one of the very first in our literature. Twenty years before Howells and Garland initiated realism in this country, De Forest had already naturalized the European novel and given it classic expression in *Miss Ravenel's Conversion*.

De Forest was a pioneer, and his book suffered the fate often reserved for trail blazers. It was a complete failure with the reading public of 1867, the year *Miss Ravenel's Conversion* actually appeared, because it was ahead of its time. Not many people in 1867 were prepared to confront the brutalities, the sectional hypocrisies, and the corruption which, in De Forest's narrative, went along with the heroism and sacrifice of the war. To be sure, a few discerning critics like William Dean Howells of the *Atlantic Monthly* praised De Forest's book, and this esteem served to keep its reputation alive in subsequent generations. In 1939, partly as a result of the national love affair with *Gone With the Wind*, *Miss Ravenel's Conversion* was at last reprinted and caused a flurry of interest.

The present-day reader, inured by Hemingway, Norman Mailer, and James Jones to the soldier's *patois*, and trained by historians to detect oversimplified versions of the Civil War, is in an even better position to appreciate De Forest's forthrightness and his keen understanding. If we can keep our own perspective and yet enter imaginatively into John De Forest's, we can find in this work not only a forgotten masterpiece of American fiction but also one of the earliest and most discerning images of the Civil War as the crisis of American culture.

In keeping with the canons of realism, *Miss Ravenel's Conversion* has a commonplace plot. De Forest asks us to imagine a family of refugees, a widower father and his blonde, blue-eyed daughter, come to New Boston, in the little New England state of Barataria, from New Orleans in the months just after Sumter. Dr. Ravenel is a mineralogist and in spite of southern birth an implacable foe of slavery. "Ashantee" is his sarcastic nickname for southern society. Lillie Ravenel, however, like most young people, is passionately devoted to her native region and openly exults in the faces of the New Bostonians at the news from Bull Run. So she has little more than a flirtation with Edward Colburne, the patriotic and athletic young lawyer who manifestly prefers her company to that of the college widows who hang like ivy on the social fringes of staid Winslow University. Lillie is attracted instead to a handsome, red-faced Virginian, Colonel John Carter. This charming, irreverent, sherry-drinking West Pointer has not followed his state into secession but is instead recruiting a Baratarian regiment.

Colburne raises a company to serve under Carter, and the scene shifts to the battlefields of Louisiana and Mississippi. Lillie and her father return to New Orleans, where the Doctor is treated as a traitor and beaten over the head one dark night. This event begins to influence Lillie's ideology. Illogically, but inevitably, she begins "to see that Secession was indefensible, and that the American Union ought to be preserved."

Equally illogical but believable is Lillie's marriage to Carter. Though she has the hair and eyes of the traditional romantic heroine, Lillie is a very different character from fictional figurines in *Godey's Lady's Book*. For one thing, she has a sense of humor. For another, she is a wife capable of sexual feeling. "It was curious," De Forest observes, "to see how slowly she got accustomed to her husband. . . . She frequently blushed at encountering him, as if he were still a lover. If she met the bold gaze of his wide-open brown eyes, she trembled with an inward thrill and wanted to say, 'Please don't look at me so!' He could tyrannize over her with his eyes; he could make her come to him and try to hide from them by nestling her head on his shoulder; he used to wonder at his power and gratify his vanity as well as his affection by using it."

La sainte passion (De Forest makes clever use of the Creole setting to employ phrases he could not have printed in English) has other devotees in the Ravenels' New Orleans household. One is Mrs. Larue, a relative by marriage. She is the dark temptress of the tale; but again, she is as unlike the conventional dark-haired, black-eyed vamp of popular fiction as Lillie is from Hawthorne's Phoebe Pyncheon. Her Creole eyes and rounded shoulders offer grave dangers to Carter. After some months of military inactivity, Colonel Carter makes an "astronomical expedition" to Washington (that is, he seeks the political patronage that will bring him a brigadier's star). Mrs. Larue conveniently takes passage on the same ship. Though Carter tries feebly to fend her off, he is no match for a woman who spouts Michelet by moonlight and drapes her bare shoulders in a diaphanous veil. The inevitable seduction soon takes place.

When the adultery is discovered by the Ravenels, Lillie and her baby son leave Louisiana and the Colonel. Carter, genuinely sorry for his error but also slightly mystified that they were making "so much of the affair; such affairs were altogether too common to be made so much of," takes to the field and leads his brigade into the battle of Cane River, where he dies, bravely and profanely, with a Minié ball in his side. Captain Colburne, matured by battle as Lillie is matured by marriage, returns at last to New Boston and wins the pretty widow. "It grieves me," the author concludes, "to leave this young woman thus on the threshold of her history. Here she is, at twenty-three, with but one child, and only at her second husband. Two-thirds of her years and heart history are probably before her. Women are most interesting at thirty: . . . then only do they attain their highest charm as members of society." As the ironic and dispassionate chronicler of domestic life and feminine psychology, De Forest is surely the superior of most of his predecessors in American fiction, and in this novel at least, he is the peer of Henry James and Howells at their best.

But *Miss Ravenel's Conversion* is much larger than a love story. The novel includes social profiles of northern and southern cities, political life in Barataria and Washington, contraband cotton intrigue, a plantation experiment by Dr. Ravenel with Negro freedmen, and a cast of characters drawn from every social class. De Forest's Negroes and Irish soldiers, his saloonkeeper-politicians, his Butternut cavalrymen from Texas, represent virtually the whole spectrum of national types. De Forest is at pains to demonstrate that our Civil War affected everyone, from the Governor of Barataria down to "Major" Scott, the leader of the ex-slaves on Ravenel's farm who has such trouble with the Seventh Commandment.

At times, to be sure, the Yankee moralist's voice drowns out that of the detached social historian. Such often happens with the theme of temperance. He still recoils from the evils of drunkenness as he came to know them in the South and in the Army. Through Edward Colburne (in some respects the author's alter ego) the novel preaches the cold-water cause. Nevertheless, De Forest is capable at times of talking like a modern sociologist. This mark of resolute honesty is most clearly manifest in his battlefield and hospital scenes. Compared to them, the bloody episodes in the novels of his more popular contemporaries ring about as true as the libretto of an operetta.

This may be most neatly observed in the case of John Esten Cooke, whose *Mohun* in 1869 so far outsold *Miss Ravenel's Conversion*. Cooke was a Virginian, and his story helped to initiate that southern conquest of the North by book, myth, and movie that began right after Appomattox and has yet to stop. Cooke knew the realities of war as well as De Forest, for he had served on General Jeb Stuart's staff, but when it came to putting them on paper he preferred the grandiose imprecisions of romanticism. Here, for example, is a typical battle passage from *Mohun*:

J W De Forest

I set out at full gallop, and soon reached the column. At the head of it rode Young, the *beau sabreur* of Georgia, erect, gallant, with his brave eye and smile.

I pointed out the enemy and gave the order.

"All right!" exclaimed Young, and, turning to his men, he whirled his sabre around his head and shouted,

"Forward!"

The Column thundered on, and as it passed I recognized Mohun, his flashing eye and burnished sabre gleaming from the dust cloud. . . .

"Charge!" rose from a hundred lips. Spurs were buried in the hot flanks; the mass was hurled at the enemy; and clashing like thunder, sword against sword, swept everything before it.

De Forest's months and years in the field had been served with the infantry, not with the cavalry, and this perhaps helps to explain the down-to-earth, anti-chivalrous accuracy of his prose. Unlike Cooke, whose episodes all run together in a welter of adjectives and repeated metaphors, De Forest makes us *see* and *hear* each moment of battle.

On went the regiments, moving at the ordinary quick-step, arms at a right-shoulder-shift, ranks closed, gaps filled, unfaltering, heroic. The dead were falling; the wounded were crawling in numbers to the rear; the leisurely hum of long-range bullets had changed into the sharp, multitudinous *whit-whit* of close firing; the stifled crash of balls hitting bones and the soft *chuck* of flesh wounds mingled with the outcries of the sufferers; the bluff in front was smoking, rattling, wailing with the incessant file fire; but the front of the Brigade remained unbroken, and its rear showed no stragglers. The right hand regiment floundered in a swamp, but the others hurried on without waiting for it. As the momentum of the movement increased, as the spirits of the men rose with the charge, a stern shout broke forth, something between a hurrah and a yell, swelling up against the Rebel musketry and defying it. Gradually the pace increased to a double-quick, and the whole mass ran for an eighth of a mile through the whistling bullets. The second fence disappeared like frost-work, and up the slope of the hill struggled the panting regiments. When the foremost ranks had nearly reached the summit, a sudden silence stifled the mus-

ketry. Polignac's line wavered, ceased firing, broke, and went to the rear in confusion. The clamor of the charging yell redoubled for a moment and then died in the roar of a tremendous volley. Now the Union line was firing, and now the Rebels were falling. Such was the charge which carried the crossing and gained the battle of Cane River.

De Forest has allowed his mighty subject to provide the emotion for the events; he has dispensed with the language of metaphor. Herein lies one of his signal contributions to American literature. If a major problem for the modern writer has been to devise ways to purify language of inherited abuses, here is an early forerunner of Crane and Hemingway who has done just that.

Implicit in De Forest's style and subject matter is a second innovation in American letters. *Miss Ravenel's Conversion* is consciously aimed at both male and female readers, at the casual magazine subscriber as well as at the serious highbrow. This attempt to widen and deepen the American novel-reading audience was singlehanded, premature, and a failure; De Forest was not able to expand the narrow and timid sensibilities of a predominantly feminine clientele wedded to books like *Mohun*. But the effort is worth our respect today, for it demonstrates one man's determination to redefine the writer's relation to society, a connection traditionally tenuous and thwarting for most of our finest nineteenth-century writers, by presenting to that society something new—a full and meticulously honest image of itself. In 1867, we are forced to conclude, American men and women did not choose to gaze into a mirror as clear and revealing as *Miss Ravenel's Conversion*.

That the candor of De Forest's style extended to other areas is demonstrated by the intelligence of his analysis of the underlying conditions and the possible consequences of the Civil War. Almost half a century before Charles Beard and the economic determinists, John De Forest had the insight to play down simpleminded abolitionist explanations and to note the importance of cotton, the spirit of capitalistic speculation, and the political party as shaping factors in the sectional conflict. He saw the war as an immensely complicated confrontation of industrial democracy and a vicious aristocracy.

Happily, the common man had triumphed and slavery had been abolished, but the two were not necessarily connected phenomena. Nor were they necessarily happy auguries for the future. Whether that struggle would impart to the reunited nation "a manlier, nobler tone" De Forest did not know. He did, however, recognize the dangers that lay ahead, and *Miss Ravenel's Conversion* has much wider significance than simply as an interesting literary curiosity. Because of De Forest's experiences, his novel literary code, and his notions of audience, his book offers an image of the Civil War peculiarly revealing of the American mind on the eve of peace. It is an image amazingly free of sectional bias. Through a realistic imagination have been filtered the common experiences of the critical years behind an uncommon vision of the troubled decades ahead.

It should not surprise us to detect in *Miss Ravenel's Conversion* that strain of nostalgia which we have come to expect in all evocations of the Civil War. It hovers most of the time in the background, but on one occasion at least finds eloquent voice. That moment comes after the description of the battle of Fort Winthrop, when De Forest ends the chapter, remarking,

Those days are gone by, and there will be no more like them forever, at least not in our forever. Not very long ago, not more than two hours before this ink dried upon the paper, the author of the present history was sitting on the edge of a basaltic cliff which overlooked a wide expanse of fertile earth, flourishing villages, the spires of a city, and, beyond, a shining sea flecked with the full-blown sails of peace and prosperity. From the face of another basaltic cliff two miles distant, he saw a white globule of smoke dart a little way upward, and a minute afterwards heard a dull, deep *pum!* of exploding gunpowder. Quarrymen there were blasting out rocks from which to build hives of industry and happy family homes. But the sound reminded him of the roar of artillery; of the thunder of those signal guns which used to presage battle; of the alarums which only a few months previous were a command to him to mount and ride into the combat. Then he thought almost with a feeling of sadness, so strange is the human heart, that he had probably heard those clamors uttered in mortal earnest for the last time. Never again, perhaps, even should he live to the age of three-score and ten, would the shriek of grape-shot, and the crash of shell, and the

multitudinous whiz of musketry be a part of his life. Nevermore would he hearken to that charging yell which once had stirred his blood more fiercely than the sound of trumpets: the Southern battle-yell, full of howls and yelpings as of brute beasts rushing hilariously to the fray: the long-sustained Northern yell, all human, but none the less relentless and stern; nevermore the one nor the other. No more charges of cavalry, rushing through the dust of the distance; no more answering smoke of musketry, veiling unshaken lines and squares; no more columns of smoke, piling high above deafening batteries. No more groans of wounded, nor shouts of victors over positions carried and banners captured, nor reports of triumphs which saved a nation from disappearing off the face of the earth. After thinking of these things for an hour together, almost sadly, as I have said, he walked back to his home; and read with interest a paper which prattled of town elections and advertised corner lots for sale; and decided to make a kid-gloved call in the evening and go to church on the morrow.

This is unusual rhetoric for a realist to employ, but its very incongruity lends the passage power to move us. Apparently, De Forest has joined hands with John Esten Cooke and the other romanticizers who manufactured the first myths about the Civil War. Actually, however, the writer has remained true to his code. For what has been more characteristic of the veteran—particularly veterans of *this* war—than to reach through the bloody horrors of the past to recapture—perhaps even to see for the first time—the glory of the war?

Mr. Stone, our guest columnist in Bruce Catton's space, is an assistant professor of English and American Studies at Yale. He will become chairman of the Department of English at Emory University in Atlanta this autumn. He is the author of The Innocent Eye: Childhood in Mark Twain's Imagination, *and is at work on a biography of De Forest.*

The Rise of the Little Magician CONTINUED FROM PAGE 51

juveniles of the far-flung Jackson clan, who constantly visited the President.

Evening callers like Van Buren ordinarily found Jackson well attended in the family sitting room. Reposing in his easy chair, puffing gently on a great Powhatan pipe whose bowl rested upon his knees, Jackson was an island of composure in a sea of chaos. Children would be romping around the room, rolling, climbing, falling, and brawling while the adults were bravely trying to read, sew, or converse. Entering unannounced, Van Buren would retire to a corner with Jackson for conversation that was continually interrupted. After finishing with the President, Van

Buren paid heed to the ladies, with whom he got on famously.

Jackson and his friend transacted most of their business not in their evening encounters, however, but in a reserved hour during the day. Every afternoon at about three thirty, Van Buren would meet Jackson at the White House, and the two would slip out the back door for a canter on horseback. Although he preferred a coach, Van Buren threw desire and comfort to the winds and acquired a trusty charger.

It was during such outings that the seed of Jackson's earlier invitation for Van Buren to function as general adviser and confidant was coming to real fruition.

Anything and everything was discussed. Legislation, appointments to office, correspondence, messages to Congress—on such instruments of policy Van Buren constantly impressed his influence. Together with Lewis and Donelson, he was also functioning as a drafter of the President's speeches and messages. Jackson, from all indications, required considerable help along these lines. His prose tended to be abrupt and disconnected, his intelligence expressing itself in judgment rather than in analysis. But Van Buren's particular forte, on which Jackson relied most, whether in speech drafting or on other occasions of decision, was his skill in political tactics and in discerning the motives of men.

To the casual observer of the political scene, Washington, in the crisp autumn of 1829, glowed with serenity. This was a condition sedulously cultivated by the two contenders for the succession. Duff Green, editor of the administration organ, the *United States Telegraph,* appears to have been instructed by his *de facto* chief, Calhoun, to scotch all rumors of discord and to chant in his columns a steady song of bliss. Van Buren reciprocated by endorsing Green's appointment to the lush post of Public Printer. Toward Calhoun personally, Van Buren was sweetness itself. He wined and dined the Vice President and his family regularly, and in all other respects their dealings persisted, in Van Buren's phrase, on "a friendly and familiar footing."

Behind the façade of official beatific calm, Van Buren was advancing his fortunes with ruthless vigor. In private sessions with Jackson he was quietly but effectively taking over a principal source of power in the new administration: patronage. With his sure touch, he pursued the policy of holding dismissals of Adams' appointees to moderate numbers, on the assumption that the incumbent clerks were generally sympathetic to his cause, while the clamoring job-seekers were decidedly disposed toward Calhoun and the western faction of Jackson supporters.

Van Buren was also launching his moves against the Calhoun camp in another locale. Being an intensely social animal, the Secretary of State had become a major figure in Washington society, a tireless party-giver and partygoer, and it was in these enterprises that he found his finest opportunities to advance his long-range purposes. The situation that worked to his greatest profit was the marriage of Secretary of War Eaton to Mrs. Margaret "Peggy" O'Neale Timberlake on January 1, 1829.

The uncommonly beautiful Peggy was the daughter of a Washington tavernkeeper and the widow of a Navy purser who had allegedly committed suicide because of her extramarital flirtations. Her wedding to Eaton, which should have been an all-out social event, was boycotted en masse by proper and indignant capital ladies. At the inaugural dinner in March they would not speak to her, and Mrs. Calhoun established the precedent, which others quickly followed, of refusing to call on her. The President, gallant and sensitive to suffering femininity, became concerned. The lady herself, meanwhile, was facing up to the situation not like a frail violet but with the ferocity of a tigress. Given Mrs. Eaton's gameness, the President's interest, and the unyielding opposition of the Calhouns, Van Buren had all the ingredients of a highly profitable situation. He lost no time in exploiting it.

He proceeded to pay, as Jackson was to term it, "the most devoted and assiduous attention to Mrs. Eaton." While other Cabinet members were bulldozed by incensed wives and squeamish daughters into slighting the wife of the Secretary of War against the President's well-known wishes, the unattached Van Buren could maneuver as he pleased. He called on Mrs. Eaton. He gave parties in her honor. He prodded his friends, the British and the Russian ministers, both of whom were bachelors, to give dances at which the Secretary's lady was treated with pointed distinction.

L'affaire Eaton, strenuously fanned by the enterprising Van Buren, quickly became a roaring holocaust. It gutted the Cabinet. The President, who was choleric on the subject, called his Secretaries together and admonished them to order their wives to be hospitable to Mrs. Eaton. At another point, he proposed to fire a Secretary whose wife was one of the shriller buglers of the crusade against her. But Van Buren managed to pull the President off; there was bigger game to bag.

In the White House the ranks were bitterly divided. Although Jackson was pure loyalty to Mrs. Eaton, the Donelsons with equal conviction deemed her a terrible blot on the social register. Not only that, Mrs. Donelson was blaming Van Buren and Van Buren alone for keeping her there, and the intensity of her feelings was becoming increasingly apparent to him. Until these recent rending events, Emily Donelson had been his favorite companion at dances and dinners. Of late, however, she had become noticeably distant.

One evening Van Buren dropped in at the White House, as was his habit, for a chat with anyone who happened to be about the sitting room. Jackson, he was disappointed to find, was not there. But Emily Donelson and several of her friends were. After some small talk, she drew Van Buren aside and with deadly candor told him that she was puzzled about his disposition toward Mrs. Eaton and would appreciate having the point cleared up. Awkwardly and ingloriously,

JACKSON DISMISSING THE CABINET.

A contemporary cartoon comments on a shake-up in one of "King" Andrew Jackson's Cabinets. Martin Van Buren can be seen in a characteristic place—safely behind the throne.

the trapped Van Buren squirmed out of the situation by declaring that he had an engagement for which he had to leave at once. Under Emily's exacting gaze, he felt compelled to add that he would be glad to discuss the subject further at their earliest mutual convenience. Emily insisted on a definite date.

At the appointed time, Van Buren and the piquant Mrs. Donelson commenced a long, lively discussion in the sitting room. Also on hand and quite alert was Emily's cousin, Mary Eastin, who shared her opinion of Mrs. Eaton. The discussion quickly became heated. Greatly affected, Miss Eastin withdrew to the embrasure of a nearby window, sobbing heavily. Alarmed by the deterioration of the situation, and even more concerned that Jackson might enter at any moment, Van Buren worked desperately to set things aright. He launched into a long, consoling monologue; the upshot was that Miss Eastin's tears were checked. Perhaps more important, Emily Donelson agreed that they should never discuss the subject again.

In the weeks that followed, Van Buren zealously plied the ruffled lady with attentions; the Donelsons, after all, were much too close to Jackson to be alienated. It worked. When Emily Donelson's first-born daughter was christened in an elaborate ceremony at the White House, the mother had the pick of Washington's manpower in selecting godfathers for her child; the two she unhesitatingly chose were the President and her recent antagonist, Mr. Van Buren.

A new and momentous issue now rose to restore Martin Van Buren's still uncertain fortunes. While the Eaton affair was running its merry pace, the country's attention was turning to the infinitely more complex and menacing issue of nullification. Nothing less than the safety and future of the Union turned on the outcome. The igniting spark had been provided by the

Tariff Act of 1828—"the tariff of abominations" it was called in the South—the last of a series of acts discriminating strongly against that region. In Calhoun's own state of South Carolina, men spoke openly of declaring the act to be null and void and making Charleston a free port; Calhoun himself was nullification's most articulate advocate.

Andrew Jackson was slow to speak out publicly on the great issue until it squarely confronted him. The occasion was Thomas Jefferson's birthday anniversary—April 13, 1830. In the four years since his death it had not been the object of any special celebration, however much Jefferson was venerated by his countrymen and the party he had founded. Now, however, Senators Thomas Hart Benton of Missouri and Robert Hayne of South Carolina proposed a grand subscription dinner, ostensibly to remedy this oversight. To Van Buren, the plot was clear. The celebration, he told Jackson, would be used as "a stalking horse" for linking Jefferson's prestige to the current doctrines expounded by Calhoun and Hayne.

When Van Buren, with Jackson and Donelson, joined the nearly one hundred celebrants in the dining hall of Brown's Indian Queen Hotel on April 13, they found the atmosphere already decidedly chilly. Van Buren quickly discovered the cause when he picked up from one of the tables a card on which had been printed the formal toasts to be offered in the course of the evening. It was clear at a glance that the banquet hall would resound with sentiments dear to the nullifiers. Only a few minutes before the arrival of the presidential party, the Pennsylvania delegation, taking one look at the toast cards, had walked out in a pique. Several other delegations were feverishly conferring on the same decision. The Marine band, meanwhile, was blaring away with extra vigor to drown out the rising tension.

Somehow the meal began and passed without incident. Then, after what seemed interminable preliminaries, the toast of the President of the United States was called for. The room crackled with expectation. The short-statured Van Buren, his view hopelessly blocked by the crowd, climbed up on a chair to observe the President. Jackson at last rose. In a voice rough with defiance, he declared, "Our Union: It must and shall be preserved." Without a word more, he lifted his glass as a sign that the toast was to be drunk standing. Chairs scraped and there was a hum of excited whispering as the company rose. Calhoun stood with them. "His glass," noticed a nearby participant, "trembled in his hand and a little of the amber fluid trickled down the side."

The fight was now in the open. A visitor to the Senate gallery observed, not long after, that the Vice President seemed "more wrinkled and careworn than I had expected from his reputed age. . . . His voice is shrill. . . . His manners have in them an uneasiness, a hurried, incoherent air." With the stealth and evil grace of the fox, Van Buren came in for the kill. His route was typically circuitous, and the weapon he counted upon to destroy Calhoun was a letter. It was a very special letter, solicited by Van Buren's trusted aide, James A. Hamilton, and written long ago by William H. Crawford while serving as Secretary of the Treasury in the Cabinet of James Monroe.

Secretary Crawford's letter centered upon a climactic episode of the Seminole Indian War in 1818, when Jackson as commanding general in the field invaded Florida without consulting President Monroe and seized the Spanish forts of St. Marks and Pensacola. To the nation, Jackson was instantaneously a hero; to the President he was arrant and insubordinate. Monroe took up the problem with his Cabinet. There, according to the Crawford letter, John C. Calhoun, then Secretary of War, forthrightly recommended that General Jackson be arrested and punished.

The letter, which had been retrieved from an old trunk in Crawford's Georgia home, reached Jackson via a number of trusted hands, including those of Van Buren's faithful White House ally, W. B. Lewis. Through Lewis, the letter finally came to Donelson and thence to the President. Jackson, to whom the disclosures were not altogether a surprise—only recently he had discussed the entire incident with ex-President Monroe himself—was still seething from the Jefferson Day dinner. The evidence is impressive that he desired to strike further at Calhoun, and Van Buren's conveniently timed skulduggery gave him a pretext for doing so. The President, accordingly, lost no time in dispatching a peremptory request to Calhoun to explain his conduct in the Monroe Cabinet. In a painstaking answer of some fifty-two pages, the Vice President freely admitted the charges, defended his own conduct, and condemned Crawford for betraying the secrets of the Cabinet. Evidently eager to keep the fight going, Jackson tartly informed Calhoun that his reply was unsatisfactory. Their break was now complete.

Although Calhoun was now in full eclipse, Van Buren's own situation was not without peril. The Cabinet was still strongly pro-Calhoun; the Eaton affair was still roaring along. Calling upon all his skill at co-ordinating seemingly disparate forces, Van Buren hit upon a bit of vivid dramaturgy designed to solve the Eaton affair, reconstitute the Cabinet, and project himself before the public as a selfless magistrate dedicated to the commonweal.

The crux of the plan entailed nothing less than his resigning as Secretary of State, ostensibly for so noble a purpose as the peace and welfare of the administration. His real object was to compel not only the resignation of Eaton but that of Calhoun's supporters in the Cabinet.

With Calhoun out of the way, he need no longer be on hand at the White House to protect his interests and could afford at least a brief absence from that arena of destiny. As a place of temporary refuge once he had resigned, Van Buren fixed his enterprising gaze upon a post outside the country, the ministership to Great Britain, rich in prestige and far from the tumult of Washington. He packed his bag of tricks and waited for an opportune moment to break the news to Jackson. He struggled unavailingly for weeks to muster his courage, so fearful was he of the General's reaction. Finally, Van Buren came to grips with fate while horseback riding with the President one afternoon through Georgetown and down the Tenallytown road. The subject under discussion was the Eatons and the disintegration of the Cabinet. Van Buren somehow managed to seize the gaping opening and blurted out nervously: "No, General, there is but one thing can give you peace!"

"What is that, sir?"

"My resignation."

The President, in Van Buren's word, "blanched." "Never, sir," replied Jackson with peremptory vigor. "Even you know little of Andrew Jackson if you suppose him capable of consenting to such humiliation of his friends by his enemies."

For hours that day and next, Van Buren sought to justify his course to the President. As the discussion wore on inconclusively into the late afternoon of the second day, the western circle—Lewis, Eaton, and Postmaster General Barry—was called in. There was more discussion, equally futile, whereupon Van Buren invited the three westerners to his home for dinner. Along the way, Eaton suddenly stopped as though transfixed. It was wrong for Van Buren, "the most valuable member of the Cabinet, to resign, he exclaimed. Then, after a breath, tumbled out the statement for which the Magician had so expertly and painstakingly built the foundations in the discussions through the long afternoon. It was he, Eaton, who should resign. He, not Van Buren, had brought the administration its woe.

For a long moment no one spoke, a hiatus that must have seemed like ages to Eaton, if he was waiting for someone to say that he was mistaken, that he too was indispensable. No one did, and Van Buren, after a decent interval, swooped in with the clinching blow.

"What about Mrs. Eaton?" he asked with quiet finality. The Secretary of War managed to mumble that he was sure she would not object. Within a matter of days Eaton sent in his resignation, and Van Buren's quickly followed. When the President and Van Buren, now the minister-designate to England, went around to the departing Eatons one day to pay their respects, Peggy was decidedly chilly.

The remainder of the Cabinet, as Van Buren had hoped, likewise resigned. As he had also calculated, the reconstituted Cabinet was predominantly loyal to himself. Thereupon he took off for England, bearing a presidential recess appointment, and fell avidly to work in London, having exceptionally long and cordial audiences with King William IV and the royal ministers. With Washington Irving, first secretary of the United States legation, he became fast friends, but best of all, he was sustained by the obvious fact that Jackson missed his counsel. "Any suggestions which your leisure will permit," wrote the President, "you may choose to make on any subject will be kindly received." And in another dispatch, "I am . . . anxious to have you near me."

Jackson's prayer for Van Buren's homecoming was suddenly, and not altogether unexpectedly, answered by no less an agency than the United States Senate. Van Buren's being a recess appointment, Jackson passed along his name to the Senate when the regular legislative session commenced in December. The titans of Capitol Hill, Calhoun, Clay, and Webster, smarting under Van Buren's unchecked rise, were sharpening their claws for vengeance. Burying momentarily their own past differences, these doughty individualists united to consign the nomination to slow death.

Three months dragged by before Van Buren's name was even referred to the Foreign Relations Committee, a step which under normal circumstances was instantaneous. In the committee and on the Senate floor, a long, mudslinging discussion ensued, linking Van Buren with every known evil of the day. A special strategy was concocted to subject the minister-designate to the most excruciating humiliation. The remaining cards were played: his nomination was reported out favorably by the Foreign Relations Committee, and when the floor vote was taken, it resulted, by careful prearrangement, in a tie.

The situation called for John Calhoun, as Vice President of the United States and President of the Senate, to cast the deciding vote. Preening himself under the clamorous encouragement of the onlooking senators, Calhoun committed his long-awaited act of revenge, and voted against Van Buren. The Senate rang with cheers, as the crowd does when the matador makes his death thrust at the fallen bull. In the exhil-

aration of accomplishment, the Vice President was heard to declare, "It will kill him, sir, kill him dead. He will never kick, sir, never kick."

But Calhoun's victory was short-lived. The stab in the back only succeeded in incensing the local party organizations, which viewed the Senate's action as a gross personal injustice and a travesty on party integrity, and all but clinched the vice presidential nomination for Van Buren. The first national convention of the Democratic party, which assembled in Baltimore on May 21, 1832, unanimously nominated Van Buren on the second ballot. The Magician, spurned in Washington, was now redeemed in Baltimore.

With characteristic foresight, Van Buren had long had in readiness a central issue for the ensuing electoral campaign. His circling eye had alighted on the mighty financial fortress of the Bank of the United States. Chartered in 1816 for a period of twenty years, the Bank was predominantly private in character, with but one-fifth of its capital subscribed by the federal government. But it was the depository of government funds; by demanding or threatening to demand specie for the state bank notes it took in, or by refusing to take them altogether, the great Bank exercised a powerful check upon state banking activity.

In terms of the political necessities of Martin Van Buren, a fight with the Bank of the United States had great allure. His popularity would surely rise. Operating free of the safety-fund requirements imposed by state law upon New York banks, and having its headquarters in Philadelphia, the Bank of the United States made that city the financial capital of the country. New York—its manufacture, trade, and population soaring—was chafing to wrest supremacy from Philadelphia. In the South, Van Buren's supporters could be counted on to jump at the opportunity to avenge their states' rights principles by exterminating a major national institution like the Bank. But to Van Buren the most valuable feature of the Bank was its unpopularity in the West, where it was hated and feared.

As early as December 8, 1829, in his annual message to Congress, Jackson had openly expressed his hostility to the Bank. Meanwhile Van Buren was assaulting it by less direct means. Although he never discussed the Bank publicly or even in his most confidential letters, his trusted lieutenant, James A. Hamilton, busied himself for weeks at Jackson's side arranging the details of a new banking structure. Van Buren himself was quietly working with Amos Kendall, a leading westerner whose influence in the administration was rocketing. A journalist with a gift for piercing invective, he occupied the nominal post of Fourth Auditor of the Treasury, but devoted most of his energies to major drafting chores around the White House.

Not all the maneuvering concerning the Bank was going on at the White House. Henry Clay, his presidential ambitions charged with a new intensity, also regarded it as a useful issue. He prodded the Bank into directing its lieutenants in the House of Representatives to introduce legislation on January 6, 1832, providing for recharter. The great Bank dispatched its shrewdest lobbyists to Washington, and Daniel Webster and John Calhoun added their might and prestige to Clay's cause. Recharter passed both houses of Congress by comfortable margins in the summer of 1832.

By this time Martin Van Buren, having lost his job in London, had returned to the United States. Indeed, he managed to reach Washington by stage on Sunday, July 8, just as the presidential veto, which Jackson had ordered prepared, was being put into final shape. The little band of draftsmen still were hard at it when Van Buren rolled up to the White House portico in his brougham. The President, who was ailing, welcomed him in his bedroom. "Holding my hand in one of his own," the anxious Van Buren later reported, "and passing the other thro' his long white locks, he said, with the clearest indications of a mind composed, and in a tone entirely devoid of passion or bluster—'the bank, Mr. Van Buren, is trying to kill me, *but I will kill it!*'" After fittingly acknowledging his agreement, Van Buren was installed as a guest in the bedroom recently vacated by Sarah Yorke Jackson, the President's favorite daughter-in-law.

The Bank's supporters contended that Van Buren—"before he could unpack his bags"—was put to work polishing up the veto for transmittal to Congress early the next morning. Plainly bearing the touch of a practiced political hand, the veto ultimately prevailed in Congress. In the subsequent presidential campaign, the Jackson-Van Buren ticket triumphed mightily.

The onrushing events in South Carolina, meanwhile, had reached a point of alarming deterioration. The nullifiers had called a special convention and swiftly passed an ordinance holding the existing tariff laws unconstitutional and not binding upon the state. Outright secession was boldly threatened. Jackson responded by dispatching a naval force to Charleston. When the more rabid nullifiers cried out for troops to be raised to "defend" the state, Jackson countered by ordering the federal garrison at Charleston alerted and dispatched General Winfield Scott to take command.

Martin Van Buren, for his part, found himself caught in a vise. At opposite and seemingly irreconcilable extremes of the nullification controversy were the two principal claimants to his loyalty, his party following in the South and Andrew Jackson. If he pleased Jackson, he would displease the southern element of his party, and vice versa.

The line Van Buren proceeded to follow was heralded by the substance of the toast he had offered at the famous Jefferson Day dinner. "Mutual forbearance and reciprocal concessions," he had said, "thro' their agency the Union was established—the patriotic spirit from which they emanated will forever sustain it." Now, late in 1832, Van Buren toiled busily applying his formula for peace. In private letters to his southern friends, he forthrightly disapproved the nullification doctrine. In counsel to Jackson, he tirelessly sought to reduce the intensity of the conflict, or at least head off measures threatening to aggravate it.

While flagging down the President, Van Buren was eyeing the tariff laws for possible reforms as the most promising solution to the nullification crisis. To avoid antagonizing the Calhounites, whose natural interests favored tariff reduction but whose zest for vengeance might tempt them to reject anything identified with himself, Van Buren worked secretly through Congressman Gulian Crommelin Verplanck, Chairman of the House Ways and Means Committee, an independent not previously identified with Van Buren's enterprises.

After weeks of intensive work, Verplanck emerged with a bill to which southerners of all camps so warmed that Van Buren began openly and confidently identifying himself as its real instigator. He stood at the brink of new fame. If the bill passed—and according to every indication it would—the Magician would surely be hailed as "the Great Compromiser." For the first time in his career he would gain a genuine national popularity among a people who desperately did not want a civil war.

The serene progress of Van Buren's plans was suddenly and unexpectedly throttled. His mighty rivals—Clay and Calhoun—met and decided that at any cost the indomitable palace politician must not become a popular hero. So anxious was Clay to block Van Buren that he put aside his long-standing high-tariff convictions and introduced his own reform bill. His object,

An early engraving shows Capitol Hill as it looked in the 1830's.

plainly, was to snatch away the accolade of "Compromiser" from the grasping hands of Van Buren. Although Clay's tariff bill called for only a portion of the cuts that Verplanck had proposed, militant southerners, led in both houses of Congress by John Calhoun, rallied around Clay. The Clay-Calhoun juggernaut swept the Kentuckian's measure into enactment.

While events were reaching their climax behind the scenes in Washington, state legislatures in both North and South were passing resolutions disavowing the nullifiers and assuring the President of their support. In conspicuous contrast, Van Buren's own state organization in Albany was discreetly tight-lipped, fearful of offending their hero's southern followers. Meanwhile, the New York Whigs, led by two wily rising politicos, William H. Seward and Thurlow Weed, put Van Buren squarely on the spot by introducing their own resolutions into the state legislature, approving Jackson's proclamation in lavish terms.

The Red Fox was trapped; the kill seemed near. Van Buren could not avoid taking a stand, and whatever he did would be ruinous. If he supported the resolution, he would break up his party and lose his status as Jackson's most likely successor. If he opposed it, he risked breaking with Jackson. As always, Van Buren chose his party. He prepared a resolution forthrightly taking issue with the "history given by the President on the formation of our Government." Accompanying it was a labored report expounding a states' rights position which would hardly fail to please his most fastidious southern supporters.

To Jackson he forwarded the resolution, the report, and a letter of explanation. Upon receiving the documents, an eyewitness reported, Jackson perused them thoroughly, drawing hard all the while on his Powhatan pipe. Then, without comment, he handed them over to his secretary for filing.

It was Van Buren's expectation and hope that the veto would bring down the curtain on the drama of the United States Bank until 1836, when its charter was due to expire. Further warfare upon the Bank would clearly invite serious dislocation of the economy and gravely endanger his own prospects for the Presidency. But his policy of passivity quickly ran into an unyielding wall: Amos Kendall. Kendall argued that the Bank, with its huge assets and far-flung branches, was capable of enormous self-interested maneuver. He proposed that the government remove its very large deposits of funds. Kendall was so convincing that Jackson in March of 1833 instructed his aide to draft a withdrawal request to the Secretary of the Treasury, Louis McLane. Encouraged by Van Buren, McLane forthrightly opposed the request.

Van Buren himself met Kendall head-on at a White House "family dinner." During the meal, the New Yorker protested with hearty candor that the removal plan would start a needless fight entailing grave risks for the administration and the party. The ordinarily mild Kendall rose from the table in great excitement. In a voice taut with anger, he said that under Van Buren's policy the Bank would surely win and that faced with the certainty of that dismal prospect, he and other administration journalists might as well lay down their pens. "I can live under a corrupt despotism as well as any other man by keeping out of its way," exclaimed Kendall, resuming his seat. As the evening wore on, Van Buren concluded that Jackson was unmistakably veering toward Kendall's plan. The Vice President of the United States found it politic to apologize fully to the Fourth Auditor of the Treasury and assume blame for the unfortunate incident.

In June of 1833, the Cabinet was reorganized. McLane stepped up as Secretary of State and handpicked the new Secretary of the Treasury, the little-known William J. Duane, primarily for his proven loyalty to Van Buren's interests. These, to be sure, had been undergoing redefinition. Convinced that Jackson was unalterably in favor of withdrawing the government's funds, Van Buren was now arguing that he should not do so until after Congress reconvened, for the statute governing removal seemed to require congressional approval. Kendall, however, in a counterthrust, proposed that removal be accomplished by executive fiat *before* Congress met, rather than risk the embarrassment of legislative defeat. The President again sided with Kendall and on June 26 ordered Duane to arrange the removal. For weeks, the Secretary ingeniously dillydallied, shielded by Van Buren. The latter's friends, Washington Irving and James Gordon Bennett, editor of the New York *Enquirer,* were convinced that Kendall was craftily employing the Bank issue to throttle Van Buren's presidential hopes.

By late summer, Jackson had come around fully to the position of Kendall and his allies, Attorney General Roger Taney and Frank Blair, a leading administration penman. The government's deposits, the President decreed, were to be removed from the great Bank well before Congress reconvened. With this policy settled and ready for launching, the support of Van Buren and his party following was imperative. It was high time to crack down, which Jackson proceeded to do by directing a strong letter to the Vice President, then sojourning in Albany. "It is already hinted," the President wrote bluntly on August 16, 1833, "that you are opposed to the removal of the Deposits, and of course privately a friend to the Bank. *This must be removed* or it will do us both much *harm.*"

Van Buren's response was mellifluously noncommittal; Jackson requested that he return to Washington at once. Van Buren, at this moment with Washington Irving on a month's tour of the old Dutch settlements on the North River and Long Island, begged off. While Van Buren pored over Long Island antiquities, the bank crisis rushed toward its climax. Duane was fired, and Attorney General Taney, who took over the Treasury via a recess appointment, promptly announced that the government would cease placing deposits in the Bank of the United States after September 30. When Congress finally reconvened, the pro-Bank majority in the Senate retaliated by refusing to approve Taney's appointment to the Treasury.

Van Buren quickly adjusted his own line to the changing situation by writing to the President, lavishing praise upon his course of action. "I now invite you here," Jackson magnanimously responded. "I have my dear Sarah's room prepared for you, until your own House can be put in order."

For all of his tempestuous interludes and narrow squeaks, the Magician emerged with the hard core of his fortunes intact. No unmendable schisms rent his following. The President still counted him as the heir apparent. Van Buren duly captured the Democratic presidential nomination in May of 1835 and swept on to victory at the polls.

On March 4, 1837, the scepter passed. The day was bright, glistening with the exhilaration of spring and the sense of renewal implicit in an inauguration. Seated side by side in the carriage Constitution, drawn by the famous grays, were the outgoing President and his confidential adviser and chosen successor. After a dignified passage down Pennsylvania Avenue, the two men on whom all interest centered appeared on the east portico of the Capitol. Below was a vast crowd wedged breathlessly together, faces upturned—"a field," said one observer, "paved with human faces." They were silent, still and reverent. The inaugural

proceeded. The Chief Justice of the United States stepped forward to administer the oath to the President-elect. The new President began delivering his message, but its urbane substance was lost in the droning monotone of his speaking style. No cheers interrupted it; the applause at the end was polite but unenthusiastic.

The old General, now divested of power, rose to descend the broad steps of the portico to take his seat in the carriage. The feelings of the crowd, so long restrained, rolled forth like a giant thunderclap. The cheers burst and burst again from three thousand hearts. The new President descended too, but he was all but unnoticed and forgotten. All eyes were on General Jackson as he uncovered and bowed, the wind stirring his silver locks. A part, indeed a substantial part, of the tribute being paid the General and his outgoing administration belonged to the unnoticed men behind him, and Jackson, more than anyone, knew it. But the crowd did not know, and never would know. Martin Van Buren, on his most glorious day, the day for which he had plotted and gambled and maneuvered and flattered for eight anxious years, was paying the price for the secrecy of his success in the palace shadows. "For once," as Thomas Hart Benton remarked, "the rising was eclipsed by the setting sun."

Louis W. Koenig is professor of government at New York University and the author of The Invisible Presidency, *a study of famous presidential confidants; this present article is based on material which appeared in the book. He is working on a book about political mavericks, among them John Randolph of Roanoke, the Copperhead leader Clement L. Vallandigham, and Senator Burton K. Wheeler of Montana.*

For further reading: An Epoch and a Man: Martin Van Buren and His Times, *by Denis Tilden Lynch (Liveright, 1929);* Martin Van Buren and the Making of the Democratic Party, *by Robert V. Remini (Columbia University Press, 1959);* The Life of Andrew Jackson, *by Marquis James (Bobbs-Merrill, 1939).*

Pictures in the Papers

CONTINUED FROM PAGE 34

Odessa bombardment from the mast of a British warship. The paper also made use of wet-plate photographs, the first time a war had been so reported. As a Christmas bonus for 1854, the editor presented his readers with a magnificent foldout drawing of the doomed charge of the Light Brigade, a scene that lived long in British hearts.

In our own Civil War the *Illustrated London News* did a great service by allowing its artist-correspondent, Frank Vizetelly, to spend most of his time with the Confederate armies. It printed 133 of Vizetelly's drawings; these are now the only extensive source for viewing the fighting from the Southern side, beginning in 1862 at Fredericksburg and ending with Jefferson Davis' flight from Richmond, in which Vizetelly took part. A few of the artist's original sketches are now at the Harvard College Library. But most of them, along with everything else in the paper's invaluable pictorial archives, were destroyed by Luftwaffe bombing raids in the dark days of the Second World War.

Herbert Ingram

The founder and genius of this wonderful paper, Herbert Ingram, had been a printer, bookseller, and news agent in Nottingham, where he noticed that people were eager to buy certain cheap weekly papers that sometimes printed small woodcuts of murders and sporting events. His own paper was in a different class from these crude predecessors which pandered to the masses; its pages prove that he was a man of fine taste and strong intelligence, as well as of extraordinary inventiveness. He was at the peak of his career when he came to America in 1860 to enjoy a well-earned vacation. At midnight on September 7 he and his oldest son Herbert went on board the steamer *Lady Elgin* at Chicago, along with four hundred other excursionists. Two hours later, about forty miles out on Lake Michigan, a schooner rammed into the *Lady Elgin,* which sank with a loss of three hundred lives. Ingram's body was washed ashore but his son was never found. There were, however, two younger sons, William and Charles, who eventually took over the management of the *Illustrated London News,* and were followed by a grandson, Bruce (now Sir Bruce), who became editor in 1900 and still holds that position today, at the age of eighty-five. Among the innovations with which he is credited is the first use in a modern pictorial weekly of photogravure and of color gravure.

In the United States, as well as in England, there were occasional pictures in some of the papers long before the appearance of true pictorial journalism. Franklin and Hall's *Pennsylvania Gazette* printed the first American cartoon—the famous *Join, or Die* divided snake—in 1754. John Peter Zenger's *New-York Weekly Journal* once published a map of the French colonial fortress of Louisbourg, and Paul Revere engraved coffins for the *Boston Gazette* after the Boston Massacre. An unusual sample of pictorial humor appeared in the *New-York Gazetteer* in 1775, when the Tory editor James Rivington printed an alleged picture of his own hanging-in-effigy; the incident actually occurred but the picture was obviously a stock cut borrowed from a book or broadside. This thrifty practice was the usual way of illustrating newspapers until the 1830's.

James Gordon Bennett's penny New York *Herald* was the first American newspaper to print any large number of genuine news pictures. Beginning in 1835 with a woodcut showing the ruins made by a great fire in downtown New York, the *Herald* published pictorial accounts of political parades and mass meetings, murder victims and murder trials, church burnings in Philadelphia, and the ball that welcomed Charles Dickens to New York. A "picture story" that was almost modern ran in the *Herald* in 1844, showing the assassination of Joseph Smith, the mobbing of a newspaper office, and other scenes of the Mormon tragedy in Nauvoo, Illinois. These pictures were engraved by Thomas W. Strong in New York, and cannot be classed as eyewitness reporting. But the Nauvoo architecture and the features of some of the participants are reasonably authentic, and were probably copied from existing prints.

In 1845 the *Herald* published the first full page of pictures ever seen in a daily newspaper—a winding procession of tiny woodcuts depicting New York's funeral honors to ex-President Andrew Jackson. Rival editors raised the cry of "Fraud!" charging that the very same woodcuts had been kicking around London and New York for years, and had already done duty in print as the coronation of Queen Victoria, the funeral of William Henry Harrison, and the Croton water celebration!

James Gordon Bennett

There was certainly a good deal of fakery, theft, and blatant misrepresentation in the lower strata of pictorial journalism during the early years. But in this instance, at least, the *Herald* made a convincing plea of not guilty. Its engraver, Strong, deposed in public that the Jackson pictures "never appeared before in any newspaper, magazine, or book published in this country or any other . . . that they were executed in my place of business, in Nassau Street . . . nor were they completely finished until after the funeral procession had taken place."

It was the *Herald* that began the practice in America of printing pictures of living persons directly involved in sensational news. This was a distinct step in enlarging the freedom of the press. But some editors thought it nothing less than criminal. In 1843 a picture was published of Miss Sarah Mercer, a young Philadelphia lady who had been seduced, and whose brother had shot and killed the seducer. The *Public Ledger* in her home town could scarcely contain its editorial rage at this invasion of privacy:

If we admit that curiosity is natural, we must insist that the eagerness, the voracity with which it is indulged, encourage a very fraudulent, as well as a very impertinent, inquisitive, eaves-dropping, scandalous spirit, in the newspapers. . . . [The young lady's] misfortunes are not enough! The afflictions of her family are not sufficiently heavy! She must bear the additional load of exposure to idle curiosity all around the country, laid upon her by a pack of mean, unmanly, low-bred, low-minded ministers to low passions! And she must bear this, to enable such vile prostitutes of the press to put a few pence in their pockets! Language is hardly adequate to express our scorn for such creatures and their detestable practices.

Bennett cared nothing for such criticism, which came his way all the time. But the *Herald* gradually stopped printing pictures as it became more prosperous. Since paper sizes and press runs were limited, Bennett preferred to give his valuable space to news and paid advertisements. After about 1850, and even during the Civil War, the leading daily newspapers of the country carried almost no news pictures. When Joseph Pulitzer revived the idea in the New York *World* in the 1880's, it was hailed as something startling and new.

Inevitably American publishers gazed longingly across the Atlantic at the tremendous success and profits of the *Illustrated London News*. But the dearth of good artists and engravers delayed the appearance of the first American picture weekly until 1851. Rather surprisingly, when it did appear, it was published in Boston. Its founder was Frederick Gleason, a self-promoting Yankee of the P. T. Barnum stripe, who had

Frederick Gleason

already made a success of a sensational story paper called *The Flag of Our Union*. The complete title of his new publication was *Gleason's Pictorial Drawing-Room Companion Devoted to Literature, Arts, Amusements, News, Etc.*

This arrangement of topics was significant. *Gleason's Pictorial* was not much more than an ordinary fireside story paper with a sugar coating of pictures. Woodcuts appeared on the front and back pages, and in alternate spreads. The rest was filled with soggy fiction and poems, generally by third-rate authors. *Gleason's* seems never to have had any system for covering news events at any great distance from Boston. Yet many interesting sketches and views were sent in by artists in other cities, and some of them made handsome engravings. Especially notable were the early views of California gold mines and unflattering portraits of miners mailed in by Daniel W. Nason, a forty-niner from New Hampshire.

Possibly *Gleason's* masterpiece was a superb drawing of Commodore Matthew Perry's squadron leaving Norfolk for the Orient in 1852. (It is reproduced in the portfolio.) By allowing the edges of this majestic picture to "bleed" almost entirely off both pages of a center spread, the editors—perhaps without intending to—provided an early example of the "Gee whiz" school of layout which is faithfully followed in the mass magazines today.

Although its national coverage was spotty, *Gleason's* early volumes are rich in attractive pictures of Boston buildings, streets, omnibuses, firemen's parades, ship launchings, political meetings, and snowstorms. Along with these are appealing bits of local color such as *Coot Shooting at the Glades, Cohasset,* and *The Learned Seals at the Boston Aquarium.* (One of these learned seals, named Ned, knew how to drill with a musket. The artist who drew him was the London-born Alfred Waud, who was soon to win fame as a combat artist for *Harper's* during the Civil War.)

An 1851 *Gleason's* picture of *The Smokers' Circle, on Boston Common,* was explained in the following caption:

It is a well known fact that—while a man may enjoy the weed by inhaling the fragrant fumes of a cigar in any other city of the Union—in Boston a *fine* is extracted from any person who presumes to smoke on the streets. Our worthy mayor, sympathizing with the oppressed . . . has had a circle of seats arrayed in a shady grove of our beautiful park; and here scores of persons resort each afternoon and evening . . . Let our readers drop round that way, and see how truthful a picture we have given them . . .

In 1855 Gleason sold the paper to his editor, Maturin Ballou, who changed the name to *Ballou's Pictorial.* Under his regime it published fewer and fewer interesting engravings, and more and more cheap fiction. Just how cheap this was became public record when the paper gave up the ghost in 1859. In a complacent farewell editorial, Editor Ballou—who had fumbled one of the greatest opportunities in the history of American journalism—added up the paper's costs during its whole nine years. His table showed that printing paper, at $423,000, was its largest expense. Drawings and engravings came next, at $161,-000. Well down on the list was the $28,000 "paid to authors for manuscripts." This averages out to $62 for each of the 451 issues. Since every issue usually had eight or ten signed stories and poems, it is obvious

Mr. and Mrs. Frank Leslie

that writing talent was no great drain on the paper's treasury.

The end of this uninspired publication is easy to explain. In its final number, for December 24, 1859, *Ballou's* carried just two sizable engravings, one showing a sleighing party in New England, and the other a rustic view on the Harlem River in New York. There is no mention whatever of the great and controversial news of the day—John Brown's raid and his public hanging, which had occurred three weeks before. In fact, under Ballou's ownership, there was almost no news in the paper at all.

Now turn to the same week's issue of *Frank Leslie's Illustrated Newspaper,* a lusty four-year-old in New York. On page one is a picture of the jail at Charlestown, Virginia, with a sentinel firing at two of Brown's men, Coppoc and Cook, as they try to escape from their death cells. The double spread in the center gives an eyewitness view of the execution of the same men, "From a Sketch by our own Artist Taken on the Spot."

The hanging took place at 1 P.M. on Friday, December 16; immediately afterward the artist left for New York, arriving late on Saturday. A staff of copy artists and engravers were awaiting him in a suite of hotel rooms near the office. They worked through the night transferring his drawing to a large sixteen-section wood block, and the presses were rolling with the picture early on Sunday morning.

Aggressive, unabashed newshawking like this was the trademark of Frank Leslie, who deserves to be called the founder of pictorial journalism in the United States. His real name was Henry Carter, and he was born at Ipswich, England, in 1821. As a young man he was thrilled by the early numbers of the *Illustrated London News,* and secretly sent some drawings to the paper, signing them "Frank Leslie" to hide such Bohemian skills from his prosperous, middle-class father. Later he went to London to work as a dry-goods clerk, but soon moved to the *Illustrated London News* office, where he was an engraver at twenty-five.

In 1848 he came to America, where Barnum gave him employment on circus posters and Jenny Lind programs. For a while he worked in the engraving room at *Gleason's,* and signed some of its best woodcuts. In 1853 he was hired by Barnum and the wealthy Beach brothers to start a new pictorial weekly in New York, the *Illustrated News.* This paper, though well financed and loudly promoted, was allowed to die in less than a year, largely because its owners grew tired of its endless technical problems.

Meanwhile Leslie was hoarding his capital in preparation for the great dream of his life—an American pictorial as bold, enterprising, and artistically excellent as the *Illustrated London News.* He launched it in December, 1855, more than a year before its arch-rival, *Harper's Weekly.* Up to the Civil War at least, *Leslie's* was by far the more interesting of the two papers. Its speed in producing and printing news pictures was phenomenal for the time; many appeared a week after the event, as compared to the four-day span which is normal for *Life* today. *Leslie's* gave sensational coverage to crimes and prize fights as well as to significant news, and its tone was always more rowdy than *Harper's.* But *Leslie's,* like its model back in London, had a fighting social conscience, and it pioneered in this country with pictorial crusades.

One of these was its successful battle, in 1858–59, against the "swill-milk" vendors of New York. Most of the city's milk then came from filthy barns in Brooklyn, where cows were fed on distillery mash. This high-powered diet, as *Leslie's* demonstrated by numerous "on the spot" pictures, gave the cows disgusting open sores, and caused their tails to rot and fall off. But the residue of alcohol in the mash stimulated their milk production almost up to the moment when they dropped dead from the "distillery disease."

There had been complaints about the milk before, but *Leslie's* pictures made the city gasp. One unforgettable front page showed a suffering cow, obviously in her last mortal throes, with her tongue dragging and

Fletcher Harper

a broken stump of tail, being held upright in a sling while a few final drops were squeezed from her udder by a nonchalant stablehand. Dead cows, covered with flies, were shown being hauled from the stables alongside open cans of milk. There was one view of a *Leslie's* artist, looking quite dapper with cape and top hat, being threatened by a mob of the so-called "milkmaids," who were actually villainous-looking males.

Leslie's followed the milk wagons on their routes and printed the names of customers whose children were drinking the "poison." It also ran midnight scenes of drivers diluting their milk at the public water pumps. The city's political bosses did their best to suppress or ignore these revelations. But public anger forced action in the state legislature, which for the first time passed a law to purify the milk supply. The grateful citizenry gave Frank Leslie a watch, with a picture of his new printing press on the lid, and a chain whose gold links were shaped to resemble the lost tails of the martyred cows.

Thus, during its first twenty years, pictorial journalism was already showing a sense of duty toward its readers, and an independent approach to the news. Most of its basic tools and techniques were already known. Photography was being widely used, to produce original pictures and to reproduce them for the engravers. Color printing from woodblocks began in the *Illustrated London News* in 1855, and in this country in the 1860's. The only really necessary invention that came later was halftone engraving, which was not perfected until the 1890's.

During the Civil War, of course, the American picture weeklies came into their own. It is impossible now to visualize that war without thinking of the pictorial reporting of Alfred and William Waud, Theodore Davis, Edwin Forbes, Winslow Homer, Joseph Becker, and their fellow artists of the battlefield and camp. A compilation recently published by the National Gallery of Art shows that *Harper's, Leslie's,* and their lesser rival, the *New York Illustrated News*

(which started in 1859), employed twenty-seven "special" or combat artists during the war, and also used the work of more than three hundred identified amateurs as well as of a great many photographers. All together, these three northern weeklies printed nearly six thousand war pictures.

(There was also a *Southern Illustrated News* in Richmond from September, 1862, to March, 1865. But it lacked able artists and engravers, and printed almost no pictures that can be classed as first-hand reporting.)

After the war Frank Leslie overextended himself and died bankrupt in 1880. His widow, a most remarkable woman, took over his paper and even his name—signing herself "Frank Leslie" henceforth—and made a financial comeback. But a much invigorated *Harper's Weekly* was the nation's top news magazine until near the turn of the century. Through the cartoons of Thomas Nast and the hard-hitting editorial policies of George William Curtis, *Harper's* exposed and did much to curb the political and business corruption of the Gilded Age. It never adapted itself very well to photography, and it lost its leadership to *Collier's,* a later arrival which developed war photography to a fine art in Cuba and the Philippines.

In the 1870's an entirely new kind of pictorial journalism arose in St. Louis and San Francisco, and then moved on to New York. It was represented at its best by Ambrose Bierce's San Francisco *Wasp* and Joseph Keppler's New York *Puck*. Both were so-called humor weeklies with serious opinions about public affairs. In *Puck* these opinions were dramatized in savage, gaudily colored cartoons, with big, ornate double spreads in almost every issue. Probably the most devastating political cartoon ever published in America was *Puck*'s "Tattooed Man" attack on James G. Blaine in July, 1884, showing the Republican presidential candidate cringing and almost nude before a tribunal of his party, with his shortcomings spelled out in tattoo across his bulging epidermis (see our next number, August, 1962). *Puck* had a number of imitators and rivals, the most effective being *Judge,* which did a good job of tormenting the Democrats with the same kind of color cartoons. A much gentler, nonpolitical type of humor was characteristic of the original *Life,* which E. S. Martin launched in 1883.

As early as 1873, New York was the home of the world's first pictorial daily—*The Daily Graphic*—which was started by a pair of enterprising Canadians. They promised to furnish every day a full budget of news told primarily in pictures. The *Graphic*

Joseph Keppler

experimented with several novel methods of printing, including some of the earliest halftones. But it never developed a vigorous news policy; subscribers had to buy other papers to find out what was going on. It disappeared in 1889, under competition from the livelier news pictures which by then were appearing in Pulitzer's *World* and Charles Dana's *Sun*.

As part of this burgeoning of the picture press came the rise of the pink paper *Police Gazette*, *The Yellow Kid* and other newspaper comics, and a furtive group of pictorial sheets whose subjects ranged from mere spice to outright pornography and blackmail. Even these have value to historians in documenting sublevels of popular taste. But very few people kept them, and they are excessively rare.

In our own century pictorial journalism, merging rapidly with television during recent years, has virtually flooded our waking hours with visual information. Through its strenuous endeavors we can now see everything, anywhere, that seems to be making history, from Congo natives fighting with spears to astronauts revolving in space. The task which the *Illustrated London News* defined back in 1842—"the necessity of etching events as they fly—of reflecting the social action of each particular week—of being alive to every point of importance, every turn of public interest or news—and, above all, of crowning the moving panorama of life, with rich, faithful, various, and abundant illustration"—is being performed in full measure and with great skill.

Whether all this outpouring helps to improve the world is really beside the point. It does keep millions of people informed, and it does help shape their opinions. The right to report in pictures, and the freedom to comment in cartoons and text, are too often taken for granted by the publishing empires that transmit the news today. But these priceless assets had to be created by the pioneers of pictorial journalism in the last century.

Roger Butterfield is the author of a best-selling pictorial history, The American Past, *and has long engaged in pictorial journalism as an editor and writer for* Life. *This article has been adapted from a paper he read last year before the American Antiquarian Society at Worcester, Massachusetts.*

Black Jack's Mexican Goose Chase

CONTINUED FROM PAGE 27

gress passed an emergency bill authorizing the Regular Army to expand to maximum war strength. And while Count Johann-Heinrich von Bernstorff in Washington did not like the looks of large-scale U.S. mobilization, he cabled his government with relief: "It seems to be increasingly probable that the punitive expedition against Villa will lead to full-dress intervention . . . We are, I believe, safe from an act of aggression . . ."

Censorship was put into effect, while the nation restlessly awaited news from the field, and the Springfield *Republican* worriedly predicted that catching Villa might after all present problems: ". . . he commanded large armies and won important battles. He was Carranza's big fist in the earlier days . . . has a certain untutored genius in war, and his brute force . . . makes many humble peons his adoring followers."

Perhaps so, but Pershing would have the ardent co-operation of the Mexican Federal Army. Or would he? For suddenly Carranza had flown into another of his famous rages. It was true, he told Wilson, that they had agreed to permit each other to chase bandits across either side of the border, but this had nothing to do with the Columbus affair. It was not supposed to be retroactive. He demanded that Wilson pull Pershing back. U.S. reaction was as might be expected from people who were only trying to be co-operative. The New York *American* sneered: "Carranza is no more President of Mexico than he is Emperor of China." A warning note was sounded by the *World*: "No complications with the Mexican Government need attend a punitive expedition, unless Carranza himself creates the complications."

In time Wilson got the First Chief's sullen consent to a temporary operation "for the sole purpose of capturing the bandit Villa." Tempers were short all around. Then followed a nasty scandal in the States when it was learned that Villa's agents were openly purchasing guns and ammunition from U.S. operators in El Paso. ("Business as usual," one typical cartoon was captioned, showing shadowy figures trading over the border.) In Chihuahua, Pancho more than ever was the sentimental favorite of the peons, for now their hero was at war with both Carranza and the United States; and dolefully they crooned:

Maybe they have guns and cannons,
Maybe they are a lot stronger,
We have only rocks and mountains—
But we know how to last longer . . .

Bitterly the citizens of Columbus buried their dead, while the Mexicans who had been killed were thrown into a mass grave. In neighboring Texas, Governor Ferguson implored the President to seize Mexico if it took "ten or fifteen years to do it." But concerning the menace to U.S. property there, the *World* opined, "Americans having interests in Mexico have backed the wrong horse. They put their money on an aristocracy instead of on democracy." And the days slipped by angrily and excitedly, amid mounting suspicions that Pershing was getting no results.

General Funston, in command of the Mexican border at Fort Sam Houston, was directed by Newton D. Baker (our new Secretary of War and another devout pacifist until the moment of his appointment; Wilson and his Cabinet were apparently riddled with pacifism) "to make all practical use of the aeroplanes at San Antonio, Texas, for observation." There were eight of them—the Provisional 1st Aero Squadron, composed of Jenny trainers—and Baker's suggestion was sound, for Villa knew every inch of the hills, the forests, the ravines, the brushlands, the mountain passes, of northern Mexico. Without air-to-ground intelligence, Pershing's chances of catching him were close to nil. Wilson was warned by Secretary of the Interior Franklin Lane that a fiasco could make us a laughing stock among all Latin Americans. And suppose Villa did accept battle and resisted somewhat too successfully? To Cecil Spring-Rice, Britain's ambassador to Washington, the thought was most distasteful, for such an event would further delay Uncle Sam's entry in the European war; and nervously he cabled London: "A check might mean a general attack, and . . . a serious war."

Ostensibly Carranza and Wilson were co-operating to put an end to Villa's outrages. A cartoon in the Cleveland *Plain Dealer*, however, mordantly epitomized this relationship; it shows Mexico in the person of Carranza seated tensely in a chair, with a tiny apple labeled "Villa" on his head; Uncle Sam is aiming a rifle at the apple and saying, "STEADY, NOW!" Again and again we patiently explained that Pershing's column was merely on police duty, to help Carranza rule Mexico competently. But scarcely had Pershing pierced the international boundary when Carranza once more became suspicious. When was Pershing going to get out? Why had there been no time limit on the agreement? Wilson placated him, but from Mexico City Carranza issued secret orders to his *Federales* in the north concerning actions to be taken if "Black Jack" should overplay his hand.

Meanwhile, Villista forces had the effrontery to raid Glen Springs, Boquillas, Eagle Pass, and Dryden in rapid succession, killing and capturing more Texans and causing further property damage. Next Villa attacked the Mexican town of Guerrero and slaughtered Carranza's entire garrison. But, it was claimed, his leg had been amputated as the result of a wound, and reportedly a brilliant maneuver had cut him and his men off from the mountains. These rumors turned out to be false. Matters were baffling, especially since *Federales* and Villistas were all mixed together in Chihuahua and looked exactly alike; and Carranza was now insisting that Pershing's troops and supplies must not ride any Mexican railway, that his men had to stay out of all towns, and that he must use only north-south roads. The General began to perceive that his was a more delicate job than anticipated. Fortunately he was somewhat acquainted with the crazy terrain, over which he had chased Geronimo years ago. As chief guide he employed Alexander Carson, a man who had once been kidnapped by Pancho and knew Chihuahua as well as any American. At the same time, Villa moved his wife and children to Cuba. Was a showdown near? By late April Pershing had been strengthened to 9,000 effectives and had reached Casas Grandes, ninety miles south of the border. As yet there had been no serious contact with the enemy—either enemy.

The ground over which Pershing led his eight cavalry regiments, five artillery batteries, and five infantry regiments, plus various ordnance, Signal Corps, quartermaster, ambulance, and engineer detachments, is a study in contrasts. To the west lie the Sierra Madre Mountains, which work southward in a broadening, almost impenetrable mass of granite. Eastward, an elevated plain 6,000 feet above sea level merges into desert country. The western plateau can be desperately hot or freezing cold or a wind-swept fury of snow and sand. On the desert nothing lives but the mesquite, the wild goose, the yucca, the tarantula, the agave, the rattlesnake, the cactus, the horned toad, and a few hapless Indians. Through this deadly wasteland ran the Mexican National Railway.

Chihuahua is (and was) the richest of the Mexican states, about twice the size of New York. It abounded in silver, lead, gold, and copper. Countless cattle grazed in the beautiful uplands, where timber, barley, cotton, beans, and wheat also grew. Its population in 1916 was 327,000. Through coercion or inclination, virtually all these souls were loyal to Pancho Villa and apathetic toward Carranza's *Federales,* who were supposed to be preserving law and order. But many Federal troops served cynically under Villa as well, on occasions that

Map labels:
ARIZONA — NEW MEXICO — U. S. A.
Columbus — El Paso — TEXAS
Nogales
Casas Grandes — Carrizal
CHIHUAHUA — Rio Grande
Guerrero — Ojos Azules Ranch
Santa Isabel
Parral — MEXICO
San Antonio
DURANGO
Mexican National Railway
Baja California
Pacific Ocean
Gulf of Mexico
Scale of Miles
0 50 100 200 300
MAIN ROUTE OF PERSHING'S ADVANCE
BATTLE or SKIRMISH
Mexico City — Veracruz

Trouble with Mexico had been brewing long before the Pershing-Villa campaign illustrated on this map. For seven months in 1914, U.S. troops had occupied Veracruz after a Mexican insult to the U.S. flag. In the intervening time the bandit Villa continued his border raids and finally, on March 9, 1916, hit the town of Columbus, New Mexico. Within a week Pershing and his men were across the border in pursuit. Only once—at Ojos Azules Ranch in May—did they encounter any sizable number of Villistas. Their clashes at Parral on April 12 and at Carrizal on June 21 were with Federal forces, who wanted them out of Mexico as much as Villa did. Finally, in February of 1917, after eleven months of fruitless march and countermarch, they were withdrawn.

promised to be interesting; and of course the civilian populace took neither side when the chips were down. No *peón* or shopkeeper cared to proffer information—especially to the gringos—unless it was his intention to commit suicide next morning anyway.

Pershing divided his men into two columns—West and East—both of which used cowboys, half-breeds, Apaches, gun fighters, and gamblers as guides. Immediately the two-timing commenced. A typical comment to any question put by an American was: "*Si,* we know Pancho. He stopped here last night. An hour ago he went to the south. *Si,* the man we saw is the *hombre* you are after. He is a big fat man with a black mustache, and Carranza says he is a bastard. *Si, Si,* we know Pancho." Pershing joined the west column and worked his way down along the edge of the Sierra Madre, using an automobile as his headquarters. He carried no equipment worth mentioning and rode with only one aide. Two other cars completed the tiny

safari of command, one of them a rattling wreck occupied by Floyd Gibbons of the Chicago *Tribune* and Robert Dunn of the New York *Tribune,* who had purchased it by signing a demand note inscribed on wrapping paper.

A buzzer telegraph line was hastily strung up as Pershing moved south, to keep him in touch with United States signalmen, and after two weeks, the General dictated his first communiqué: "Our troops seem to be pressing him, but I won't hazard any predictions. Villa is no fool—it may be that the campaign has just started." A scout sitting nearby commented, "As I figure it, General, we have got Villa entirely surrounded on one side."

Nothing much, really, had happened in a military sense. There had been occasional brushes with Villa's men, and the 7th Cavalry had just scattered some raiders and wounded Villa in the leg. The crack 10th (Negro) Cavalry was swinging south through the dry belt, followed by Major Frank Tompkins and his 13th.

There were plenty of rumors. Some natives brought Pershing a pair of bloody boots and a bullet-riddled shirt; Villa, they announced solemnly, was dead. A few days later he was also killed in Santa Ana. He had also been crippled by a Carranzista in Juárez. The *peones* told the disgusted Americans dozens of other silly yarns. For observational purposes, Pancho had transformed himself into an agave plant. He was a little brown dog that yipped at the heels of U.S. cavalry mounts. He put horse shoes on backward, so that Pershing's scouts would go the wrong way. He was disporting with the *señoritas* of Ojos Àzules while Pershing's men were only a few miles away—the only report which had a ring of truth. For on the night of March 30, as Pershing made camp near San Geronimo, 7,500 feet up in the Sierra Madre, in a blinding snowstorm, the fact was that Villa was traveling in a buggy toward Durango with 140 men. He had not been able to stay away from the expedition. It had fascinated him. He had kept scouting it, teasing it; and finally it had fetched him a bullet above the right knee, putting him out of action for weeks.

Much as the Mexicans resented foreign troops pouring into their country, business did boom. Prices soared and café windows carried the un-Mexican sign "Open All Night." Along the lines of march Chinamen set up little booths and sold souvenirs to the Americans. The men chewed on syrupy cactus candy, pink tamales, and big black Mexican cigars; they tried out "Mex" cigarettes like Alfonsos and Belmontes; they drank Mex beer and mescal and *sotol* and tequila until drunkenness came to be a problem. Some of them sickened from the mouldy meat and dysentery-laden water. And business was exceptionally good for the perfumed Mexican prostitutes in little towns along the trek southward. Best of all, the gringos often paid in silver coin—not in the wretched paper currency which Villa and Carranza forced down the throats of their subjects. On the other hand, there was much resistance to official U.S. receipts; with them horses, cattle, flour, and other commodities were purchased until the Mexicans learned that it could take many months to work their way through U.S. red tape and get their cash.

In the Sierra Madre foothills, icicles hung from the whiskers of men and horses, and the water in canteens froze solid. Horseshoes and nails were so scarce that the men picked them up in any condition and saved them in oiled bags. Cash was short: Colonel W. C. Brown of the 10th Cavalry spent $1,680 of his own money on regimental supplies. "Other officers have advanced several hundred dollars," he wrote Pershing plaintively. "How and when we will ever be reimbursed is problematical." Under the blinding sun exhaustion became chronic, and there was seldom enough boiled water to drink. Scores of horses died. During rest periods the men were sometimes ordered to remain standing, for there was no rousing them if they lay down to sleep. At dusk darkness came to the canyons as though by the flick of a switch; the trails became a twisting nightmare; but each dawn the packmaster rattled his bells, the horses and mules drifted sleepily together, the expedition moved southward once more, and the men sang:

> We left the border for Parral
> In search of Villa and Lopez, his old pal.
> Our horses, they were hungry,
> And we ate parched corn.
> It was damn hard living
> In the state of Chihuahua
> Where Pancho Villa was born.

All eight biplanes of the 1st Aero Squadron were cruelly squandered delivering messages between Pershing and his far-flung units, rather than being properly employed in reconnaissance duties as ordered. The fliers had no parachutes, their planes lacked replacement parts, gusty winds made desert landings risky, and soon only two planes were left. Lieutenant Benjamin Foulois flew one to Chihuahua City with a conciliatory message from General Pershing. Upon landing, he was astounded to find himself under attack from natives, who threw stones at him, fired at him, and ripped portions of the plane fabric with knives. Somehow he and his observer managed to stagger aloft and return to Pershing's headquarters. Soon Foulois' plane and the other remaining Jenny also cracked up, terminating the aerial phase of the expe-

dition only five weeks after it had begun. This was a blow. Without air intelligence the punitive columns could only flounder around northern Mexico, irritate the populace, infuriate Carranza, amuse Villa, and accomplish nothing which bore the slightest resemblance to the lofty purposes enunciated by Mr. Wilson.

Would the cavalry ever come to grips with Villa? Early in April, Pershing helplessly asked Major Tompkins, who had rejoined the western column, "Tompkins, where is Villa?"

"General, I don't know, but I would like mighty well to go find out where he is . . . I would head for Parral and would expect to cut his trail before reaching there."

"Why?"

"The history of Villa's bandit days shows that when hard pressed he invariably holes up in the mountains in the vicinity of Parral."

"How many mules do you want?"

"Twelve."

The General next day called for Tompkins and said, "Go find Villa wherever you think he is." Tompkins departed with five days' rations, five hundred silver pesos, and Troops K and M of the 13th Cavalry. On April 12 he halted near Parral, four hundred miles south of the New Mexico border. At all costs his problem was to avoid the wrong war with the wrong enemy. That meant staying friendly with the Federal cavalry, which by now was ominously arrayed along both sides of Pershing's slender line of communications and had been scouting Tompkins himself all the way down from San Geronimo.

Tompkins entered the city and found it occupied by Carranza's troops under a general named Lozano, who rode up and told him politely to get out. Simultaneously shopkeepers barred their doors, children left the streets, and citizens proceeded to revile the Americans verbally and with gestures. Tompkins retired slowly toward the outskirts. As he did so, Carranzistas massed on a hill to the south of town began outflanking his command. Firing broke out. In accordance with ancient folklore having to do with relative casualties suffered by U.S. and native troops (" 'I got one at 800 yards, Major.' The Mexicans must have concluded that that kind of shooting was too good for them so they fell back . . ." etc.), the Carranzistas allegedly lost forty killed as against two Americans. But as many U.S. newspapers uneasily noted next morning, the first real collision of the campaign had been against our so-called friends.

There was another fight in May at Ojos Azules, when a squadron of the 11th Cavalry actually did engage part of the Villa band. This time the proportion of casualties reached mathematical infinity, for according to the record, we suffered not a single man killed or even wounded, while the Villistas "lost 44 killed and had a large number wounded." The Americans had also been outnumbered five to one, it was said.

For several weeks the two columns and various detachments of the American army, including a dozen unhappy civilians who had been talked into driving trucks for the expedition, meandered south. No amount of money could hire a native guide. By June Pershing was hopelessly bogged down, while in Washington he was being knifed in the back by individuals who opined that he had mishandled everything. Mr. Wilson had become disillusioned. To Secretary Baker he spoke of "his shame as an American over the first Mexican War . . . his belief in the principle laid down in the Virginia Bill of Rights that a people has the right to do as they damn please with their own affairs." Sadly he estimated that to pacify that huge nation, we would need "five hundred thousand men at least."

Suddenly it was late spring, General Villa had recovered from his wound, and again he was leading his riders around the invader. U.S. newspaper and magazine reports had diminished; those which appeared were muted in tone. They spoke of the disciplinary action which was accomplishing its purpose, and of the disruption of Villa's army; and in this there was truth, for Pershing had temporarily split the raiders into fragments. These fragments dared not attack the American army, now 12,000 strong, but they could coalesce as soon as the gringos withdrew. Fully 150,000 National Guard troops were now barracked at El Paso, Nogales, and Brownsville. Although forbidden to cross the border, they gave President Carranza something to think about. But in the heat and monotony of the summer, they did nothing but drill and languish and drink and curse the day they had been summoned to prepare for thrilling adventures in pursuit of Pancho Villa.

The next bombshell came from Carranza's commander in the north, General Jacinto Trevino, who advised Pershing that the show was over, that U.S. troops would not be permitted to move south, west, or east. In other words, unless they went home or sat exactly where they were they would be considered at war with Mexico. Pershing replied that he would take orders only from his own government. "DRIFTING TOWARD INTERVENTION IN MEXICO" headlined the *Literary Digest,* and the Houston *Chronicle* observed that "the United States of America has no moral right to permit a people, living next door, to destroy itself." The implication was clear enough. In Washington our General Staff put the final touches on plans for a full-scale invasion.

Trevino's ultimatum was followed by a military shock, compounded (in the words of one colonel) by "one of the most amateurish performances of American professional troops . . . ever recorded," plus the low cunning of General Villa. (His agents had deceived Pershing into believing that he could be taken at Carrizal. When part of the 10th Cavalry arrived there, Villa, a few miles away, was watching everything through binoculars.) The commander of the detachment, a Captain Boyd, had been told to engage Villa but to stay out of Carrizal. Upon nearing the town, Boyd noticed a large body of *Federales* taking up defensive positions, and Mexican infantry began flowing into entrenchments along the lefthand approach to the town. Several Mexican officers asked Boyd to leave, whereupon he moved his line several hundred yards forward. There followed further squabbling, during which the Mexicans worked themselves comfortably around both flanks, set up three machine guns, put more riflemen in an irrigation ditch, and waited for Boyd to make his move.

When finally he ordered his reluctant force across two hundred yards of open plain, he was killed almost instantly; so was his second in command, and so was the next lieutenant in line. Troop C's left flank was turned. Troop K fell back. One machine gun was captured by the Negroes in a head-on rush. Many Americans were trapped, and what stunned the U.S. was not that ten of our men had been killed and ten wounded but that twenty-three had been captured. Worse yet, the defeat had been administered by Mexican regulars with whom we were supposedly in partnership. To

North Americans, who generally assume that the presence of our troops on foreign soil is reassuring to the natives thereof, the incident proved what had long been suspected—that all "greasers" were treacherous, regardless of which army they belonged to.

Earlier, in a blistering 5,000-word note, President Carranza had demanded that all U.S. troops clear out of Mexico. To this Mr. Wilson wired back: "The United States cannot recede from its settled determination to maintain its national rights and perform its full duty in preventing further invasions . . ." Mr. Baker had then ordered the seizure of the international bridges over the Rio Grande. Somewhat alarmed, Carranza backed down, released the U.S. prisoners, and reiterated his intention of co-operating in the pursuit of the ineffable Villa. But who could any longer believe this frenetic jingo whose plain policy was to badger Uncle Sam so as to promote support for his feeble government?

Whatever it all meant politically, Pershing settled down to policing Chihuahua by districts, although it was not clear how this would chastise Villa or prevent further border raids—which, by the way, continued that summer. U.S. cavalrymen patrolled the countryside running centrally through the state (it was impossible to keep the mountains and desert under surveillance), became almost friendly with the peasants and landowners of the area, and awaited orders that would get them out of that godforsaken land.

Late in June Pershing retracted his expedition to 150 miles south of the border. Once he thought absent-mindedly of going home to his wife and family, and then with some pathos wrote a friend, "One *never, never* can get over it." His command was now holding one rigid line from Columbus to Casas Grandes. That former town, once so somnolent, was his only supply depot and had become transformed into a frontier madhouse, as though gold (rather than death) had been struck on Main Street March 9. With nothing else to do, Pershing instituted a systematic training program. For seven months the Americans drilled on Mexican soil while Carranza boiled. "The hardest part of all," observed Secretary of the Interior Lane, "is to convince a proud and obstinate people that they really need any help . . . that we do not want to take some of their territory . . ." The Mexican state of Sinaloa independently and with solemn formality declared war upon the United States. From Funston's border headquarters came a call to the War Department for 65,000 additional National Guardsmen to stand off a possible invasion of Texas. Was the General serious?

U.S. newspapers screamed at Carranza for his "treachery," while one cartoonist showed Uncle Sam facing Mexico with a rifle in his right hand and "civilization," "education," and "peace" in the other. The similarity to the Philippine insurrection was exact. But in Rio de Janeiro the *Gazeta de Noticias* noted: "The severity and contempt with which Washington looks upon the revolution of the neighboring countries are neither just nor Christian." From the Pope in Rome emanated a plea to both sides to avoid war.

Wilson offered to arbitrate, whereupon a joint commission of Americans and Mexicans began talking in New London, Connecticut; Secretary Lane was chairman of the U.S. delegation. Months passed in bickering, and Lane was driven to assert that the impasse was all due to Mexico's obstinate First Chief: "Carranza is obsessed with the idea that he is a real god and not a tin god, that he holds thunderbolts in his hands instead of confetti, and he won't let us help him . . ." It was the same old story: these people preferred to operate in their own incompetent way; they didn't seem to *want* to be helped; and Carranza kept insisting that we get out of Mexico once and for all, especially since any child could see that Pershing was never going to catch Villa. We were on the brink. If war should come, Theodore Roosevelt feverishly announced, he was ready to offer his private but nonexistent army of three brigades equipped with artillery, machine guns, and airplanes.

Came autumn, and a rumor that Pancho had organized a new army of 18,000 men. German small arms were reaching him via coffins and other absurd camouflage. Most of Pershing's expedition (the "perishing expedition," it was now being called) was encamped listlessly near Casas Grandes, fighting off swarms of flies and enduring high winds and dust storms, severe evening cold-snaps, and a morass of mud each time it rained. Recreationally there was nothing for the troops to do. And at last the Mexican-American commissioners came to conclusions which, one suspects, might have been reached at their first meeting. Pershing would withdraw. Normal diplomatic relations would be restored. U.S. troops would patrol the border, and the Mexican government would be held responsible for future raids on our soil.

Indubitably General Pershing was relieved; yet his so-called punitive expedition had punished nobody; Villa was still at large; despite admirable tact, Pershing had barely escaped full-scale war; and over one hundred U.S. battle casualties had been suffered. But he asserted in his memoirs:

After we had penetrated about four hundred miles into Mexican territory and overtaken Villa's band . . . the increasing disapproval of the Mexican Government doubtless caused the administration to conclude that it would be better to rest content that the outlaw bands had been severely punished and generally dispersed, and that the people of northern Mexico had been taught a salutary lesson . . .

Still, Villa's army had not been caught and brought to battle. The outlaws had hardly been punished. The common people of Chihuahua had had nothing to do with the affair and had learned, perhaps, a lesson somewhat different from the one Pershing had in mind. General Hugh Scott concurred, however, by stating that Pershing had "made a complete success . . . from the War Department's point of view." But if the United States border was secure, Pancho was back in action elsewhere with a vengeance. As late as January 7, 1917, he raided Santa Rosalia and killed 300 people, mostly Chinese and Federal soldiers, including an officer's wife who, according to an eyewitness, "took a pot shot at Villa while he was killing off the Chinamen. The Chinese, trying to escape, would say, 'Don't shoot me standing; shoot me running.' . . ."

On January 28 the War Department announced that Pershing's expedition would withdraw. On February 5 the last American soldier shook the dust of Chihuahua from his boots.

The expedition may not be entirely brushed off as a failure. Since Carranza enjoyed little control over northern Mexico and could not stop the killing of U.S. citizens on U.S. territory, we could hardly be expected to fold our hands and piously accept our losses. Financially, Villa stood worse than before. Hundreds of his men had gone back to the farm. About a thousand U.S. officers had been given field experience, which they would utilize to grim advantage. The United States had proved that it was not out to grab territory. The expedition furnished last-minute tests and training for "Black Jack" Pershing. American national pride had been assuaged. On the other hand, we had manifested a harsh unilateralism, an alarmingly swift plunge into militarism, and an emotional instability counteracted only by Wilson's refusal to kick Mexico when she was down. The cost of the adventure came to $130,000,000.

Pancho Villa made peace with the new Mexican government after the assassination of his arch-enemy Carranza in 1920 and retired in splendor to a 25,000-acre ranch near Parral. But now that he was no longer in contact with the masses, derogatory stories began to be told about his past; and this sarcastic rhyme, referring to two notorious massacres, was sung to plucked guitars in fly-specked taverns and over many a campfire:

> Hurrah for Villa, boys!
> Fix the machine guns.
> Listen, Francisco Villa,
> What does your heart tell you?
> Don't you remember, brave one,
> That you attacked Paredon?
> Don't you remember, brave one,
> That you took Torreon?

On July 19, 1923, in his Dodge touring car, he visited his lawyer in Parral in order to dictate a new will. Armed with two Colt .45's, Villa was at the wheel. To his right sat a guard similarly equipped. Another in the back seat carried a carbine. As he proceeded slowly down the Calle de Gabino Barreda, eight riflemen cut loose at the car from ambush. Almost instinctively the stricken Villa pressed the accelerator and roared toward his murderers. The Dodge struck a tree and turned over. With Villa sprawled in the dust, the gunmen kept firing until his body contained forty-seven bullet wounds. Then came the newspapermen, the snapshots of Villa and the death car, the sightseers, the public display of his body at the Hotel Hidalgo, the picture postcards . . .

For years many simple *peones* remained unconvinced, and swore that they saw him and his revolutionary bandit-riders sweep by their cottages at night. "No, he is not dead, señor; they only try to trick us . . ." The leader of the killing squad, Jesus Salas Barrazas, a congressman from Durango, had once been pistol-whipped by Villa in an argument over a woman. Sentenced to twenty years in jail, he was released after six months. In the Parral cemetery, Pancho Villa still rests under a small gray slab.

Leon Wolff is the author of In Flanders Fields, *an account of Haig's World War I campaign, and of* Little Brown Brother, *a history of the Philippine insurrection, which recently won the Francis Parkman prize of the Society of American Historians.*

For further reading: Great River *(Volume II), by Paul Horgan (Rinehart, 1954);* Woodrow Wilson and the Progressive Era, *by Arthur S. Link (Harper & Brothers, 1960).*

Sacco Guilty, Vanzetti Innocent? CONTINUED FROM PAGE 9

cation, gunpowder, nitroglycerine, dynamite, high explosives, blood and other stains, causes of death, embalming, and anatomy.

In 1915 Hamilton had come a cropper when he appeared as an expert for the prosecution in the New York trial of Charles Stielow, accused of murdering his housekeeper. According to Hamilton's testimony, a bullet taken from the housekeeper's body could only have come from Stielow's revolver. Principally because of this testimony Stielow was found guilty and sentenced to death. Yet later he was pardoned after it was shown by more competent experts that the death bullet could not have come from this revolver.

Hamilton's career survived even this devastating reverse. When he appeared in Boston to testify in the Proctor-Hamilton motion, he had the respectable assistance of Augustus Gill, a professor of chemical analysis at the Massachusetts Institute of Technology. Hamilton now claimed that by the measurements he had made under the microscope he was able to determine that the test bullets offered in evidence at the trial had been fired from Sacco's pistol but that Bullet III had not. Professor Gill corroborated this opinion. Hamilton also maintained that the hammer in Vanzetti's revolver was not new, since an essential screw did not show marks of having been removed.

In answering for the prosecution Captain Van Amburgh had become much more positive than he had been at the trial. He displayed his strip photographs, declaring that he was now "absolutely certain" that Bullet III and Shell W had been fired in Sacco's pistol.

Toward the close of the hearing, Hamilton appeared in court with two new .32 caliber Colt automatics that he said he wanted to compare with Sacco's pistol. Before Judge Webster Thayer and the lawyers for both sides, he disassembled all three pistols and placed their parts in three piles on a table in front of the judge's bench. Then, picking up various parts one by one, he explained their function and pointed out their interchangeability. Finally he reassembled the pistols, putting his own two back in his pocket and handing Sacco's to the clerk of court.

Just as Hamilton was leaving the courtroom Judge Thayer called him back and ordered him to hand over the two pistols in his pocket to be impounded. He did so. Two months later when Van Amburgh was again examining Sacco's pistol, he noticed that the barrel, previously fouled with rust, appeared bright and sparkling as if it were brand-new. At once he realized that there had been a substitution of barrels and that if the gun were now fired it would produce very different markings on the bullets. He notified Assistant District Attorney Williams, who went at once to Judge Thayer. After a private hearing Thayer ordered an investigation. This was held in the following three weeks with only Van Amburgh, Hamilton, the district attorney, and a defense lawyer present.

At the opening of the investigation the three pistols were brought in. The briefest examination made it clear that Sacco's Colt had acquired a new barrel. Its original fouled barrel was now found to be in one of Hamilton's pistols. Everyone in the room was aware that Hamilton must have made the substitution when he disassembled the three guns in court, and the district attorney now accused him of trying to work up grounds for a new trial. Unabashed, Hamilton maintained that someone connected with the prosecution had made the switch. At the conclusion of the investigation Thayer passed no judgment as to who had switched the barrels but merely noted that the rusty barrel in the new pistol had come from Sacco's Colt. In concluding he ordered this barrel replaced and the three pistols delivered into the clerk's custody "without prejudice to either side." The prejudice, however, was not so easily erased. To the end Hamilton was a detriment, expensive, untrustworthy, and untrusted.

In the six years that had elapsed between the conviction of Sacco and Vanzetti and the passing of the death sentence on them in 1927, the case had expanded from its obscure beginnings to become an international issue of increasing turbulence. Finally in June, 1927, the governor of Massachusetts appointed a three-man committee headed by President A. Lawrence Lowell of Harvard to review the case.

The ballistics issue had remained dormant since Judge Thayer's rejection of the Proctor-Hamilton motion. Just before the Lowell Committee hearings, still another expert, Major Calvin Goddard, arrived in Boston with a comparison microscope, with which he offered to make without charge what he maintained would be conclusive tests on the Sacco-Vanzetti shells and bullets. The prosecution had no objections. William Thompson, the conservative Boston lawyer who had taken charge of the defense, would not approve of the tests but agreed not to try to prevent them.

Goddard made his tests June 3 before Professor Gill, a junior defense lawyer, an assistant district attorney, and several newsmen. His findings were:

1. That Shell W was fired in the Sacco pistol and could have been fired in no other.

2. That the so-called "mortal" bullet, Bullet III,

was fired through the Sacco pistol and could have been fired through no other.

Professor Gill, after spending some time looking through the comparison microscope, became convinced of the parallel patterns of Bullet III and a test bullet, but felt that these would have shown more clearly if Bullet III could have been cleaned of its encrusted grime. Thompson, for the defense, refused to give permission to have this done. Shortly afterward Gill wrote to Thompson that he now doubted his testimony at the Hamilton-Proctor motion and wished to sever all connection with the case. His disavowal was followed by another from the trial defense expert James Burns.

Goddard's findings, though unofficial, undoubtedly had much influence on the Lowell Committee. When Thompson later appeared before the committee, he made the novel accusation that the prosecution had juggled the evidence by substituting a test bullet and cartridge fired in Sacco's pistol for the original Shell W found in the gravel and Bullet III taken from Berardelli's body. As an indication of this he pointed out that the identifying scratches on Bullet III differed from those on the other bullets, being wider apart and uneven—as if made with a different instrument.

The year after Sacco and Vanzetti were executed, Thompson spoke out even more bluntly and emphatically, accusing Captain Proctor of having made the shell and bullet substitution just before the evidence was offered at the trial. After the substitution, according to Thompson, Proctor's conscience had bothered him to the point that he had just before his death signed the affidavit expressing his doubts.

The certainty that Goddard had hoped to bring to the ballistics evidence was made to seem less than certain in the autumn of 1927 by his findings in the Yorkell murder case in Cleveland. A few weeks after Yorkell, a bootlegger, had been shot down in the street, the police arrested a Frank Milazzo, who was found to be carrying a revolver similar in type to the one that killed Yorkell. Two bullets taken from Yorkell's body and several bullets test-fired from Milazzo's pistol were sent to Goddard for examination. After viewing the exhibits through his comparison microscope Goddard announced that one of the bullets found in Yorkell had been fired from Milazzo's revolver. In spite of Goddard's findings Milazzo was shortly afterward able to prove that he had bought the revolver new a month after the shooting. Goddard attributed the mistake to a mix-up of bullets at police headquarters. The Cleveland police denied this. Supporters of Sacco and Vanzetti have used the incident to question the infallibility of the comparison microscope. What apparently happened was that Goddard, instead of comparing a murder bullet and a test bullet, had compared the two Yorkell murder bullets with each other. They, of course, matched. Who was at fault it is impossible to say, but the comparison microscope itself was in no way discredited.

In July, 1927, the Sacco-Vanzetti guns and bullets were brought to Boston from the Dedham Courthouse, where they had been in the custody of the clerk of court since the trial, to be examined by the Lowell Committee. Then they disappeared. When in 1959 I tried to see them, they were nowhere to be found. The Dedham clerk of court had a record of their having been sent to Boston but no record of their return. The Massachusetts attorney general's office had no idea where they were, nor did the Commissioner of Public Safety at state police headquarters.

It took me six months of poking about before I finally managed to discover where they had gone. Apparently, after they had been examined by the Lowell Committee, they were sent to the ballistics laboratory of the state police and placed in the custody of Captain Van Amburgh. He put all the exhibits, each triple-sealed in its official court envelope, in a cardboard box and locked them away. The box remained there almost twenty years. Then when Van Amburgh retired he took several ballistics souvenirs with him, among them the box of Sacco-Vanzetti exhibits.

Van Amburgh—who died in 1949—was succeeded in the laboratory by his son. The son in turn retired in 1951 to Kingston, a small town near Plymouth, about forty miles from Boston. When I telephoned him to ask about the Sacco-Vanzetti exhibits, he refused at first to say whether he had them or not. But after I had persuaded the Boston *Globe* to run a feature article on the missing exhibits, he admitted to reporters that he did have them but regarded himself merely as their "custodian." The *Globe* story was a Sunday sensation. Among the paper's early readers was the Commissioner of Public Safety, J. Henry Goguen. The Commissioner at once sent two state troopers to Kingston to demand the surrender of the exhibits. The next day the guns and bullets, still in their box, were back in the state police laboratory.

When I at last saw the exhibits at the laboratory they were relatively free from corrosion, although the clips that fastened them in their triple envelopes had rusted into the paper. Apparently they had not been disturbed since 1927. What I first planned to do was to have comparison tests made of Bullet III and a bullet fired from Sacco's pistol, and similar comparisons made with Shell W. Then I hoped to determine whether or not the other bullets and shells had been fired from a single gun.

Yet I knew that even if Bullet III could be proved

A Corroborative View

A quite similar view of the Sacco-Vanzetti case—concluding that Sacco was very probably guilty and Vanzetti probably innocent—is contained in James Grossman's stimulating article, "The Sacco-Vanzetti Case Reconsidered," in the January, 1962, issue of Commentary. After reviewing the facts of the crime and examining the ballistics evidence, Mr. Grossman goes on, in the excerpt reprinted below, to discuss the characters and beliefs of the principals.

Sacco and Vanzetti's defenders have always urged as their strongest argument that it is impossible for these two men to have committed this sordid crime; it is utterly inconsistent with their characters. . . . In part perhaps because it seems to fit in with their characters, Sacco and Vanzetti are often regarded as holding a harmless, mildly eccentric, utopian belief in the natural goodness of man and as being completely opposed to violence in all forms and under all circumstances. These views . . . are not the views they actually held. Sacco and Vanzetti were followers of Luigi Galleani ["the Nestor of the Massachusetts anarchists"], who approved not only of the traditional propaganda of the deed, killing kings and heads of state, which we associate with some anarchists, but who also justified robberies and thefts if they were committed for the cause. . . .

When we turn . . . to the conditions existing in 1920 we find that they are the very conditions which [Sacco and Vanzetti believed] would justify violence on behalf of themselves and their friends. The White Terror [their term for Attorney General Palmer's roundup of radicals during the Red Scare] was for them not a propaganda phrase but a reality. It was reported to them almost daily that their friends were being persecuted, arrested, held incommunicado . . . They had the right to defend themselves; and defense was bound to be expensive. . . .

While the Braintree murder is unthinkable as a personal theft of Sacco's, I am suggesting that it is possible to understand it as an act of war, a step in the raising of a defense fund. . . . The figure of speech, war, which taken fairly literally seems to be

© LOW, ALL COUNTRIES

the clue to the Braintree deed, may also explain how Sacco, if he was guilty of the deed, can be so sincere and convincing in his claim of innocence and never for a moment in his public statements in court or in his private letters seem to be a conscious murderer. For if he did commit the deed, he would no more feel guilty of murder than would a soldier defending his country. . . .

In the court proceedings, and in speaking to his supporters, Sacco, of course, did something more than assert innocence in general terms; he claimed he was in Boston and not in Braintree on the day of the murder. . . . [But] in writing to his comrades and his friends, publicly or privately, Sacco never in any letter that I have seen specifically denies the killing. . . . No word of his innocence was spoken at the solemn great moment of his death, when he cried out long life to anarchy and bade farewell to his wife, children, and friends . . .

Vanzetti's letters throughout, his statements on being sentenced and afterward, to the very moment of death, are startlingly different from Sacco's in the unmistakable explicitness of Vanzetti's assertions of innocence and denials of guilt. . . . When his words are general he excludes all possibility of revolutionary ambiguity: "I am utterly innocent in the whole sense of the word." And at the moment of death . . . he uses his most moving formulation; to those present he said, "I wish to tell you that I am an innocent man. I never committed any crime, but sometimes some sin." . . . The sense, whether true or false, of Vanzetti's innocence radiates so profusely through the pages of his fine letters and magnificent statements that we read Sacco's in their light. . . . Sacco has been parsimonious [in expressions of] innocence and generous only in the use of terms that do not necessarily imply it. . . .

Vanzetti's statements . . . seem to me affirmative proof of his innocence. But if we ignore them entirely, the evidence against him is not strong. . . . For in Vanzetti's case there is no strong evidence, like the bullet in Sacco's, requiring an almost irrefutable defense to overcome it.

beyond dispute to have come from Sacco's pistol, there still remained the question raised by Thompson of bullet substitution. There was at least the possibility that the bullets might still test for blood. If it could now be demonstrated that all six bullets had traces of human blood on them, then the evidence would be overwhelming that there had been no bullet substitution. If on the other hand Bullet III showed no trace of blood, whereas the other five bullets did, the presumption would be strong that Proctor or someone connected with the prosecution had substituted one of the bullets fired into sawdust.

I thought there would be no difficulty in arranging these tests, but when I discussed the matter with Commissioner Goguen I found out otherwise. Even in 1959, it seemed, the Sacco-Vanzetti case was still an explosive political issue—as the spring legislative hearings requesting a posthumous pardon for the two men had demonstrated—and the Commissioner wanted to stay out of it. Each time I asked for permission to have properly qualified experts conduct ballistics tests, he postponed any definite answer, telling me to come back in a month or two. At last, after a year, he announced flatly that he would allow no tests.

Not until Goguen's term of office expired and his successor, Frank Giles, took over was I able to arrange for the tests. Finally on October 4, 1961, Professor William Boyd of the Boston University Medical School examined the six bullets for blood. Unfortunately, because of slight oxidization of the bullets, he was unable to determine whether any blood traces remained. However, after Bullet III had been washed I was able to examine the base under the microscope. Previously the bullet had been covered with some foreign substance that obscured the markings on the base. With this removed I could see the three scratched lines clearly. Although they were farther apart than the lines on the other bullets, this could have been because Bullet III had a concave base whereas the bases of the remaining bullets were flat. In any case as I looked through the microscope successively at Bullets I, II, III, and IIII, I could see no notable difference between the scratches on Bullet III and those on the rest.

A week after Professor Boyd had made his blood tests, two firearms consultants came to Boston to make the ballistics comparisons: Jac Weller, the honorary curator of the West Point Museum, and Lieutenant Colonel Frank Jury, formerly in charge of the Firearms Laboratory of the New Jersey State Police. On October 11, 1961, Weller and Jury conducted their tests in the laboratory of the Massachusetts State Police. Sacco's pistol, they found, was still in condition to

be used. After firing two shots to clear the rust from the barrel, Colonel Jury fired two more shots which he then used to match against Bullet III in the comparison microscope. Making independent examinations, Jury and Weller both concluded that "the bullet marked 'III' was fired in Sacco's pistol and in no other." They also agreed, after comparing the breechblock markings of Shell W and a test shell (see opening photograph), that Shell W must have been fired in Sacco's pistol. The other five bullets, they concluded, were fired from a single unknown gun, probably a semiautomatic pistol. It is to be presumed that the three shells, also from a single gun, came from the same weapon as did the five bullets—although this, as Jury and Weller pointed out, cannot be demonstrated.

I spent some time myself looking through the microscope at the cross-sections of Bullet III and the test bullet. The striations fitted into each other as if the two bullets were one. Here was a matter no longer open to question. But there still remained Thompson's question: was this Bullet III a substitution?

Even though nothing could be proved by blood tests, Jury and Weller felt that there had been no substitution. They maintained that a bullet fired into oiled sawdust would have shown characteristic marks on it. No such marks were on Bullet III. Theoretically, they pointed out, it would have been possible to have fired a test bullet into a side of beef, but this would have involved many problems, such as the purchase of the beef and keeping the experiment secret.

Besides the reasoning of Jury and Weller I had reasons of my own that made me feel there had been no bullet substitution, that the theory itself evolved out of Thompson's despair. There was, of course, the coincidence that Bullet III with its obsolete cannelure was duplicated by the six Winchester bullets found on Sacco when he was arrested. According to the autopsy report of April 17, 1920, Bullet III had been fired into Berardelli as he was in a prone position. Dr. Magrath identified Bullet III at the trial by the scratches he had originally made on it:

As I found it [he testified], it lay sideways against the flat surface of the hip bone, and in my opinion the flattening of the bullet was due to its striking that bone side on.

This peculiar flattening would have been almost impossible to duplicate in a substitute bullet. When Thompson in 1927 accused the prosecution of substituting Bullet III, the assistant district attorney offered to call Dr. Magrath before the Lowell Committee to reidentify the bullet he had marked, but the defense showed no interest in this.

Beyond the physical evidence of the bullet itself, the substitution theory breaks down when the trial record is examined. There Captain Van Amburgh on the stand had been most tentative in identifying Bullet III as having been fired from Sacco's pistol. Captain Proctor was even more ambiguous and later admitted that he never believed that Bullet III came from that particular Colt. If, however, Bullet III had been a substitution, the two captains would have *known* that it came from Sacco's Colt, since they themselves had fired it. Doubts they might have had as to their conduct, but none at all about the bullet.

When the case first came to trial, it was no earth-shaking issue for District Attorney Katzmann or for the state police. Katzmann, if he had lost, would still have been re-elected district attorney. The case could not have been worth the risk of detection and disgrace to forge the evidence for a conviction.

In the light of the most recent ballistics evidence and after reviewing the inquest and autopsy reports, as well as the trial testimony, I felt I could come to no other conclusion than that the Colt automatic found on Sacco when he was picked up by the police was the one used to murder Berardelli three weeks earlier. About the gun found on Vanzetti there is too much uncertainty to come to any conclusion. Being of .38 caliber, it was obviously not used at South Braintree, where all the bullets fired were .32's. There is at least the possibility that it may have been taken from the dying Berardelli, but there is an equally strong if not stronger possibility that this is not so. A Harrington & Richardson was a cheap, common revolver, and there were several hundred thousand of them being carried at the time Vanzetti was arrested. No one today can be certain whether Berardelli's Harrington & Richardson was of .32 or .38 caliber, whether it had a broken spring or a broken hammer, whether it was ever called for at Iver Johnson's, whether in fact Berardelli had a gun with him the day he was murdered. Jury and Weller found it impossible to determine if the hammer of Vanzetti's revolver had been replaced.

Whether Sacco himself pulled the trigger of his automatic that day in South Braintree, whether he was even present, cannot be established definitely. But if he did not fire it, and if in fact he was not there, then one of his close associates must have been the murderer. The ballistics evidence leaves no alternative.

When a few years ago I wrote an article, "Tragedy in Dedham" (AMERICAN HERITAGE, October, 1958), I was convinced that the two men were innocent, victims if not of a judicial frame-up at least of an ironic fate. But after the ballistics tests of 1961 I felt that, at least in the case of Sacco, I could no longer hold to my opinion. It has been pointed out that Vanzetti, just before he died, solemnly proclaimed his inno-cence. Sacco, however, when he took his place in the electric chair, gave the traditional anarchist cry—"Long live anarchy!"

Whatever my altered views about Sacco, I still continue to feel that Vanzetti was innocent. Besides various subjective reasons, and convincing talks with Vanzetti's old friends, I found what seemed to me the clinching evidence in the statement of the New York anarchist leader, Carlo Tresca. Tresca, a luminous and vivid personality, became the most noted anarchist in the United States after the deportation of Luigi Galleani in 1919. He was the admired and trusted leader to whom the anarchists confidently turned when they were in trouble. It was he who had selected the original trial lawyer for Sacco and Vanzetti. His influence remained vast over the years, not only among the dwindling anarchists but throughout the whole New York Italian colony.

During World War II the anti-Soviet Tresca was so successful in keeping the Communists out of the government's overseas Italian broadcasts that a G.P.U. killer known as Enea Sormenti was imported to eliminate him. Tresca was shot down on a New York street in 1943. Several weeks before he died he happened to be talking with his long-time friend Max Eastman, who had earlier written a "Profile" of him for the *New Yorker*. The subject of Sacco and Vanzetti came up, and Eastman asked Tresca if he would feel free to tell him the truth about them.

Without hesitation Tresca replied: "Sacco was guilty, but Vanzetti was not." At that moment some people came into the room, interrupting the conversation, and Eastman never saw Tresca again. Yet the reasons for Tresca's answer must have been profound. He could easily have avoided the question or even denied his comrade's guilt. And if any man should have known the truth of the case, Tresca was the man.

To my mind the most that can be said against Vanzetti is that he must have known who did commit the Braintree crime. Sacco, if he was guilty, was so out of no personal motive. But anarchist deeds of robbery and violence for the sake of the cause were not unknown. If he actually participated in the South Braintree holdup, it was to get money to aid his imprisoned fellow anarchists, and he must then have seen himself not as a robber but as a soldier of the revolution. But if someone else of his group was guilty, someone from whom he had received the murder pistol, he would have preferred death to betraying a comrade.

As far as the guns and bullets in the Sacco-Vanzetti case are concerned, the evidence is in, no longer to be disputed. The human problem remains.

FOR ONE DAY ONLY!!!
JOICE HETH,

Now on her return to the SOUTH, where she must arrive before cold weather, will, (at the urgent requests of many ladies and gentlemen) be seen at

CONCERT HALL
FOR ONE DAY ONLY.

This is positively the LAST OPPORTUNITY, which can ever be afforded to the citizens of New England, of seeing this most wonderful woman.

JOICE HETH is unquestionably the most astonishing and interesting curiosity in the World! She was the slave of Augustine Washington, (the father of Gen. Washington,) and was the first person who put clothes on the unconscious infant who in after days led our heroic fathers on to glory, to victory and freedom. To use her own language when speaking of the illustrious Father of his country, "she raised him." JOICE HETH was born in the Island of Madagascar, on the Coast of Africa, in the year 1674 and has consequently now arrived at the astonishing

Age of 161 Years!

She weighs but *forty-six ponnds*, and yet is very cheerful and interesting. She retains her faculties in an unparalleled degree, converses freely, sings numerous hymns, relates many interesting anecdotes of *the boy* Washington, the red coats, &c. and often laughs heartily at her own remarks, or those of the spectators. Her health is perfectly good, and her appearance very neat. She was baptized in the Potomac river and received into the Baptist Church 116 years ago, and takes great pleasure in conversing with Ministers and religious persons. The appearance of this marvellous relic of antiquity strikes the beholder with amazement, and convinces him that his eyes are resting on the oldest specimen of mortality they ever before beheld. Original, authentic and indisputable documents prove however astonishing the fact may appear, JOICE HETH is in every respect the person she is represented.

The most eminent physicians and intelligent men in Cincinnati, Philadelphia, New-York, Boston and many other places have examined this *living skeleton* and the documents accompanying her, and all *invariably* pronounce her to be as represented 161 *years of age!* Indeed it is impossible for any person, however incredulous, to visit her without astonishment and the most perfect satisfaction that she is as old as represented.

☞ A female is in continual attendance, and will give every attention to the ladies who visit this relic of by gone ages.

She was visited at Niblo's Garden New York, by *ten thousand persons* in two weeks.———Hours of exhibition from 9 A. M to 1 P. M. and from 3 to 6 and from 7 to 9 P. M.—Admittance 25 cents—Children 12½ cents.

☞For further particulars, see newspapers of the day. ☞Over

"I had hired Joice in perfect good faith"

Joice Heth

If we are to believe P. T. Barnum's autobiography—and some people will believe anything—he made his debut in show business with the imaginative humbug described in this old broadside. He was 25, and had been a drummer, a boardinghouse keeper, and very nearly a barkeep; he was a partner in a grocery when, in 1835, opportunity knocked. It took the form of tiny, toothless, pipe-smoking, prevaricating Joice Heth, whose proprietors offered her to Barnum for a mere $3,000. He beat the price down to $1,000, and began exhibiting her. She grossed $1,500 weekly. The public and most of the press swallowed Joice whole; after all, there was the bill of sale signed by Augustine Washington. Could the father of the Father of His Country tell a lie? When the old woman died a little later, and the examining doctors concluded that she was scarcely eighty, Barnum offered no argument to the cries of fraud. He had taught her none of her tall tales, he protested, but "had hired Joice in perfect good faith." The return on his capital had been satisfying, and he had discovered a great principle of show business—that even exposure makes good publicity. With smug piety, he buried Joice at Bethel, Connecticut.